Ralph thinks his life couldn't be more **perfect**. He has his **best friend**, Vanellope—who he hangs out with every night—and his own **You're My Hero** medal, which she gave him. What else could he want? *Not* the Internet, that's for sure!

VANELLOPE

Vanellope used her ability to **glitch** to become the best racer in *Sugar Rush*. But as much as she loves her game and spending time with Ralph, she can't help **wondering** if there's **something else** out there for her.

KNOWSMORE

The Internet is a busy place with endless websites. Luckily, there's KnowsMore! He runs a **search bar** to help users find exactly what they're looking for in only seconds. Just watch how fast his **autofill** works!

SPAMLEY

Spamley **pops up** when you least expect it. While he's used to being ignored, Ralph and Vanellope take note of his sign, which advertises ways to **get rich** by playing video games.

GORD

Gord might not be a netizen of many words, but he's Spamley's **loyal assistant**. He's always there to lend a **helping arm** or two.

SHANK

Shank is the **coolest**, toughest leader of a racing crew in the very popular Internet game *Slaughter Race*. Vanellope is in **awe** of Shank's driving skills.

Yesss runs the hip, **trendy** BuzzzTube website. She knows how to turn videos into viral sensations—and how to get them as many **hearts** as possible!

FELIX & CALHOUN

While Ralph and Vanellope explore the Internet, Felix and Calhoun realize they will need more than **his hammer** and **her armor** when a group of *Sugar Rush* kids come to live with them!

ISBN 979-11-86701-95-9 14740

Longtail Books

Chapter 1

For six years, **Wreck**-It Ralph and Vanellope von Schweetz had been the best of friends. Every day, they worked as characters inside **arcade** games at Litwak's Family Fun Center and Arcade. Ralph played the Bad Guy in *Fix-It Felix Jr.*, while Vanellope **race**d go-karts[1] in a game called *Sugar Rush*. But each evening, after all the players had left and Mr. Litwak had closed the arcade, Vanellope and Ralph left their games behind and met

---

1 go-kart 고카트. 주로 어린이가 타고 노는 소형 자동차. 지붕과 문 없이 프레임과 1인승 좌석이 있다.

up in Game Central **Station**. They would spend the rest of their time **hang**ing **out** and **goof**ing around together.

One night, as the two sat on their favorite **bench**, they played a different kind of game while other characters walked by.

"Okay, I **spy**[2] with my little eye . . . something yellow and round, and . . . it eats **dot**s," said Ralph.

"Seriously, Ralph?" said Vanellope.

"Of course I'm serious."

Vanellope knew exactly which character he was **refer**ring to.

"Why is that **obvious**?" Ralph asked.

Vanellope shook her head, **amaze**d by Ralph's thought **process**.

Ralph and Vanellope **hop**ped off the bench and walked through Game Central Station, **making their way** over to their favorite restaurant. Moments later, they were **guzzling** down soda at the **counter**, **chat**ting about random things.

---

2 ㅣ spy 한 명이 눈에 보이는 사물을 나타내는 첫 글자나 색 등을 말하면 나머지 사람들이 그것을 추측해 내는 놀이. 보통 'I spy with my little eye'라는 표현으로 시작한다.

"Then he's like, 'Stop stealing my food, Ralph.' And I go, '*Your* food? I don't see your name anywhere on these chili dogs.[3]'"

"But *were* they his chili dogs?" asked Vanellope.

"Of course they were his chili dogs," Ralph said.

After finishing their sweet drinks, the friends rode the train over to another video game. Along the way, they played rock, paper, scissors. On "shoot," Vanellope made the scissors **sign** and Ralph held out both **pinkies**.

"What is that?" asked Vanellope.

"Pinky lasers,[4]" said Ralph. "And pinky lasers destroy rock, paper, and scissors every time." Ralph pretended to **fire** his **imaginary** lasers. "*Pew-pew-pew-pew.* You lose."

"*You're* a **loser**," **joke**d Vanellope.

"Nicest thing you ever said to me," Ralph **declare**d with a smile.

Once they got to the video game, Ralph and Vanellope continued to goof off. The game was set inside a **swamp**, and there were lots of **log**s for them to roll on.

---

3 chili dog 빵과 소시지 사이에 칠리, 고기, 강낭콩 등을 넣은 스튜를 부은 핫도그.
4 laser 레이저. 증폭기 안에서 유도 방출을 반복하여 증폭된 빛 또는 그러한 빛을 내는 장치.

"**Abandon** ship! Man **overboard!**" shouted Vanellope. She laughed as she jumped to a **nearby** log, causing Ralph to **flail** and **plunge** face-first into the swamp.

Later, Ralph and Vanellope went for a visit inside a football game.

"Do you **realize** we're **basically** just zeroes and ones **float**ing around the **universe** like **tiny specks** of **dust?**" asked Vanellope. Ralph and Vanellope looked up at the sky as they hung out on the fifty-yard[5] line, **toss**ing a football **back and forth.** "Like, doesn't the very **nature** of our **existence** make you wonder if there's more to life than this?"

"Why would I wonder if there's more to life when the life I got is perfect?" replied Ralph. For a moment, he thought back to before he met Vanellope, when he was wrecking buildings in *Fix-It Felix Jr.* and had no friends. "I mean, sure, it doesn't look so hot on paper. Y'know, I *am* just a Bad Guy who wrecks a building. And, yes, for twenty-seven years, I basically lived like a dirty **bum**

---

5 yard 길이의 단위 야드. 1야드는 약 0.91미터이다. 미식축구에서 50야드 라인은 필드를 두 구
   역으로 나누는 선으로, 골라인으로부터 50야드(약 46미터) 떨어져 있다.

without any friends . . . but now I got a best friend who just happens to be the coolest girl in this whole arcade."

Vanellope smiled. "Aww, thanks, **pal**."

Ralph **punch**ed the ball with his giant **fist** and it flew through the **goalpost**s. "Home run!" he **cheer**ed. Then he turned to Vanellope. "Let's go watch the sunrise."

As the sun began to **peek** over the **horizon** behind Litwak's, Vanellope and Ralph sat in Game Central Station, watching its light through an open **socket**, just like they did every morning.

"So you're saying there's not one single, **solitary** thing about your life that you would change?" asked Vanellope, still thinking about what Ralph had said on the football field.

"Not one. It's **flawless**," answered Ralph. "Think about it—you and me get to goof off all night long. Litwak shows up. We go to work. The arcade closes. Then we get to do it all over again. Only thing I *might* do different in that **scenario** would be not having to go to work. Other than that, I wouldn't change a thing." Just then, the outside light disappeared. "Hey, where'd our sunrise go?"

BEEP! *BEEP! BEEP!* A loud **alarm blare**d. Litwak had just **plug**ged something into the last remaining **outlet** in the power **strip** close to where Ralph and Vanellope sat.

Vanellope **gasp**ed. "That's the plug-in **alert**. Let's go see what it is!"

Chapter 2

Inside the **arcade**, Mr. Litwak **stretch**ed **awkward**ly as he **bent** to **plug** a new **cord** into the power **strip**.

A **burst** of excitement **rush**ed through Game Central **Station** as the video-game characters began to **chatter**. Everyone was eager to see what the new game was. They all **dash**ed toward the plug to try to catch a **glimpse**.

"Hey, Felix, Calhoun—whadda we got gettin' plugged in here?" Ralph asked.

"Well, Sonic[1] thinks it's going to be a new pinball

---

1 Sonic 소닉. 비디오 게임 캐릭터인 파란색 고슴도치로, 음속으로 달릴 수 있다.

machine,[2]" Felix said. Then he turned to Calhoun. "What do you think, ladylove?"

"I **bet** you a shiny nickel[3] it's a photo **booth**," Calhoun replied.

"Please be a **racing** game, please be a racing game," **chant**ed Vanellope.

Everyone watched as the **marquee** above the plug finally lit up: WI-FI.

Ralph read the word aloud: "'Whiffee? Wifey?'"

A **hedgehog** from a video game smiled at Ralph. "It's actually **pronounce**d 'Why-Fie,' Ralph," he said.

"I know," Ralph said **defensive**ly.

"And Wi-Fi is the Internet," continued the kind hedgehog. "Which I've heard is an online community where human beings go to shop and play games and **socialize**. It's said to be a **wondrous**, **miraculous** place."

"Fun!" Vanellope said.

Surge Protector[4] stepped up with a **stern** look on his

---

2 pinball machine 핀볼 머신. 핀볼은 오락실 게임 중 하나로, 버튼을 눌러 금속 공이 기계 아랫 부분으로 떨어지지 않고 위로 계속 올라가게 하면서 점수를 많이 얻는 게임이다.
3 nickel 니클. 미국·캐나다의 5센트 동전

face, **capturing** everyone's attention. "Oh, no, it is not. That **sign** right there says 'Wi-Fi.' What it *should* say is 'DIE-Fi.'" Surge **pause**d, waiting for the **crowd** to laugh, but everyone was silent. "Take the **joke**, guys," he said. "But really, the Internet is nothing to **laugh at**. It is new and it is different; therefore, we should fear it. So **keep out**. And get to work. The arcade's **about to** open."

Vanellope and Ralph **linger**ed a bit as the crowd **disperse**d. "**Figure**s," Vanellope said with a **sigh**. "We finally get something new plugged in and we're not even allowed to go there."

"Totally not **fair**," said Ralph.

"A new racing game would have been cool," she said with a **shrug**.

"Something wrong with your game?" asked Ralph.

"No," said Vanellope. "It's just—every **bonus** level's been un**lock**ed. I know every **shortcut**. **I'd kill for** a new **track**."

---

4 Surge Protector 과도한 전압의 유입으로 인해 발생되는 전자 기기와 전자 부품의 파손, 소프트웨어의 손상 등을 막기 위한 장비. 여기에서는 게임 세상을 보호하는 경찰관 같은 역할을 한다.

"New track?" said Ralph. "You've already got three options."

"Yeah, I know. But don't you ever wish something new and different would happen in your game?"

"No," he answered **immediate**ly. He didn't even have to think about it.

"Well, **agree to disagree**," said Vanellope.

"I don't want to disagree," said Ralph.

"No, it's just something you say to end an argument."

"We're arguing? I don't wanna argue."

"Relax, relax. You're making it worse. Go to work. I'll see you tonight, dung merchant,⁵" said Vanellope, turning away.

"All right," said Ralph. They both walked off toward their games, but then Ralph looked back, thinking about what Vanellope had said. "She wants a new track—she'll get a new track." Ralph smiled as a great plan fell right into his brain. He knew just what to do.

---

5 dung merchant 의역하자면 '똥싸개'라는 뜻으로 쓰였다.

Chapter 3

Later that day, a girl named Swati and her friends were playing in the arcade at Litwak's. Swati put a few quarters[1] into *Sugar Rush* and sat in the driver's seat. Her friend Nafisa watched as she prepared to play.

"Pick Vanellope," Nafisa said. "She's got the best super power."

"Yeah, the **glitch**," said Swati. "I love her."

Inside *Sugar Rush,* Vanellope's name was **plaster**ed

---

1 quarter 쿼터. 미국 · 캐나다의 25센트 동전.

all over the leaderboard.[2] It seemed she won every time!

Vanellope sat in her car at the starting line along with Taffyta and the other racers. The *Sugar Rush* **announcer**'s voice spoke up as the girls prepared to **compete**: "Drivers, start your engines."

"You're gonna lose today, princess," said Taffyta, giving Vanellope a **nasty** look.

"While I am **technically** a princess, Taffyta, I'd rather you just think of me as Vanellope—the racer who**'s about to** kick your **butt**," said Vanellope.

The announcer spoke again, ending their conversation. "Three, two, one . . . GOOOOOOO!"

The racers hit their **pedal**s and were off! Taffyta took the lead as Vanellope glitched her way through **traffic**, disappearing and reappearing farther and farther ahead of the rest of the **pack**.

"Scuse me, pardon me, coming through," Vanellope said as she passed one racer after another with ease. When she approached the Gumball[3] **Challenge**, everything

---

2 leaderboard 리더 보드. 경기장에 설치된 전광판으로, 경주 도중의 주회수(周回數)나 선수들의 순위 등을 표시한다.

happened as usual. Huge gumballs rolled down a **steep** hill straight for her, but because she **knew** the **track inside and out**, it wasn't challenging at all. "One, two, and three gumballs." She **effortless**ly **made her way** around each one.

Taffyta still had the lead, but Vanellope easily **caught up**. When Taffyta **spot**ted her, Vanellope **lean**ed back in her seat and **snore**d loudly. Then she **perk**ed up and said, "I'm sorry. I must have fallen asleep. Am I winning?" With a **grin**, Vanellope **blast**ed past Taffyta.

Taffyta **wail**ed as she fell to second place.

Vanellope safely rounded a turn out of the Gumball Challenge.

"And that's Vanellope with a huge lead!" said the announcer. "No one's gonna catch her now!"

In the **meantime**, Ralph, hidden away in the **distance**, was working on a new track. "Here she comes," he said to himself excitedly. "She's gonna love this. Right **on time**."

Soon Vanellope **notice**d three billboards.[4]

---

3 gumball 사탕같이 생긴 껌.
4 billboard 빌보드. 고속도로 등에 세운 대형 광고판.

The first one read LOOKING FOR SOMETHING NEW?

The second said AND DIFFERENT?

And finally: THEN TAKE THIS TRACK. . . .

Vanellope smiled as she read each one. She knew right away it was the **handiwork** of her best friend. "Ralph, you old son of a gun!⁵" she said **gleefully**. "I'd say I've got time for a little **detour**." She **steer**ed her car toward the new track.

In the arcade, Swati noticed she was heading for something she'd never seen before. "Hey, look. I think I un**lock**ed a new track!"

Vanellope went **off-road** onto Ralph's **bumpy homemade** track. There were candy-cane⁶ tree **obstacle**s in **unexpected** places and super-dangerous jumps. As Vanellope went over the track, she **howl**ed with **delight**. "*Wa-hoo!* Thank you, Ralph!"

"You're welcome!" Ralph **yell**ed, **thrill**ed that Vanellope was enjoying his creation.

---

5 son of a gun '나쁜 녀석' 또는 '골칫덩이'라는 뜻의 속어로 남자끼리 친근감을 나타내는 표현이다.

6 candy-cane 빨간색과 흰색 줄무늬로 이루어진 지팡이 모양의 사탕. 주로 크리스마스에 먹는다.

In the arcade, Nafisa **urge**d Swati on. "Get back up there—you're going to lose!"

Swati **yank**ed the **wheel** hard to the left, trying to get Vanellope back onto the regular track, but it wasn't working. "What's wrong with this thing?" she said, **struggling** to control the Vanellope racer. She pulled hard at the wheel again, and this time the whole thing came right off!

Vanellope rounded another turn and **rocket**ed over the new track, **hoot**ing the entire way. *"Wa-hoooooo!"* She was **having the time of her life** . . . until suddenly, her tire hit a **bump** wrong, causing her to **crash**! Her car **tumble**d into a **ditch** and **land**ed in a **puddle** of mud.

"Kid!" Ralph shouted, running to her. "Oh, man. I'm so sorry!" he said. "Are you okay?"

"Oh my gosh," Vanellope said. "That was so much fun! What an **amazing** track! Thank you, thank you, thank you!" She hugged Ralph tightly, still **exhilarate**d by the new course.

Ralph smiled and took his hero medal out from underneath his shirt. "You're welcome. You know I take my duty as your hero very seriously."

"You took a serious doodie[7] *where?*" Vanellope joked.

Taffyta appeared on a hill above them with her hands on her **hip**s. "Vanellope, get up here," she said in a serious **tone**. "We have a situation."

In the arcade, Swati held the steering wheel up **apologetic**ally to Mr. Litwak as other kids stood **nearby** watching her.

"Mr. Litwak, the Vanellope racer wasn't working, and I think maybe I turned the wheel too hard," Swati said. "I'm real sorry."

"Oh, it's okay, Swati," said Litwak, taking the steering wheel from her and stepping toward the game. "I think I can get it back on pretty easily."

Inside *Sugar Rush,* Vanellope and all the other racers stood around nervously talking to each other. Taffyta turned to Ralph. "What did you do?" she said angrily.

"He was just trying to make the game more exciting.

---

7 doodie 응가. 'duty'와 발음이 비슷한 단어를 사용해서 농담을 하고 있다.

Leave him alone," said Vanellope.

Ralph **poke**d his head onto the game screen to see what was going on in the arcade. "Yeah, why don't you relax, Taffyta. Litwak will fix it."

"All right, on you go . . . ," said Mr. Litwak as he began to put the wheel back on the game. But when he tried to **force** it, the wheel broke—into two pieces!

"Um. Okay," said Ralph inside *Sugar Rush*. "Still not a problem. **Obvious**ly, he'll just order a new part."

Outside the game, Mr. Litwak**'s face fell**. "Well, I'd order a new part," he said to the **crowd** of kids now **gather**ed around, "but the company that made *Sugar Rush* **went out of business** years ago."

The kids were **aghast**.

"I'll try to find one on the Internet," said one kid, looking down at his phone.

All the kids dropped their heads as they began to do the same, searching their phones for a new steering wheel.

"Good luck," Mr. Litwak said. "That'll be like finding a **needle** in a—"

"I found one," said Swati **cheerful**ly. "See, eBay[8] has a wheel, Mr. Litwak." Swati held her phone up to show him.

"Really? Great," he said.

"See?" said Ralph inside the game. "Those kids have it under control."

Mr. Litwak **adjust**ed his glasses as he read the information about the steering wheel on the phone. "Are you **kid**ding me?" he **scoff**ed. "*How* much? That's more than this game makes in a year." Mr. Litwak **sigh**ed. "I hate to say it, but my **salvage** guy is coming on Friday, and it might be time to sell *Sugar Rush* for parts."

The kids **groan**ed as Mr. Litwak headed around to the back of the machine.

Ralph's eyes **pop**ped. "Litwak's gonna unplug your game!" he shouted. "Go. Run, run, run!" Ralph, Vanellope, and everyone else hurried out as **chaos** filled *Sugar Rush*.

Mr. Litwak yanked on the plug, trying to remove it.

Out in Game Central Station, **Surge** Protector was

---

8 eBay 이베이. 인터넷 경매 사이트로 출발해 지금은 세계 최대의 종합쇼핑몰 및 전자상거래 중개 사이트로 성장한 미국 회사.

whistling to himself when suddenly the **stampede** of *Sugar Rush* characters tumbled out, filling the station in a **flash**.

"**Gangway!**" a couple of donut **cop**s named Winchell and Duncan shouted as they **trample**d over Surge.

"What are you doing out of your game, for Peter's **sake**?" asked Surge, shocked and **confuse**d. "The arcade's open!"

"*Sugar Rush* is getting unplugged," Ralph explained.

Stressed *Sugar Rush* **citizen**s continued to run every which way as Mr. Litwak **jiggle**d the plug to get it out of the **socket**.

"We're **homeless!**" cried the donut cops.

"Calm down! Calm down!" said Surge, trying to **collect himself**.

"Oh, jeez.[9] I'm **freak**ing out hard," said Sour Bill, who, even when **panic**ked, spoke in a low, **deadpan** voice.

"I've never seen this many gameless characters!" said Surge.

---

9 jeez '이런!', '맙소사!'라는 뜻의 감탄사로 'Jesus Christ(예수님)'에서 파생한 단어.

Vanellope stepped up to Surge. "Where are we supposed to go?"

"Stay here, I guess, until the arcade closes," he said. "Then we'll **figure out** where the heck[10] we're gonna put you."

Worry and fear filled Vanellope, and she began to glitch. Different parts of her started disappearing and then reappearing **rapid**ly. She couldn't believe it. Her game was gone.

---

10 heck '젠장', '제기랄'이라는 뜻으로 당혹스럽거나 짜증스러운 감정을 강조하는 속어.

Chapter 4

Later that night, Vanellope sat on the **rooftop** inside *Fix-It Felix Jr.*, resting her **chin** in her hands and **staring** out into the dark, quiet arcade. It was **depress**ing to see the *Sugar Rush* **console** sitting by the front door, waiting to be picked up by Mr. Litwak's **salvage** guy.

Ralph **bumble**d onto the **roof** carrying food and camping **supplies**. "Okay, here we go," he said **cheerful**ly. "I **raid**ed Gene's **fridge**. Good news—he has pie! Oh, and I took a **bunch** of his **pillow**s and **junk**. I'm thinking we can make a **fort** up here. Or a yurt.[1] Or we could

stack the pillows and make an igloo.[2] A pillow igloo. A pigloo!" He began stacking pillows. "So whaddya think, kid? Fort, yurt, or the obvious best choice, pigloo?"

But Vanellope didn't respond. She continued to stare out at her game, sad and **lost in thought**. Finally, she said quietly, "I can't believe I don't have a game anymore. What am I gonna do all day?"

"Are you **kid**ding?" said Ralph. "That's the best part. You **sleep in**, you do no work, then you **hang out** with me every night. I've **literal**ly just described **paradise**."

"But I loved my game," said Vanellope.

"Oh, come on," said Ralph. "You were just **bellyaching** about the tracks being too easy."

Vanellope looked up at her friend. "That doesn't mean I didn't love it. Sure, it was **predictable**, but still . . . I never really knew what might happen in a race. And it's that . . . it's that feeling—the not-knowing-what's-coming-next feeling—that's the **stuff**. That feels like life to me,

---

1 yurt 유르트. 가죽이나 펠트로 만든 둥근 천막. 키르기스족이나 시베리아의 유목민들이 사용한다.

2 igloo 이글루. 이누이트족이 얼음과 눈으로 만드는 반구 모양의 집.

and if I'm not a racer anymore . . . who am I?"

"You're my best friend," said Ralph.

"That's not enough," said Vanellope.

"Hey," said Ralph, **wound**ed by her words.

"No, I just . . ." Vanellope started to **glitch**.

"Are you—are you okay?" asked Ralph, **concern**ed.

"It's fine. I'm fine. It's nothing." Vanellope took a few deep breaths and managed to stop glitching. "I'm sorry," she continued. "I know I'm being **weird**. I think maybe I just need to be alone right now." Vanellope **hung her head** and turned away.

"Oh," said Ralph. "Okay. I'll meet you over at our favorite restaurant in a little while." He watched **helpless**ly as she walked away.

Down below, Felix and Calhoun's apartment was **pack**ed with *Sugar Rush* characters, as well as some characters from other games.

Felix **address**ed the group. "All right, we've found good homes for so many of our **chum**s from *Sugar Rush*. And we're just hoping a few more of you will open your doors and your hearts to those in need."

Gene pointed at Sour Bill as he **stir**red his drink. "That large green olive will fit in nicely with my **décor**," he said.

"I'm a sour ball,[3]" said Sour Bill **blunt**ly.

"Well, **beg**gars can't be choosers, can they?" said Gene. "Come along, **condiment**." He **gesture**d for Sour Bill to join him.

"Mmm-kay," said Sour Bill as he followed Gene out of the apartment.

"**Marvelous**," Felix replied. "That just leaves the racers, ten **spirited youngster**s looking for a home." He knew Vanellope would stay with Ralph.

The *Sugar Rush* racers lined up against the wall.

"We're, like, **adorable**," Taffyta said in the most un**convincing** way.

"So, any takers?" asked Felix. Silence fell across the room as the remaining characters **avert**ed their eyes. No one was **willing** to take the colorful racers. "Anyone?" he repeated.

---

3 sour ball 사워 볼. 새콤한 맛이 나는 딱딱하고 둥근 사탕.

Calhoun **grab**bed Felix's hand and smiled at him. "Felix, I know we've never really talked about a family before. . . ."

"I know," said Felix, understanding what Calhoun was suggesting. "And it does feel like the kind of thing you just **jump into with both feet** and **nary** a plan."

Just like that, they'd made their decision. Calhoun turned to the others and **announce**d, "Felix and I will give them **sanctuary**!"

Surge Protector nearly **spit** up his drink. "Can I have a word with you two?"

Felix and Calhoun looked at each other and then followed Surge into the kitchen. He closed the **blind**s and turned to them **dramatic**ally. "I get it. You've been married six years; you're looking to **spice** things up. But trust me, this is the wrong kind of spice. Those things are **basically feral**."

Calhoun stepped up to face Surge. "Pardon me, sir, but those youngsters are **lamb**s in need of two kind, caring **shepherd**s."

"How hard can **parenting** be?" Felix asked. "You **treat** the child like your best friend, you give them everything they want, and you just love **their** little **socks off**. Right, Tammy?"

"Darn tootin',[4]" said Calhoun.

They turned away from Surge and opened the kitchen door. Out in the living room, the kids had **take**n **over**, **knock**ing over furniture and **bouncing** around.

Taffyta, **irritate**d, held up a **remote** control. "Your **dumb** TV doesn't work, Mommy."

Felix and Calhoun looked at each other, suddenly **uneasy** about their decision.

Surge **pop**ped out. "I told you so. . . ." Then one of the kids threw a **trophy** across the room and **struck** him on the **forehead**. "Ow!"

"Eee-oh, boy," said Felix. At that moment, Felix and Calhoun **realize**d they were entering a strange new world.

---

4 darn tootin' '네 말이 맞아'라는 뜻으로 동의할 때 쓰는 감탄사.

Later that night, Ralph sat alone at the **counter** in the restaurant with an empty **stool** beside him. "Hey—" he started to say to the waiter.

"No, Ralph," the waiter **interrupt**ed. "I haven't seen Vanellope. Not since the last time you asked, thirty seconds ago."

"Sorry," said Ralph. "I'm just worried about her. She's glitching like crazy and acting super **insecure**. And get this—she said being friends with me wasn't enough for her. I mean, that's crazy. I'm a great friend."

"Who's being insecure, Ralph?" asked the waiter. "Come on, the kid just loves her game. **Give** her **a break**."

Ralph sighed and **nod**ded as the waiter walked off to help another customer.

Just then, the door opened and Felix entered. He stepped up to the empty stool beside Ralph. "Is this seat taken?" he asked.

Ralph was surprised to see him. "Felix? Since when do you drink soda?"

"Oh," replied Felix, looking at the soda in front of him. "Since tonight."

"I hear that. This one was supposed to be for Vanellope," said Ralph, nodding to the soda. "I guess you can have it."

"Oh, thank you," said Felix. He took a **sip** and **wince**d, nearly **choking**. "**Smooth**."

"Why do I have to **screw** everything **up**?" said Ralph with a sigh. "I mean, it **figure**s, just when my life was finally perfect . . ."

"Mine too," said Felix. "But hey, now I'm a father of ten. Isn't that just a **bless**ing?" Felix **swung** his head back as he **chug**ged down the rest of his drink and **cough**ed. "Eee-oh, boy!" he **croak**ed, **slam**ming the empty glass onto the counter.

Ralph turned to Felix. "Wait, what'd you say, Felix?"

Felix looked at Ralph, **confuse**d. "Um, isn't that just a blessing?" he repeated.

Ralph shook his head **vigorous**ly. "No, no, the weird sound thing."

"Eee-oh, boy?" asked Felix.

"Eee-oh, buh?" repeated Ralph as something in his brain began to **click**.

"Eee-oh?" said Felix.

"Eee-buh?" said Ralph.

"Eee-oh, boy," said Felix.

"Eee-oh, boy! EBoy! EBoy!" Ralph shouted.

"What're you getting at there, Ralph?" asked Felix, still lost.

Ralph was excited. "That kid out in the arcade said there was a **steer**ing **wheel** part in the Internet at something called eBoy, or . . ." He grabbed his head as he tried to remember. "No, it was e*Bay*. **That's it**—eBay!" he **exclaim**ed.

"Ralph, are you thinking about going to the Internet and finding that part?" asked Felix.

"Getting that part's the only thing that's gonna fix the game, and that's the only thing that's gonna make Vanellope happy again."

Felix smiled. "And if *Sugar Rush* is fixed, all those **lovable scamp**s living in my house—and destroying my **sanity**—will have homes of their own again!" Felix placed a hand on Ralph's shoulder. "Ralph, this is an important **mission**. A **noble** mission. I'll **cover** for you."

"Thanks, **pal**," said Ralph, heading for the **exit**.

"Ralph, what about your **tab**?" called the waiter. "You **owe** me for the soda."

"Oh, Felix is gonna cover for me," said Ralph. Then he turned to the crowd in the bar. "Felix is paying!"

The crowd **cheer**ed.

"Eee-oh, boy," said Felix.

Chapter 5

Ralph ran back into his video game, where he found Vanellope trying to build a go-kart out of **brick**s. She kicked it in **frustration** and the whole thing fell apart.

"**Boo**!" Ralph shouted.

He **startle**d Vanellope so much that she jumped up and glitched. "Ralph! What is wrong with you?"

"Start **churn**ing butter and put on your church shoes, little sister, cause we're about to **blast** off!" said Ralph excitedly.

"What are you even talking about?" Vanellope asked.

"We're going to the Internet." Ralph told her he wanted to find the part so they could fix her game.

"Really?" said Vanellope, shocked. "Oh my gosh! Really?"

"Yeah, I probably should have just said, 'We're going to the Internet.' We're going to the Internet! C'mon!" The two friends ran off together, feeling more **energize**d than they had since Vanellope's game was un**plug**ged.

Moments later, they approached Surge in Game Central **Station**. Surge was **stoic**ally **patrol**ling the **barricade**d Wi-Fi plug.

"Hey, Surge," said Ralph. "Are we glad to see you." Ralph **made up** a lie that there was trouble over at another game.

"Yeah, we saw some **undesirable**s causing a real **donnybrook** over there," added Vanellope.

"Oh, heck, no. Not **on my watch**," said Surge. "**Appreciate** the **tip**."

Ralph and Vanellope quietly **giggle**d as Surge **dash**ed off. Then they **snuck** into the plug. "So all we gotta do is find this eBoy place," said Ralph.

"eBay," Vanellope corrected him.

They **hop**ped onto a moving **sidewalk** inside the router[1] plug and **chat**ted as they traveled **upward**.

"Right, eBay," said Ralph. "We go there, get the wheel, and have it delivered to Litwak before Friday. He fixes your game. Everything goes back to the way it was. **Boom**. Happily ever after."

"This is a shockingly **sound**, well-thought-out idea for you, Ralph," said Vanellope. "No **offense**."

"I know. And none taken."

The moving **walkway** neared its end and Ralph **announce**d, "Ooh, here it comes. Ladies and gentlemen, boys and girls, I give you . . . the INTERNET!"

They entered the router and looked around, expecting to see something amazing. But the space around them was mostly empty. There really wasn't anything going on.

"Huh, the Internet is not nearly as **impressive** as how the **hedgehog** described it," said Ralph.

"Yeah. I gotta admit, I'm **underwhelmed**," agreed

---

1 router 라우터. 서로 다른 네트워크를 연결하는 장치.

Vanellope. "I wonder where they keep their eBay."

"Hello, anybody home?" said Ralph.

"Hello!" called Vanellope. "We're looking for eBay!"

"Didja hear that?" asked Ralph. "Sweet **echo**. Listen, this'll be super cool." Then, he said as loudly as possible, *"Ka-kaw, ka-kaw!"*

Vanellope smiled and joined in the fun, calling, *"Hoo-lee-hoo! Hoo-lee-hoo!"*

Meanwhile, Mr. Litwak sat at his office desk, **staring** at his computer screen. He moved the mouse across the **pad**. "Okay, connect to network," he said, searching for the Wi-Fi icon[2] on the menu bar. "**Bingo**. Password is HighSc0re, with a zero instead of an *O*. And we . . . are . . . online!" Mr. Litwak **click**ed on an icon. Suddenly, what appeared to be a little man who looked just like Mr. Litwak traveled at light speed from the computer to the Wi-Fi router. It was his avatar.[3]

Ralph and Vanellope were still **squawk**ing like birds

---

2 icon 아이콘. 컴퓨터에 제공하는 명령을 문자나 그림으로 나타낸 것이다.

3 avatar 아바타. 아바타는 분신(分身) 또는 화신(化身)을 뜻하는 말로, 사이버공간에서 사용자의 역할을 대신하는 캐릭터이다.

and enjoying their echo fun when a green light turned on nearby.

"Oh, Ralph, look!" said Vanellope.

"Whoa, cool," said Ralph. "**Mood** lighting.[4]"

Litwak's avatar appeared before them and Ralph screamed. "Aaaah! That's a gremlin![5] Stay away!"

"It looks like a **tiny** Mr. Litwak," said Vanellope.

The little Mr. Litwak avatar turned and moved down a **platform**.

"Come on, Ralph, let's follow him," Vanellope said, and ran after the tiny Litwak **figure**.

Ralph and Vanellope watched as Litwak's avatar was **encase**d in a small **capsule**. A voice read out a computer address with some numbers, and the friends **gaze**d in **awe** as the capsule suddenly blasted through a **tube, zoom**ing away.

Vanellope glitched onto the **launch** pad, ready to go after him, and Ralph followed. "Whoa!" said Vanellope as she was **enclose**d in a capsule of her own. "Cool!"

---

4 mood lighting 무드 조명. 실내의 온화한 분위기를 조성할 목적으로 하는 조명 방식.
5 gremlin 그렘린. 기계에 고장을 일으킨다고 알려진 요정.

Just like Litwak's avatar, she was **catapult**ed into the net.

"Wait for me," said Ralph. "Come on, I want to go." He stepped up toward the launch pad but **trip**ped and fell. Soon he was **encapsulate**d, too, but because he was so big, his **pod** looked like it might **burst**. "Hey! I can't breathe!" Ralph screamed, but his voice was **muffle**d by the tight fit.

Ralph and Vanellope flew like **lightning** through the **cable**s. They were on their way to the Internet!

Chapter 6

"**R**alph!" cried Vanellope, **thorough**ly enjoying the wild ride. "Isn't this great?"

"No, it's not!" said Ralph, hating every second. The **pod** seemed to get tighter and tighter around his body, like it was **strangling** the life out of him.

When they finally stopped, they were **release**d at the browser's[1] home page.

"Sweet mother of monkey milk![2]" said Vanellope,

---

1 browser 브라우저. 인터넷을 검색할 때 문서나 영상, 음성 등의 정보를 얻기 위하여 사용하는 프로그램. 대표적인 브라우저로 익스플로러, 크롬, 파이어폭스 등이 있다.

landing on her feet. Her eyes **widen**ed as she looked around. Bright lights, **skyscraper**s, and **crowd**s were everywhere. Vanellope was completely **entrance**d. It was like nothing she had ever seen before.

Ralph **splat**ted onto the floor, then slowly got up and looked around. "Holy cow.[3] Kid, I don't think we're in Litwak's anymore."

"We most certainly are not, friendo. We are in the Internet! C'mon, Ralph!" Vanellope excitedly **dash**ed off and Ralph followed. They reached an **overlook** and stood **gazing** down on millions of websites, **awestruck**. Each **site** looked like its own island city, and they were all connected by a **float**ing, **sprawl**ing **superhighway** that **stretch**ed out in every direction as far as they could see. Avatars **roam**ed in and out of the websites. The entire thing looked like a **futuristic** mall!

"Wow," said Ralph. "Look at all this **stuff**."

"This is the most beautiful miracle I've ever seen,"

---

2 sweet mother of monkey milk 놀라움이나 실망 등을 나타내는 표현인 'sweet mother of Jesus'를 바꿔서 사용했다.
3 holy cow '이런!', '맙소사!'라는 뜻으로 놀라움이나 곤혹 등을 나타내는 표현.

said Vanellope.

"Yeah, it's really something," agreed Ralph.

"But it's too big. It goes on forever and ever," Vanellope said, nervously glitching. "How are we possibly gonna find eBay out there?"

"It's okay," Ralph said, trying to calm her. "Not to worry. I'm sure there's someone who can give us directions. Um . . ." Ralph looked around and **notice**d an egg-shaped character wearing glasses and a **graduation** cap.[4] "Oh, that little egg guy has on one of those hats that smart people wear. Maybe he can help us."

KnowsMore, an **upbeat**, eager **know-it-all**, stood behind a search bar. He lit up as users approached via their computers. "Welcome back to the search bar, madam," he said. "I hope you were able to find a **satisfactory** breakfast burrito[5] based upon the search results I provided this morning. What can KnowsMore help you find now?"

---

4 graduation cap 학사모. 대학교의 졸업식에서 착용하는 네모난 모양의 모자.
5 breakfast burrito 토르티야 안에 미국에서 흔히 아침식사로 먹는 재료인 감자나 계란, 베이컨 등을 넣은 부리토를 말한다.

On a quiet **tree-lined** street in **suburbia**, a woman **sip**ped coffee as she stared at her computer screen. The letter *B* **blink**ed as she began typing the word "ballet" on her keyboard. She spoke aloud as she typed, "Where can I find ballet—"

"Ballet shoes? Ballet classes? Ballet folklorico?[6]" KnowsMore **blurt**ed, eagerly trying to guess the rest of her request.

"Ballet TIGHTS,[7]" said the woman as she continued to type. "Girls' size small," she added.

"Oh, little Madeline's trying ballet now, is she?" said KnowsMore. "I hope this **last**s longer than the soccer **phase**."

The woman clicked the return button[8] on her keyboard, and tons of results from KnowsMore's search popped up on the screen. "I found twenty-three million results for 'ballet tights, girls' size small,'" said KnowsMore.

As the woman clicked on one of the results, a pod

---

6 ballet folklorico 멕시코의 지역 민속 춤에 발레의 요소가 가미된 춤.
7 tights 타이츠. 허리 부분에서부터 다리 부분까지 몸에 꼭 붙는 스타킹 모양의 긴 바지.
8 return button 애플의 맥 키보드에 있는 키. PC 키보드에 있는 엔터(Enter)와 같다.

formed around her avatar. A **split second** later, she was **whisk**ed off onto the information superhighway and taken to a **specific** website without so much as a word.

"They never say thank you," KnowsMore said to himself after she left.

As the woman **depart**ed, Ralph and Vanellope stepped up. "Oh, hello, sir," KnowsMore said to Ralph. "Welcome to the search bar. What can KnowsMore help you find today?"

"Um . . . ," Ralph said, trying to think of how to **phrase** his question.

"Umbrella," said KnowsMore, guessing Ralph's request. "**Umbrage**. Umami.[9] Uma Thurman.[10]"

"No—" Ralph said, and he was **interrupt**ed again.

"Noah's Ark.[11] No Doubt.[12] Nordstrom **Rack**.[13]"

---

9 umami 우마미. 인간이 혀로 감지할 수 있는 단맛, 신맛, 짠맛, 쓴맛 외의 제5의 미각으로 감칠맛을 나타낸다.

10 Uma Thurman 우마 서먼. 미국의 영화배우.

11 Noah's Ark 노아의 방주. 구약성서 《창세기》에 나오는 이야기로, 노아가 하나님의 계시로 배를 만들고 그의 가족과 동물들을 배에 태워 대홍수를 피할 수 있었다.

12 No Doubt 노 다웃. 미국의 록 밴드.

13 Nordstrom Rack 노드스트롬 랙. 미국의 백화점인 노드스트롬이 소유한 온라인 쇼핑몰을 말한다. 백화점의 이월 상품 등을 판매한다.

KnowsMore continued shooting out guesses.

"*Rrrrrgh,*" Ralph **grow**led, **frustrate**d.

"Ergonomics,[14]" continued KnowsMore. "Urban Outfitters.[15] Urkel,[16] played by Jaleel White.[17]"

"Looks like no one put Humpty Dumpty[18] together again," said Ralph, **lean**ing over to Vanellope. "This guy's a little soft-**boil**ed."

"I'm pretty sure he's just trying to guess what you're gonna say," said Vanellope.

"Yes, I'm sorry. My **autofill** is a **tad aggressive** today," explained KnowsMore, **embarrass**ed.

"Lemme try," said Vanellope. She typed in "eBay Sugar Rush steering wheel." She pushed the return button.

"Oh, I only found one result for your **query**. Hmm, isn't that interesting," said KnowsMore as a photo of the

---

14 ergonomics 인체 공학. 해부학, 생리학, 심리학 등과 같이 인간과 관련된 여러 학문 분야를 연구하여 인간이 다루는 기구, 기계, 설비를 인간에게 알맞게 제작하기 위하여 연구하는 학문.

15 Urban Outfitters 어번 아웃피터스. 의류, 신발, 액세서리 등을 판매하는 미국의 의류 브랜드.

16 Urkel 미국의 시트콤 《Family Matters》에 등장하는 인물인 스티브 얼클(Steve Urkel)을 말한다.

17 Jaleel White 잘릴 화이트. 미국의 배우로 위에 나온 스티브 얼클을 연기했다.

18 Humpty Dumpty 험프티 덤프티. 영국의 전래 동요와 루이스 캐럴의 동화 《거울 나라의 앨리스》에 나오는 달걀 캐릭터로, 담벼락에서 떨어져 깨져버린 달걀을 의인화한 것이다.

Sugar Rush steering wheel on sale at eBay popped up.

"How did you . . . ?" asked Ralph, **dumbfounded**.

"Oh, the Internet is very **intuitive**," said Vanellope with a **grin**. Then she clicked on the result. She and Ralph were **instant**ly **encase**d in a pod.

"**Redirect**ing to eBay," said the **robotic** voice.

"Thank you, Mr. KnowsMore!" Vanellope shouted before they were whisked away.

"Oh, I *like* her," KnowsMore said. "What a **delightful** girl."

Vanellope and Ralph **zip**ped along the superhighway. As the pod moved forward, Ralph and Vanellope stared **wide-eyed** through its **translucent** walls, gazing at all the **sight**s.

They **whip**ped by Google. "Guess we know where to go if we ever need **goggle**s," said Ralph. "There's a whole building full of them."

"There it is!" **screech**ed Vanellope, pointing out the **sign**. "eBay!"

The friends cheered, more than ready to get the steering wheel and save Vanellope's game.

Chapter 7

The pod **drop**ped them **off** at eBay's plaza, where avatars and **netizen**s **rush**ed in every direction. Vanellope and Ralph tried to stay focused as they **made their way** toward the **entrance**, but a variety of **pop-up**s **surround**ed them, shouting out their advertisements and **distract**ing Ralph.

"Get rid of **belly fat** using this one **weird trick**!" said one.

"Ooh, I like weird tricks," said Ralph.

"**Sassy housewives** want to meet you!" another pop-up said.

"They do?"

Before he could ask for more information, a pop-up was right in his face. "**Congratulation**s—you're a winner!"

"Really?"

Another **pop**ped up and said, "These ten child stars went to **prison**. Number six will **amaze** you!"

"That sounds interesting," said Ralph.

A pop-up named Spamley appeared and asked, "You wanna get rich playing video games? Click here to find out how."

"For real?"

"Raa-alph, come on!" shouted Vanellope, eager to get to eBay.

"But there's a lot of cool **stuff** here," said Ralph.

"I'll be right here if you change your mind, brother," said Spamley. Then he turned his attention to another **nearby** avatar as Vanellope **drag**ged Ralph away.

Vanellope and Ralph entered eBay to find a giant **bazaar** that looked like a **flea market**. Avatars stood at different **counter**s, calling out **bid**s as **auctioneer**s **rattle**d **off** numbers.

"Next up is a black velvet painting[1] of a **sorrowful kitten**," said an auctioneer. "Bidding starts at twenty-five." The **fuzzy feline** painting hung behind him, staring out with **oversized**, sad eyes against a black velvet background.

At the next counter, another **announcer** stood by a **stuffed** beaver,[2] calling, "Fifty for the beaver, the beautifully taxidermied[3] beaver—"

Ralph and Vanellope walked slowly, **taking** it all **in**. Some people were even bidding on an **artificial hip**! Then the friends stopped to watch an **auction** for a potato **chip** in the shape of a **celebrity**.

"Fifty-fifty-fifty. Now, who will gimme two fifty?" **bark**ed the auctioneer.

"Four hundred!" shouted a bidder.

"Going-once-going-twice-and-sold![4]" shouted the

---

1 velvet painting 벨벳 페인팅. 캔버스나 종이와 같은 재료를 대신하여 표면에 연한 섬유털이 치밀하게 심어진 직물인 벨벳을 바탕으로 삼아서 그림을 그리는 것을 말한다.

2 beaver 비버. 갈색 또는 검은 갈색을 띠고 넓고 편평하며 비늘로 덮힌 꼬리를 가지고 있다. 뒷발에 물갈퀴가 발달하여 헤엄을 잘 친다.

3 taxidermy 박제술(剝製術). 동물의 가죽을 곱게 벗기고 썩지 않도록 처리한 뒤에 솜 등을 넣어 살아 있을 때와 같은 모양으로 만드는 기술.

4 going-once-going-twice-and-sold 경매에서 경매인이 한 품목에 대한 경매를 마치기 전에 외치는 표현으로 '응찰을 할 사람 없습니까, 없습니까, 네 팔렸습니다!'라는 뜻이다.

auctioneer.

The winning bidder jumped up and down **joyful**ly.

Ralph looked over at Vanellope, **utter**ly **confuse**d. "Are you understanding how this game works?"

"I think all you have to do is **yell** out the biggest number and you win," replied Vanellope.

Ralph shook his head and told Vanellope it was the weirdest game he'd ever seen. He was focused, though, and told Vanellope to **glitch** up onto his shoulders. From there she had a better chance of **spot**ting the **steer**ing **wheel**.

"Let's see, there's a **bunch** of sports **memorabilia**," Vanellope said, still searching. "Oh, there's a **row** full of old video-game **junk**!" She pointed excitedly. "There it is! I see it! Whoa, someone else is trying to win it. Hurry, let's go!"

With Vanellope still on his shoulders, Ralph **race**d through the crowd, **knock**ing avatars out of the way. "Move!" he shouted.

A hologram[5] of the *Sugar Rush* wheel appeared

---

5 hologram 홀로그램. 3차원 영상으로 된 입체 사진.

behind the auctioneer. A clock was **tick**ing down, with only thirty-five seconds to go, and one avatar had already put in a bid!

"Two-and-two-and-two-and-two-and-two-seventy-five," said the auctioneer. "And with thirty seconds left in this auction, we have two seventy-five. Do I hear three-and-a-three-and-a-three-and-a-three?"

Ralph and Vanellope arrived, and Ralph **blurt**ed, "I'll give you three! Right here! Three!"

"I heard three, three, three, I heard three!" shouted the auctioneer.

"Three oh-five," said the other bidder.

"Three oh-five—who'll gimme three ten?" said the auctioneer.

"Three ten," said Ralph.

The other bidder offered 315, and Ralph offered 320. Then the bidder offered 325. Ralph leaned toward Vanellope and **whisper**ed, "Oh, man. This guy's good."

The auctioneer shouted, "I have three and a quarter. Do I hear three fifty?"

Vanellope **elbow**ed Ralph and said, "Watch this."

Then she shouted, "One thousand!"

"We now have a bid of one thousand," said the auctioneer.

"**Smooth** move!" said Ralph, **impress**ed by Vanellope's skills. Vanellope thanked him, and then Ralph said, "**Check** this **out**." He eyed the auctioneer **shrewd**ly and shouted, "Fifteen thousand!"

"Fifteen thousand. Do I hear fifteen-five?" said the auctioneer.

"Fifteen-fiver!" shouted Ralph, feeling like he was really **getting the hang of it**.

"Sixteen!" shouted Vanellope.

The two friends continued to shout out higher and higher numbers, enjoying the game, all the way up to twenty-seven. Just before the timer **ran out**, Ralph made one last bid: "Twenty-seven and one!"

"And—sold!" shouted the auctioneer. "For twenty-seven thousand and one to the **barefoot hobo** in the broken **overall**s."

"Hey, that's me!" said Ralph, **beam**ing with pride.

"We won!" **cheer**ed Vanellope.

"Congratulations. Here is your **voucher**," said the auctioneer, handing Ralph a **slip** of paper. "Please take it to **checkout** for **process**ing."

Ralph and Vanellope exchanged a **celebratory fist bump**[6] and headed off to the checkout area, **victorious**.

---

6 fist bump 서로의 주먹을 툭 부딪치는 인사.

Chapter 8

Ralph and Vanellope arrived at the **checkout** and were **greet**ed by a **straight-faced clerk** named Elaine.

"So," she said, looking over Ralph's **voucher**. "We are set to ship one *Sugar Rush* steering wheel to Litwak's Family Fun Center in Los Aburridos, California. With **expedite**d shipping, that should arrive Wednesday morning."

"That's two whole days before Litwak **scrap**s your game. We're way ahead of schedule," said Ralph.

"We **rule**," said Vanellope.

"I'll just need a **credit** card number," said Elaine.

"Sorry, what's a cacca-nummah?" asked Ralph.

"A credit card number, please," said Elaine, an **impatient tone creep**ing into her voice.

Ralph and Vanellope exchanged a worried look. "Number," said Ralph. "Right. Uh, seven?"

Elaine **frown**ed. "Excuse me?"

"Sorry, no—that's, you're right, that's **ridiculous**. I meant eleven," said Ralph.

"Those aren't credit card numbers," said Elaine, now very **annoy**ed.

"I'm pretty sure they are," said Ralph.

Elaine **narrow**ed her eyes at Ralph. "How exactly do you intend to pay for this item, sir? You **owe** twenty-seven thousand and one dollars."

Ralph was completely **stun**ned.

"Dollars? Dollars, like money?" asked Vanellope.

"Yes, and if you don't have a credit card, we also accept PayPal,[1] Venmo,[2] ProPay,[3] Square Cash,[4] and BuzzzyBuxxx," explained Elaine.

"You're gonna laugh," said Vanellope. "Okay, so this

big **galoot**, he left his wallet at home."

"Yeah, yeah, I did leave my wallet at home, in my wallet room," said Ralph, **go**ing **with** Vanellope's story. "And the door's **lock**ed."

"Look," said Elaine, tired of **deal**ing with their ridiculous behavior. "If you don't pay within twenty-four hours, you will be in **violation** of the unpaid-item **policy**, you will **forfeit** the **bid**, and you will lose this item." Elaine leaned around them and shouted toward the line, "Next!"

Ralph and Vanellope walked away, both feeling **disappoint**ed, but Ralph was also **fuming** mad. He **rant**ed to a passing avatar, "Hey, **buddy**, you going to eBay? I got some free advice for you: don't. What a **scam**!" He tried to **punch** a sign that read BARGAIN OF THE DAY, but it was a hologram, so his giant **fist** just **slip**ped right through

---

1 PayPal 페이팔. 온라인 상에서 개인과 기업 간의 송금, 구매 및 판매, 기부 등 결제 시스템을 제공하는 사이트.

2 Venmo 벤모. 미국에서 주로 사용하는 모바일 송금 시스템. 개인 간 모바일 결제와 소셜네트워크의 기능이 통합되어 있는 것이 특징이다.

3 ProPay 프로페이. 개인 사업자나 소규모 사업자가 신용 카드 거래를 이용할 수 있는 결제 방식.

4 Square Cash 스퀘어 캐시. 미국의 모바일 결제 기업인 스퀘어(Square)가 출시한 모바일 결제 및 송금 시스템.

it. "Look, their signs aren't even real!" he screamed. He **yank**ed the sign out of the ground and **hurl**ed it as hard as he could. It **crash**ed right into a nearby avatar and knocked her down.

In a studio apartment[5] outside the Internet, a woman frowned at her computer screen, annoyed that she was just **kick**ed **off** eBay. "What the heck. I was gonna bid on lipstick," she **whine**d.

Feeling **powerless**, Ralph **collapse**d into a **heap**. Then he noticed Vanellope glitching worse than he'd ever seen before. He got up and **rush**ed over to her. "Hey, come on, kid," he said gently. "What's going on? What's wrong?"

"This was our only chance and we **blew** it," Vanellope said. "There was only one wheel in the whole Internet, and we blew it. We blew it."

"Hey, calm down. We came here to save your game. That's what we're gonna do," Ralph said **confident**ly.

Vanellope took a deep breath. "Okay . . . okay."

"There you go. See. All we gotta do is **figure out** a

---

5   studio apartment 우리나라에서 흔히 '원룸'이라고 부르는 형태의 집으로, 방 하나에 화장실, 주방이 붙어 있는 1실형 주거.

way to earn a little bit of moola.[6]"

"We're video-game characters, Ralph. We don't *have* moola. Unless you can think of some **magical** way to get rich playing video games."

They looked at each other—they suddenly remembered one of the **pop-up**s they had seen earlier: Spamley! They hurried off to find him.

"Wanna get rich playing video games! **Click** here to find out how," said Spamley to avatars as they passed him.

"Back off, pop-up!" said a pop-up **block**er, punching Spamley and knocking him to the ground.

"Oof," said Spamley, **brush**ing himself off. "Dang[7] pop-up blockers. Why's everybody gotta be so mean?"

"Oh, there you are," said Ralph, walking up to him. "**Thank goodness** you're still here. Me and my friend here, we got twenty-four hours to make twenty-seven

---

6   moola '돈'을 의미하는 속어.
7   dang '빌어먹을', '젠장'이라는 뜻의 'damn'을 완곡하게 표현한 말.

thousand and one dollars or she loses her game."

"Yeah, so, can you please tell us how to get rich playing video games?" asked Vanellope.

"You **bet**!" said Spamley, more than happy to help. "Come on, click right here. I'll take you to my website."

Ralph clicked, and he and Vanellope were **encase**d in Spamley's strange, **rickety** pod, which had some trouble lifting off because of Ralph's size.

"You got an **ample carriage** there, **buster**," Spamley said. "Causing quite a **drag**."

As they rose up onto the **superhighway**, Spamley's pod headed toward a **steep drop-off** and Ralph **panic**ked.

"You're getting close to the **edge**," he said. "You see that? That's the edge. That's the edge. Ahhh!"

The pod fell into the drop-off but managed to **barely** stay **afloat** as it continued on its way.

"By the way, my name is JP Spamley,[8] and I'd like to welcome both of you to the Spamley family."

They landed minutes later, and Spamley led them

---

8 JP Spamley 세계에서 가장 오래된 금융 기업 중 하나인 JP 모건과 미국을 대표하는 투자 금융 회사인 모건 스탠리의 이름을 합치고, 여기에 'spam(사기)'을 합성해서 만든 이름.

to his **site**. **Stack**s of paper, **garbage**, and empty food **containers** were everywhere. It looked more like a **hoard**er's[9] home than a **professional workplace**. Ralph and Vanellope **recoil**ed from the **rotten stench**.

"So this is your website?" asked Ralph, feeling **doubtful**.

"I know what you're thinking, and it is a bit of a **mess**," Spamley said. Then he turned and shouted, "Hey, Gord!" He focused his attention back on them and continued, "But I do have a system here, if I could just find that list . . . ." He turned and shouted again. "GORD!"

Suddenly, a short, round guy in a brown **chunky** sweater appeared behind Ralph and Vanellope, **startling** them. Spamley told Gord that they were looking to make some money by playing video games, and Gord handed them each a stack of what looked like **Wanted poster**s.

Ralph read each aloud as he looked at it. "'Fishwife's **amulet**, *Wizard Quest*, three dollars. Foxhole hammer, *Zombie*[10] *Crusades*,[11] five dollars.'"

---

9 hoarder 호더. 물건을 버리지 못하고 모아두는 강박장애를 겪는 사람.
10 zombie 좀비. 원주민의 미신과 공포 이야기에 나오는 되살아난 시체를 말한다.
11 Crusades 십자군. 중세 유럽에서, 기독교도가 팔레스타인과 예루살렘을 이슬람교도로부터 다시 찾기 위하여 일으킨 원정 혹은 그 원정대를 말한다.

"Now, those are some of your more **commonplace**, low-dollar items," said Spamley.

"Can you **back up** a sec, Mr. Spamley?" asked Vanellope, reading one of her **sheets**. "You're saying if we find the golden cleats[12] from *Pro League Soccer*—if we find those and bring them back here—then a human being in the real world will pay us fifteen dollars?"

"Yes, ma'am," answered Spamley.

"So this is a real thing?" asked Ralph. "People actually do this?"

"What're ya, **soft in the head**?" said Spamley with a **chuckle**. "Of course they do."

Ralph was completely shocked.

"Here's the thing," said Vanellope. "We need, like, a ***buttload*** of money. Do you have any more **lucrative** items, **perchance**?"

"GORD!" shouted Spamley. Gord appeared and handed over another sheet of paper. "Is forty thousand dollars lucrative enough for you?" asked Spamley.

---

12 cleats 밑창에 미끄러짐을 방지하는 징이 박힌 운동화.

"It's more than enough!" **exclaim**ed Ralph.

"Then all's you gotta do is bring me Shank's car from a game called *Slaughter Race*."

Ralph and Vanellope exchanged a look of excited **disbelief**. "Wait, a racing game?" said Vanellope.

"That's right," said Spamley. "*Slaughter Race* is the most popular online racing game out there. However, it is **wicked** dangerous."

"Don't worry, the kid's the best racer in the world," said Ralph. "We'll get you that car, no problemo."

Feeling **hopeful** again, Ralph and Vanellope hurried over to *Slaughter Race*.

Chapter 9

Moments later, Ralph and Vanellope walked through *Slaughter Race*. A car **explode**d beside them and Vanellope smiled, **giddy**. "Okay, this game is kind of amazing," she said, looking around.

"Yeah, the attention to detail is **impressive**. I've never been to a game with **smog**," said Ralph, feeling a little **uneasy**. A **ferocious**-looking dog appeared, **growl**ing and **baring** its teeth. "Ahhh!" screamed Ralph. "Nice **kitty** . . ."

"Easy, boy," said Vanellope as they slowly backed up.

"Easy . . ."

The dog **lunge**d at Ralph, but just before it reached him, a great white shark **emerge**d from the **sewer** and **chomp**ed down! Just like that, their dog problem was solved, and the shark quickly **retreat**ed back into the sewer.

Ralph breathed a huge **sigh** of **relief**. "Let's just find Shank's car and get outta here," he said.

"Agreed," said Vanellope, **nod**ding.

Ralph and Vanellope found a **warehouse** and climbed up onto an outside **ledge**. They **snuck** inside through a broken window and **survey**ed from above. Down below, they could see Shank's car!

"Whoa," said Vanellope **admiring**ly. "That car is **gorgeous**. No wonder it's worth so much."

But before Ralph and Vanellope could make a move, avatars for two players **crept** into the warehouse.

One of the players, Jimmy, sat in his bedroom, while the other player, Tiffany, was in her living room.

"Thirty-one hours of **continuous** game play, and we've finally found Shank's car," Jimmy said into his headset.

"Come on, let's **jack** this ride."

"Oh, it's on," said Tiffany.

Jimmy's grandmother called to him from **downstairs**, "Jim! Jimmy? You're not playing that **horrible** game again, are you?"

"No, Gramma, I'm doing my homework," he answered. Then he **whisper**ed into his headset. "Okay, like I was saying . . . let's jack this ride."

Inside the game, the two players headed toward Shank's car.

A group of **scary**-looking characters in the warehouse **surround**ed Jimmy and Tiffany **threatening**ly. Shank **saunter**ed in like it was **no big deal**, keeping her cool.

"Well, well, well," she said. "While the cat was away, these mice tried to play."

"Hey," whispered Ralph, "I think that might be Shank."

"Listen up, *mice:* anyone who tries to play with this cat's ride is gonna **get** *got,*" said Shank.

"You're going down, Shank," Jimmy said, pulling out a board with **nail**s in it.

"Pyro," ordered Shank. "Give these **punks** the works."

Pyro, a member of Shank's **crew**, pulled two **flamethrowers** off his back and **dramatic**ally **ignite**d them. Then he **narrow**ed his eyes and approached the avatars with his **weapon**s.

In an **instant**, END OF THE ROAD appeared on Jimmy's screen in his bedroom over a **burn**ed image of his avatar and Tiffany's.

"Aw, gosh dangit!" said Jimmy. "Now we gotta start all over."

Ralph **immediate**ly turned to leave and Vanellope asked him where he was going.

"I'm **scare**d," said Ralph. "If we get burned up in here, we're dead, we're gone. So I think we should get out of here right now."

Vanellope stopped him. "I have an idea." She led Ralph to another area of the warehouse.

With the avatars gone, Shank and her **gang hung out** discussing their game. Pyro turned to Shank and asked **thoughtful**ly, "Do you ever **reckon** we're going too **hard on** the players?"

"I have felt that way before," admitted Shank. "But the way I look at it, making life difficult for the players— that's our **calling**. It's why we're programmed the way we are."

Another crew member, named Felony, said, "Yeah, but to Pyro's point, I mean, those players worked so hard to get here."

"**I hear you**, Felony, but imagine a game without **challenge**s. The same **predictable** thing every single time—who would want that?"

"Shank's right," said Butcher Boy. "You know, I just saw a really **insightful** TED[1] Talk, and I can't really remember what the guy said—it's more about how he made me feel—but I think, **ultimate**ly, the point was **honor** your **journey**, guys. . . ."

"And I honor you, Butcher Boy," said Shank **sincere**ly.

Butcher Boy thanked her, and a girl named Debbie spoke up. "Hey, Shank. Didja ever wonder what it would

---

1 TED 기술(Technology), 엔터테인먼트(Entertainment), 디자인(Design)을 의미한다. 미국의 비영리 재단으로, "세상을 바꿀 아이디어, 퍼뜨릴만한 아이디어를 공유하자"는 취지 아래 정기적인 강연회 및 세계 최고의 명사들이 참여하는 강연회를 개최하고 있다.

be like if someone actually got your car?"

"Well, I know one thing—whoever does will have to be the best of the best," said Shank.

KNOCK! KNOCK! KNOCK! Suddenly, someone was **bang**ing on the warehouse door. Shank and the crew **snap**ped to attention, **grab**bing their weapons and putting their **game face**s back on, ready to play.

Butcher Boy opened the door, **reveal**ing Ralph, **gulp**ing nervously.

"Good day to you, madam," Ralph said to Shank.

"Who are you?" asked Shank.

"I'm here from the, ah, **Department** of Noise? And the thing is, we've been getting some **complaint**s down at HQ[2]—uh, Larry's the one who takes the calls. . . ."

While Ralph **distract**ed them, Vanellope **tiptoe**d into the warehouse and **hop**ped into Shank's car. "Whoa, this is nice," she said to herself. "Where have you been all my life?" She **settle**d into the driver's seat as Ralph continued.

---

2 HQ '본사', '본부'를 의미하는 'headquarters'의 약어.

"Anyway, someone told Larry that we've been hearing a lot of gun sounds and screaming sounds and **what-have-you**. That sort of thing."

"Yeah, you mean the everyday sounds of this game?" said Shank. She took a step toward him and asked, "Who did you say you were again?"

"Oh, I'm . . . Larry?" said Ralph, failing **miserably** at his act.

"You said Larry took the call," said Shank.

Ralph **stutter**ed as Vanellope **stomp**ed on the **gas** and headed straight for the *Slaughter Race* gang, **forcing** them to **dive** out of the way. Vanellope **ram**med the car into Ralph, **plaster**ing him to the **hood** as she **sped** off. Luckily, Ralph was so big that it didn't hurt him at all. He rolled into the **passenger** seat.

"Good job, Larry!" said Vanellope.

"Yeah, **work**ed **like a charm**!" said Ralph.

The car **blast**ed out of the warehouse, **whip**ping past Jimmy's avatar, who had just appeared again in a **brand-new** car with Tiffany's avatar.

"Aw, someone got Shank's car," he said, **envious**.

Shank grabbed Jimmy's avatar by the neck and **yank**ed him out. "And I need yours," she said as she hopped into the driver's seat.

"I'll just go," said Tiffany's avatar, jumping out and running off.

Back in his house, Jimmy threw his **controller** onto the floor. "This is the worst day of my life!" he shouted.

Jimmy's grandma called, "You having trouble with your algebra,[3] Jim?"

Inside the game, Vanellope drove the stolen car down the highway. "It's a **shame** we have to leave so soon. This game is cool," she said, enjoying the **thrill** of driving through **uncharted territory**.

"Just get us out of here," said Ralph. He was not enjoying the ride.

"No problem," said Vanellope, focusing on the road.

But they were **interrupt**ed when Butcher Boy appeared **out of nowhere** and raced up behind them. "You **mess** with the **bull**, you get the **horn**s!"

---

3 algebra 대수학. 수학의 한 분야로 수 대신에 문자를 사용하여 방정식의 풀이 방법이나 대수적 구조를 연구하는 학문.

Vanellope pulled a **slick** move, causing Butcher Boy to crash into a wall. They thought they were **in the clear**, but then Ralph spotted Shank in Jimmy's car.

"Oh, no, it's that Shank lady," said Ralph. "She looks **upset**."

"Don't worry. I'll lose her," Vanellope said coolly. She took a **curb** and jumped off the road into a dry river **basin**.

"Where are you going?" yelled Ralph over all the **commotion**. "Kid, get back on the **track**. I'm gonna **lose my cookies!**"

"There is no track. I can drive anywhere!" Vanellope said **gleefully**. She **hit the gas**, turned the wheel, and disappeared into a **tunnel**.

Surprisingly, Shank stayed on their **tail**! "I believe you have something of mine," she said.

"Yeah, come and get it," **taunt**ed Vanellope. She **spiral**ed around Shank and **zip**ped out of the tunnel.

"This kid can drive," said Shank, **impress**ed.

"Whoa, Mother Hubbard,⁴ this lady can really drive," said Vanellope. As hard as she tried to lose her, Shank was able to **keep up**.

Vanellope continued to **expertly maneuver** the car, but after making a turn, she found herself in trouble. She **was about to** crash into a huge **pile** of burning buses! The **sight** of the **flame**s made Ralph scream.

"Kid, you see them. We're not gonna fit!" yelled Ralph, white-**knuckling** the **dashboard**. "**Dead end!** Dead end!"

Vanellope took a deep breath and **grin**ned. "Not for me. Bye-bye, Shanky," she said, **confident** in her plan. She glitched right through the burning buses!

"Whoa! You got the glitch under control!" said Ralph, relieved.

"Yeah, cause I feel like me again! One **exit**, straight ahead!" cheered Vanellope.

"You're not gonna lose me that easy," said Shank, appearing next to them **out of the blue**.

Vanellope couldn't believe it! "Wha—? How did you—?"

---

4   Mother Hubbard 원래는 영국의 자장가에 등장하는 주인공의 이름이지만 '빌어먹을', '젠장할'
이라는 뜻의 속어를 완곡하게 표현할 때 사용하기도 한다.

"Uh, you might wanna keep your eyes on the road," said Shank. Then she **rev**ved her engine, drove up a **load**ing **ramp**, and **launch**ed herself into the air. She **land**ed directly in front of Vanellope. Ralph screamed as Vanellope **spun** out to avoid **colliding** with her. When they finally stopped, Shank and her crew stepped out of their cars and approached the two friends.

"Yo!" yelled Shank. "Department of Noise! Get out of my car."

Vanellope glitched as she and Ralph **realize**d they were **trap**ped, wondering what was going to happen next. They began to fear the worst.

Chapter 10

Ralph turned to Vanellope. "You just **stay put**. Don't panic. I'm gonna talk to her," he said.

"Ralph, be careful," said Vanellope, worried.

"It's fine. This is what heroes do." He started to get out of the car but realized he was **stuck**. He was **squeeze**d in too tightly! He **struggle**d, **wiggling** left and right, and finally managed to squeeze out of it. "Oof. That is not designed for a big boy," he **mutter**ed, getting up and **dust**ing himself off.

"You guys thought you could just steal my car?" said

Shank. "Let me tell you what's going to happen now—"

"Wait," said Ralph, interrupting her. "We aren't normally **criminal**s. See, my friend here, she's a candy-kart[1] **race**r. You should see her racing around her sweet little **track** in her cookie-wafer[2] car that we built together. . . ."

Vanellope's **gaze** fell to the ground. She wished she could disappear while Ralph **embarrass**ed her in front of Shank.

Shank looked at Vanellope and then back at Ralph. Tears filled Ralph's eyes.

"And the thing is," said Ralph, "her perfect little game broke." He was now **wail**ing **uncontrollably**. "And that's partly on me, so we're here to fix it, but we need money to do that, and someone was gonna pay us money for your car, and—"

"Okay, okay, you can stop crying," Shank said, **cut**ting him **off**. "Though I do **respect** your **outward display** of **vulnerability**."

---

1 kart 'go-kart'의 약어.
2 cookie-wafer 우리가 흔히 웨하스라고 부르는 과자로, 밀가루, 우유, 달걀노른자 등을 잘 혼합해서 묽은 반죽을 만들어 얇고 바삭하게 구운 것이다.

"Thank you," said Ralph, trying to **pull** it **together**.

"Yeah, I mean, I get it. I do. **Friendship** is everything to us, too—right, guys?" Shank turned to her **crew**, and they all nodded in agreement.

"Word.³ We're like family," said Felony.

"I **honor** your **journey**s, guys," Butcher Boy said softly.

"That's really great," said Ralph. "So does this mean we can keep your car?"

"Absolutely not," said Shank. "But I do want to help. Felony, you got your phone on you?"

"You know it," replied Felony.

Shank told her to start recording and **gesture**d for her to film Ralph. "Pyro, hit big boy with the **blow**-and-go," ordered Shank.

Before Ralph could **react**, Pyro started up a **powerful** leaf blower⁴ and pointed it directly at Ralph's face. The **intense** wind made Ralph's **cheek**s **billow** and shake as he screamed, "What are you doing?"

"Say something—first thing that comes to your

---

3 word 동의하거나 긍정의 말을 할 때 사용하는 속어.
4 leaf blower 낙엽 청소기. 바람을 내보내 떨어진 잎이나 깎은 잔디를 청소하는 기구.

mind!" **yell**ed Shank.

"I'm gonna **wreck** it!" said Ralph.

"Good, good," said Shank. She turned to Pyro and told him to turn off the blower.

"What the heck did you do that for?" asked Vanellope.

"There are much better ways to make money on the Internet than stealing cars. Here," said Shank, taking the phone from Felony and handing it to Ralph. "Such as becoming a BuzzzTube star."

"Am I supposed to know what that means?" asked Ralph.

"I just started an **account** for you, Larry," Shank said. "Now lemme **post** the video." She clicked a few buttons on the phone. "There we are. If this thing goes **viral**, you can make a lot of money."

"Wait, for real?" Vanellope asked, surprised.

"Yeah. Friend of mine—**chick** named Yesss—she's the head algorithm[5] over at BuzzzTube. Tell her I sent you. Yesss will **hook** you **up**."

---

5 algorithm 알고리즘. 어떤 문제의 해결을 위하여, 입력된 자료를 토대로 하여 원하는 출력을 유도하여 내는 규칙의 집합을 의미한다.

"Wow," said Vanellope. "That's so nice of you."

"Not sure 'nice' is the right word," said Ralph, **rub**bing the pain from his cheeks.

"Thank you," said Vanellope.

"I should be thanking *you*, little sister. That race was fun," said Shank.

"Oh. Thank you. Again," Vanellope said, shocked to hear such high **praise** from Shank. "Um, say, while we're **talk**ing **shop**—what move did you do to get through those **burn**ing buses? Was it a power drift[6] into a drift jump, maybe?"

"Maybe," said Shank **coy**ly. "If you ever want to come back for a **rematch**, I'd be happy to kick your **butt** again." She jumped into her car, and Vanellope watched in **awe** as she **zoom**ed away.

"Whoa," Vanellope said, **admiring** Shank's exit.

"**Show-off**," said Ralph, **roll**ing **his eyes**. "C'mon, kid." He started walking away, but Vanellope wasn't following. He turned back to see her **linger**ing inside

---

6 drift 드리프트. 자동차가 최고 속도로 달리면서 살짝 뒷바퀴가 옆으로 미끄러지게 하면서 커브를 도는 기술.

Slaughter Race. Once they were outside it, he looked at her. "Man, that game is a **freak** show."

But she was **bouncing** with excitement. "I know!" she exclaimed. "I love freak shows, don't you?"

"No," Ralph said **firm**ly.

"Come on—tell me that Shank lady wasn't the coolest person you've ever met," said Vanellope, still **reel**ing from the game.

"Cool? Name one thing that's cool about her."

Vanellope quickly **rattle**d **off** a list. "She looks cool. She talks cool. Her hair is cool. She drives cool. Her car is cool."

"Are you saying my hair isn't cool?" Ralph asked **defensive**ly.

Vanellope looked **confuse**d. "Wha—? No," she said, wondering why he was suddenly talking about himself. "I'm just sayin' that game was next level. The racing was **awesome**—and there's no one telling you what to do or where to go."

Ralph and Vanellope reached an **intersection**, and while Ralph headed one way, Vanellope went the other.

Ralph asked her where she was going.

"To BuzzzTube," she explained.

"No," Ralph said. "We're going back to Spamley's. He can give us some easier **loot** to find."

"What about Shank's algorithm friend?"

"Please," said Ralph **sarcastic**ally. "I don't trust Shank."

"Well, I do."

"Well—" But before Ralph could finish, a small boy appeared **out of nowhere**.

"Hello, mister," said the eBoy.

"Ah! Who are you?" Ralph asked.

"I'm your **friendly** eBay **alert** messenger," the eBoy said.

"Huh," Ralph said. "An actual eBoy."

The eBoy continued, "Just here to let you know your bid **expire**s in eight hours."

"Eight hours?" Ralph **gulp**ed. There wasn't any time to **waste**. "Oh, man. Thanks, eBoy."

"You got it!" the eBoy said, disappearing as quickly as he'd arrived.

Vanellope looked at Ralph. "Chumbo,[7] if we **nickel-**

and-dime it with Spamley, it'll take us twenty years to make enough money."

Ralph considered what Vanellope was saying and sighed. He knew she wasn't wrong. "All right, fine," he said. "We'll do it your way. But I'm telling you right now, this BuzzzTube is a terrible idea."

---

7   chumbo '이봐' 또는 '친구'라는 뜻으로 육중한 덩치를 가진 남자를 부르는 말.

Chapter 11

Moments later, Ralph and Vanellope entered the main floor of BuzzzTube. Thousands of random video **clip**s appeared, **float**ing before them.

"Who knew the world had so many babies and cats," Ralph said, trying to **take** it all **in**.

"Hey, look," Vanellope said, pointing to Ralph's video. "There's yours." They both watched as a **netizen suck**ed up users' hearts with a big **hose**. A number **measuring** the amount had **tick**ed **up** to 723,000.

"Why are they giving your video all those hearts?"

Vanellope asked.

"Cause **obvious**ly they love me," he replied. "I toldja this place was a good idea."

"Doofus,[1]" said Vanellope with a **giggle**.

"Now, who are we s'posed to see about getting paid again?" asked Ralph.

"The head algorithm," Vanellope said. "Her name is Yesss."

Yesss sat in her office at her desk, **frown**ing as she **sift**ed through a **stack** of videos. Her **assistant**, Maybe, stood **nearby**. "NO!" she yelled. "NO. NO. NO! Un**inspire**d, **cliché**d, YouTube's[2] got this one. . . ." Suddenly, she stopped and pulled up a video so Maybe could see it. The video showed a man in a Chewbacca[3] mask. "Chewbacca *Dad?* Really?"

"Yah, it's like Chewbacca Mom,[4] but it's a daddy?"

---

1 doofus '얼간이' 또는 '멍청이'라는 뜻의 속어.
2 YouTube 유튜브. 구글이 운영하는 동영상 공유 서비스로, 사용자가 동영상을 업로드하고 시청하며 공유할 수 있는 사이트.
3 Chewbacca 츄바카. 영화 《스타워즈(Star Wars)》에 나오는 캐릭터로 키가 크고 털이 많으며, 카쉬크 행성의 우키족이다.
4 Chewbacca Mom 2016년에 인터넷에서 인기를 끈 동영상. 텍사스에 사는 엄마 캔디스 페인이 입을 벌리면 괴성이 나오는 츄바카 가면을 쓰고 이를 즐기는 자신의 모습을 촬영한 것이다.

said Maybe **cautious**ly.

"NO. I need next-level **genius**, not this **drivel**," said Yesss.

"Hey-o!" said Ralph, appearing in the **doorway**. Yesss **peer**ed over her sunglasses to see Ralph and Vanellope approaching. "Are you the head of Al Gore?[5]"

"I am the head ALGOrithm of BuzzzTube, which means I **curate** the **content** at the Internet's most popular video-sharing **site**," explained Yesss. "Which means I don't have time to **trifle with** every shoeless **mouth-breathing hobo** that **trundle**s into my office. Yo, Maybe, call **security**."

"Yes . . . But, Yesss," said Maybe, reaching for his phone, "he's the leaf-**blow**er guy. His video has one point three million hearts."

"Well, that is different," Yesss said, completely changing her **tone**. "Why didn't you tell me I was in the **presence** of a genius?" Yesss got up and approached

---

5 Al Gore 앨 고어. 미국 45대 부통령을 지냈으며 퇴임 후 환경운동가로 활발한 활동을 펼치고 있다. 환경 문제 해결을 국제적인 문제로 부각시킨 공로를 인정받아 2007년 노벨 평화상을 받았다. 본문에서는 알고리즘과 앨 고어의 발음이 유사한 것으로 말장난을 하고 있다.

Ralph while Maybe brought him an iced **beverage**.

"Yeah, this lady named Shank told us to come see you," Vanellope said.

"*Slaughter Race* Shank? No wonder your video's so **dope**. Shank is for-real cool," Yesss said.

"Right?" said Vanellope. "She's like the coolest person I've ever met."

"*Pfft*, she is not," Ralph said. "I'm the cool one getting all the hearts from my famous video."

"That's right, baby," Yesss said. "What'd you say your name was?"

"Ralph. Wreck-It Ralph."

"Well, Wreck-It Ralph, you are **trend**ing! And these are for you," Yesss said. Then she began **chant**ing, "Heart, heart, heart, heart, heart, heart, heart!"

Ralph was confused, but he joined in. "Heart, heart, heart, heart, heart!"

"Um, not to **buzzkill** the heart-**fest**," Vanellope said, "but Shank kinda told us that **viral** videos can make actual money?"

"Oh, hearts *are* money, honey. Here," Yesss said,

handing Ralph and Vanellope each a Buzzzy **device**. "Your Buzzzy **account convert**s hearts into dollars, see?"

Ralph looked at his account and saw the number forty-three. "Forty-three thousand dollars! We only needed twenty-seven thousand and one! Oh my gosh, kid. We did it!"

Yesss looked at Ralph. "That's forty-three dollars. As in, **nowhere** near twenty-seven thousand and one."

"But that's how much we need to save Vanellope's game," Ralph explained.

"And we only have eight hours left," Vanellope added, **emphasizing** their **deadline**.

"Oof, I hate to say it, but that ain't happening." Yesss looked at the phone. "In fact, your video's **tap**ped **out**."

"Wait, I thought I was **trench**ing?" Ralph said.

"Trending," Vanellope said, correcting him.

"You were, but that was fifteen seconds ago. Now you're not. Bye." Yesss turned and walked back toward her desk.

Ralph looked at Vanellope **desperate**ly. "What're we gonna do?"

"Calm down, **pal**," said Vanellope. "I **bet** if we asked really nice, Shank would let us take her car, or—"

"No," Ralph said immediately. He did not want to go back to Shank or anywhere near *Slaughter Race*. He stepped up to Yesss's desk. "What if you made a whole **bunch** of videos of me doing different things?"

"You mean **saturate** the market," Yesss said, thinking. "That could get you a lotta hearts fast."

"What exactly do you plan on doing in these videos?" Vanellope asked him.

"I'll just copy whatever's popular," he answered.

"Genius," said Yesss. "Yo, Maybe. What's trending right now?"

"Ah, let's have a lookie-loo,[6]" said Maybe as he brought up a series of videos. "As usual, human suffering is number one." They watched a video of a man **trip**ping and falling. "Followed by babies sucking on lemons, cats becoming **frighten**ed by **zucchini**s . . . oh, screaming **goat**s are back, **hot pepper challenge**s, video-game **walk-**

---

6 lookie-loo '구경꾼'이라는 뜻의 속어.

throughs, unboxings, **makeup tutorial**s, cooking demos,[7] and—lastly—bee **pun**s."

They watched a video of an **animate**d bee **buzz**ing around a daisy.[8] "Let's *bee* friends," it said. The flower **wink**ed at it.

"Ugh," Ralph and Vanellope said in **unison**.

"All right, you don't have to do any bee puns," Yesss said.

"Oh, I'm doing a bee pun," Ralph **retort**ed. "And I'm eating a hot pepper and I'm putting on makeup. I'm doing all those things." He was **determine**d to earn hearts and make the money they needed.

"This is what the Internet was **invent**ed for," Yesss said excitedly. "I love you."

"Kid! We're totally gonna save your game!" Ralph **exclaim**ed.

"And I know just how to start!" said Yesss. The three quickly got to work.

---

7 demo 'demonstration(시범 설명)'의 약어.
8 daisy 데이지. 하얀색 또는 붉은색 등의 여러 가지 꽃으로 봄부터 여름까지 오래도록 핀다.

Later that day, in an office **cubicle**, a **laid-back employee** named Lee **scroll**ed through BuzzzTube at his computer, looking bored. "Seen it. Saw that one. Seen it. Huh?" He **notice**d one of Ralph's videos, **click**ed on it, and watched it play. He let out a small, **goofy** laugh and turned to one of his office **mate**s. "Yo, McNeely, remember Wreck-It Ralph?"

"That bad guy from the old video game?" asked McNeely.

"Yeah, exactly. I'm gonna send you a super-random video. **Check** it **out**, **dude**." He clicked on a heart, giving the video some love, and sent it off.

Inside BuzzzTube, Lee's avatar appeared, **toss**ing a heart at Ralph's video. McNeely's avatar threw a heart as well.

In one video, Ralph ate a hot pepper that was so **spicy**, it sent him **bang**ing around the kitchen. In another, he presented a cooking tutorial, during which he burned a pie and his hair caught on fire! With each **ridiculous** video that users watched, they continued to give Ralph hearts. It seemed the plan just might work! But the truth was . . . they were **run**ning **out** of time.

Yesss had one more idea.

Chapter 12

Yesss **paced** as she **address**ed an **army** of **pop-up**s like a **drill** sergeant.[1] "This man is **on fire. Literal** and **figurative** fire," she said. "But this **genius** still needs two hundred million hearts in the next five hours or this child loses her game." Yesss pointed to Vanellope, who **nod**ded **solemn**ly. "That's why I'm on to **phase** two: you, my **elite** pop-up army. I need you out there **pop**ping up and getting **click**s at all the social media and **entertain**ment websites.

---

1 drill sergeant 군대의 직급인 훈련 담당 하사관.

I'm talking Tumblr,[2] Instagram,[3] Mashable[4]. . . . This isn't just a marketing **campaign**! This is an **all-out viral assault**! Let's get this man his hearts!"

The pop-ups **march**ed out of the **hangar** as Vanellope stepped up to Yesss. "That looks like fun. Hey, Yesss—I wanna go, too."

"Hmmm, I don't know," said Yesss. "Can you be **annoy**ingly **aggressive**?"

Vanellope began **poking** her **nonstop**. "I don't know. Can I? Can I? Can I?"

"Yeah, you're perfect." Yesss handed her a pop-up **sign**. "Here."

"Hey, I wanna go!" Ralph said.

"No, baby. You have to stay here and make the videos," Yesss told him.

"Yeah, Ralph," Vanellope said. "That's kinda the whole point."

"Okay, but . . . ," said Ralph. "I just don't know if it's

---

2 Tumblr 텀블러. 글이나 사진을 친구와 공유할 수 있게 하는 단문 블로그 서비스.

3 Instagram 인스타그램. 사진 및 동영상을 공유할 수 있는 소셜 미디어 플랫폼.

4 Mashable 매셔블. 기술, 디지털, 문화, 그리고 연예 등에 대한 내용을 공유하는 소셜 미디어 플랫폼.

a good idea for you to go out on the Internet by yourself."

"What exactly is the issue here? You think I can't take care of myself?" she said.

"No, but if we're being honest, I sometimes have to question your **judgment**," said Ralph. "You **tend** to have bad **taste** in friends."

Vanellope **pause**d, confused. "What? YOU are my best friend."

Ralph nodded. "**Case in point**."

Vanellope looked at him. "Ralph, come on. It's my game we're trying to save. I wanna help."

Ralph didn't like the idea at all. "But the Internet is really big. What if you get lost?"

"She won't," said Yesss. "She'll be in my personal web-**browsing limo**, which has GPS.[5] And your app[6] **come**s **with** BuzzzFace, so you can **keep in touch** anywhere on the Internet." With that, she **usher**ed Vanellope toward her limo.

---

5 GPS 'Global Positioning System'의 약어. 인공위성을 이용하여 자신의 위치를 정확히 알아낼 수 있는 시스템이다. 개인의 위치 확인에서부터 비행기, 선박, 자동차의 항법 장치, 측량, 지도 제작 등에 쓰인다.

6 app 앱. 스마트폰 등에서 사용하는 응용 프로그램. '애플리케이션(application)'을 줄인 말.

"I don't know," Ralph said, still **hesitant** about the plan.

"Ralph, I'll be fine," **reassured** Vanellope.

"But we've never really been apart in six years."

"*You'll* be fine," said Vanellope. "It's just a few **measly** hours. Focus on what's important: getting that **wheel**."

Her words brought Ralph back to **reality**. "Yeah, you're right."

Vanellope **hop**ped into the limo. "You and me, we'll be **celebrating** this time tomorrow," she said to Ralph as the doors closed. Then she turned to Maybe. "All right, Jeeves!⁷ Take me to where the action is."

The limo **blast**ed off, leaving Ralph and Yesss behind. Ralph turned to Yesss. "Where are you sending her?"

She pulled up a **holographic globe** of the Internet that **glow**ed brightly. "Since candy girl comes from an **arcade** game, I'm thinking she'd be good in the gaming **district**."

Ralph's eyes **widen**ed as he saw the *Slaughter Race* icon appear on the map. That was the *last* place he wanted

---

7 Jeeves 지브스. 영국 작가 P. G. Wodehouse의 단편 소설 시리즈에 나오는 등장인물로 재치 있고 유능한 집사이다.

her to go. "Actually, why don't you send her somewhere a little more . . ." Ralph **spun** the globe, searching for the best and safest site for Vanellope. "How 'bout fan sites? She is **technically** a princess, so maybe you could send her to this one with the castle."

"Good call," said Yesss. "I'm **redirect**ing our newest little pop-up to the happiest place online."

A little later, Vanellope gazed around the busy site called OhMyDisney.com. "Wow, this place is **bonkers**!" she said. Avatars **flit**ted around characters of all shapes and sizes, clicking on everything around them. "Sheesh,[8] is there anything this Disney **joint** *doesn't* own?" she said to herself.

"If there is, they'll buy it **eventually**," answered Eeyore[9] in his deep **monotone**. The gray **donkey** looked

---

8 sheesh '쳇' 또는 '세상에'라는 뜻으로 놀람이나 불만 등을 나타내는 감탄사.
9 Eeyore 이요르. A. A. Milne의 동화 Winnie-the-Pooh에 나오는 늙은 당나귀 인형의 모습을 한 캐릭터. 회의적이고 비관적인 성격이 특징이다.

at Vanellope with his sad eyes and then slowly moved on.

Vanellope turned around to see a quiz **taking place** nearby.

An **announcer** said, "Your last question—'My friends would describe me as . . .'"

In the real world, a girl read the options: "'Smart, funny, kind, brave.'" She thought it over before clicking on her answer. "Um, I guess kind."

"Based on your answers," said the announcer, "your princess BFF¹⁰ is . . . Snow White!"

Everyone **applaud**ed as Snow White stepped forward and took her place in the **spotlight**.

"I do believe our **friendship** shall be the **fair**est of them all!" Snow White said sweetly.

Vanellope followed an avatar looking to click on something and said, "Wanna meet *my* BFF? It's Wreck-It Ralph. Click here to see his newest video."

"Is Wreck-It Ralph a Disney character?" asked the princess avatar.

---

10 BFF '영원한 가장 절친한 친구'라는 뜻의 'Best Friends Forever'의 약어.

"Sure," said Vanellope. "Why not."

The avatar clicked on Vanellope's pop-up and was **immediate**ly **whisk**ed away in a **pod** to BuzzzTube.

Vanellope headed over to another **crowd** and managed to get more avatars to click. "It's almost too easy," she said to herself. But as she spun around to find more avatars, a **security guard** stopped her.

"Hey, do you have a **permit** for that pop-up?" asked the guard.

"Urm . . ."

"That's un**authorize**d click**bait**,[11]" said another guard. "You're coming with us."

"Uh, click here," said Vanellope. Just as the guard **grab**bed for her, she hit him with her sign and he **zoom**ed off to BuzzzTube.

Vanellope turned and **bolt**ed as more guards appeared, joining in the **chase**. She ran through the site, **desperate**ly looking for an escape **route**, until she found herself **trap**ped in a **corridor**.

---

11 clickbait 인터넷에서 자극적인 제목이나 이미지 등을 사용해 가치가 떨어지는 콘텐츠의 클릭을 유도하는 행위.

Vanellope looked left and right, but there was **nowhere** to run.

Chapter 13

With the **guard**s right behind her, Vanellope pushed against the only door in **sight**—a **lock**ed one **label**ed PRINCESSES. She **struggle**d for a moment, trying to **glitch** inside.

By the time the guards arrived, she was gone. "Any **sign** of her?" one asked.

"No—maybe she went down to the *Air Bud*[1] **pavilion**," said the other. They **set out** to continue their search.

---

1 Air Bud 농구를 잘하는 개 버디를 주인공으로 한 가족 영화.

On the other side of the locked door was a lovely **dressing room** where Vanellope came **face to face** with the Oh My Disney princesses!

"Uh, hi," Vanellope said **awkward**ly.

The princesses **leap**ed into action, ready to protect themselves. Mulan held her **sword**, Rapunzel **grip**ped her frying pan, and Belle **clutch**ed a book. Cinderella **smash**ed her glass **slipper** and **wave**d its **jagged edge**— just **in case**.

"Whoa, whoa, ladies! I can explain," said Vanellope, holding up her hands. "See, um, I'm a princess, too."

"Wait, what?" said Anna.

"Yeah, Princess Vanellope von Schweetz of the, uh, *Sugar Rush* von Schweetzes. I'm sure you've heard of us. It'd be kind of **embarrass**ing if you haven't."

"What kind of princess are you?" asked Pocahontas.

"Do you have magic hair?" asked Rapunzel.

"No," answered Vanellope.

"Magic hands?" asked Elsa.

"No."

"Do animals talk to you?" Pocahontas, Jasmine, and

Cinderella asked **simultaneous**ly.

"No."

"Were you **poison**ed?" Snow White asked **dramatic**ally.

"No."

"**Curse**d?" asked Aurora and Tiana.

"No."

"**Kidnap**ped or **enslave**d?" asked Rapunzel, Belle, Cinderella, Elsa, and Anna.

"NO! Are you guys okay? Should I call the police?" asked Vanellope.

"Then I have to **assume** you made a **deal** with an **underwater** sea **witch** where she took your voice in exchange for a pair of human legs?" said Ariel.

"No! Who would do that?"

"Have you ever had true love's kiss?" asked Snow White.

"Ew! Baaaarf!" said Vanellope, **gag**ging.

"Do you have daddy issues?" asked Jasmine.

"I don't even have a mom," said Vanellope.

Nearly every princess in the room **squeal**ed, "Neither do we!"

"And now for the million-dollar question,[2]" said Rapunzel. "Do people assume all your problems got solved because a big strong man showed up?"

"YES!" Vanellope shouted without **hesitation**. "What is *up* with that?"

"She *is* a princess!" they all exclaimed. Snow White **trill**ed with **delight**.

Cinderella eyed Vanellope's **outfit**. "Who made your **gown**?" she asked. "I've never seen anything quite like it."

"Oh, this old thing?" Vanellope said, looking at her **casual** clothes with a **shrug**.

"Oh, I'd so love to have one of my own," said Cinderella. The other princesses agreed, shouting, "As would I!"

"Oh, I want one, too, you guys!" said Ariel.

"I'll get my mice on this," said Cinderella.

A few moments later, all the princesses were enjoying pure **comfort** as they relaxed in **hoodie**s, **sweatpants**, and **fluff**y **boot**s. Each one had their hair tied up in a **sloppy knot** or ponytail.[3]

---

2 million-dollar question 굉장히 중요하거나 가치 있는 질문이라는 뜻으로 사용되는 숙어.
3 pony tail 포니테일. 긴 머리를 위쪽에서 묶고 머리끝을 망아지 꼬리처럼 늘어뜨린 머리 스타일.

"So this is love," said Cinderella. "All **hail** Princess Vanellope, the queen of **comfy**!"

The princesses **cheer**ed, "Yay, Vanellope!"

"Of all the thingamabobs[4] in this entire world, I never thought I'd get to wear a real . . . what's it called again? Oh, yeah. Shirt." Suddenly, Ariel broke into song: *"I once had a dream that I might wear a shirt—"*

Vanellope's face **twist**ed in **confusion**. "Whoa, whoa, whoa, what is going on?" she asked.

"She's singing," said Jasmine.

"Yeah, duh. But there was, like, music and a **spotlight**. You all saw it, right?" asked Vanellope.

"That's what happens when a princess sings about her dreams," explained Tiana.

"I **assure** you, that has never happened to me. Not once," Vanellope said.

"Well, why don't you try right now?" said Rapunzel. "What is it that you really want? Sing about that."

"Okay, sure. Let's see . . . um . . ." Vanellope **clear**ed

---

4 thingamabob '뭐라던가 하는 것'이라는 뜻으로 물건의 명칭이나 사람의 이름이 기억나지 않거나, 모를 때 사용한다.

her throat and began to sing **stiff**ly, *"Oh, steering wheel. Oh, steering wheel. Yes, I want a steering wheel. . . ."*

The princesses **wince**d as they listened to her out-of-**tune** attempt.

"Well, there's a lot to **unpack** there," Belle finally said. "So, this steering wheel you sing of—that's a **metaphor**?"

"No," Vanellope replied. "No metaphor. I **literal**ly meant a steering wheel. I think the issue is I'm a **lousy** singer."

"Sometimes your song can't start until you go somewhere to **reflect**," offered Mulan.

"What works for some of us is finding a body of water and **staring** at it," Pocahontas said, agreeing with Mulan.

"What?" Vanellope asked.

"Oh, yes!" Snow White exclaimed. "I stare at a wishing **well**!⁵"

"I stare at the ocean," Moana said.

Mulan raised her hand. "Horse **trough**," she **confess**ed.

"Soap **bubble**s!" Cinderella said.

---

5 wishing well 동전을 던진 사람의 소원을 이루게 해 준다는 우물을 말한다.

"Wait," said Vanellope. "You're saying if I just stare at some water—"

"*Important* water," Ariel **clarified**.

"Right, of course," said Vanellope. "Important water. I stare at that and somehow **magical**ly I'll start singing about my dream? I don't think so, ladies."

"You'll see," Belle said.

As Vanellope let their words **sink in**, there was a **knock** on the dressing-room door. "Five minutes, princesses!" a voice **announce**d. "Another Which Disney Princess Are You? quizlet starts in five minutes."

"I guess it's back to the gowns, girls," said Tiana with a **sigh**.

"Lovely to meet you, Vanellope," said Aurora.

"Best of luck finding your song," said Belle.

"And may a mouse never leave your girnal[6] with a **teardrop** in his eye, and may you always be just as happy as wish you to be," Merida said.

"Uh-huh . . . ," Vanellope said. Then she **lean**ed over

---

6 girnal '곡물 저장고' 또는 '창고'라는 뜻의 스코틀랜드어.

and asked the others, "What did she just say?"

"We don't know," Moana replied.

"We can't understand her," said Tiana.

"She's from the other studio," Anna added.

Vanellope politely smiled and left the princesses. Her mind was heavy as she **depart**ed. She couldn't stop thinking about the song. Could her new friends somehow be right?

Chapter 14

Meanwhile, Ralph and Yesss were busy working on creating a whole new video.

"Hey, guys. **Wreck**-It Ralph here with a little box I'm gonna open. Let's see," Ralph said as he **inspect**ed the box. "Got a little **heft** to it. Something **wobbling** around inside. Let's open it up, and—"

But before Ralph could finish his sentence, a **swarm** of **buzz**ing bees flew out of the box and he **screech**ed!

"Open sesa-*bees!*[1]" said a voice.

Ralph and Yesss **edit**ed the video in her office.

"All right," said Yesss, looking at her computer. "**Upload**ing. Who knew a bee **pun** would be the thing to put us over the top? **Genius**."

Then the eBoy appeared in front of Ralph. "Hey, mister!" he said **cheerful**ly.

"Oh, hi, eBoy," said Ralph.

"Just here to let you know your **bid expire**s in thirty minutes."

Ralph thanked him, and the eBoy disappeared.

"You hear that, Yesss? We don't have much time," said Ralph.

"Oh, no, oh, no, no, no, no, no, no," said Yesss, her eyes fixed on her computer screen. A bright rainbow-colored wheel[2] appeared, spinning and spinning. "OH, *NO!*" she shouted, **frustrate**d.

"Why are you angry at that **lollipop**?" asked Ralph. "What's going on?"

"The file's not **load**ing," Yesss answered. "If this

---

1   open sesa-bees 동화 《알리바바와 40인의 도적》에서 도적들이 보물을 숨겨 놓은 동굴 문을 여는 말인 '열려라 참깨(open sesame)'에 'bee'를 넣어 말장난을 하고 있다.
2   rainbow-colored wheel 맥 OS에서 응용 프로그램이 오류를 일으킬 때 나타나는 아이콘.

thing doesn't load, we're not gonna **make it**. You don't have enough hearts."

Ralph immediately started to run for the door.

Yesss called out, "Where are you going?"

"I'm going down to the floor to get some hearts!" he shouted as he left the office.

"That's a genius idea," Yesss said. She turned back to her computer, and when the file still hadn't uploaded, she screamed, "Someone get me **tech support**!"

Ralph **wander**ed around the main floor of BuzzzTube and found himself staring at a video monitor that was showing a popular meme[3] of a large, **fluff**y cat **stuck** inside a small pickle **jar**. Tons of users were watching it, so Ralph decided to **replace** it with his own video, **forcing** the users to watch that instead.

"Here you go! Right here," he shouted. "This is the one you wanna watch." Then he grabbed a **hose** from a **netizen** and started **suck**ing up all the hearts he could.

As he was collecting hearts, Ralph **notice**d a group

---

3   meme 밈. 특정 메시지를 전하는 그림, 사진, 또는 짧은 영상으로 재미를 주는 것을 목적으로 한다.

of avatars walking by. He wanted to get their attention to direct them to his video, so he **chase**d them through a door **label**ed COMMENTS.

"Anybody in here?" he said. "Hey, come out here and give me some hearts!" But the room was completely empty.

As Ralph looked around, he wondered if he had **stumble**d **into** a library of some sort. He **spot**ted his name on a wall and went over to look at it, only to **realize** the wall was full of comments from various users.

He began reading aloud: "'Wreck-It Ralph is back.'" He laughed and said, "Oh, they're talking about *me*."

Ralph kept reading. "'Wreck-It Ralph? Seriously?'" He was confused, and said to himself, "Darn tootin', I'm serious."

He looked at another: "'*Fix-It Felix Jr.* was my favorite game.'" Ralph smiled and said, "Mine too."

Then he moved on to a different comment. "'Ralph's videos **stink**.'" His smile **fade**d as he stared at those three words. Yet another user commented with "'So stupid.'" He continued to read one bad comment after the other, even the one that had his name **misspell**ed—"'Ralf is

THE WORST' "—and, finally, "'I HATE HIM.' "

Ralph couldn't believe it. The people giving him hearts weren't laughing *with* him at all. They were **laugh**ing *at* him. Every single comment was **cruel**.

Yesss entered, looking for Ralph. It broke him out of his **spell**. "Yo, Ralph! You in here, **dude**? I gotta show you—"

Ralph turned around and Yesss **instant**ly saw the sadness in his eyes.

"Oh, Ralph. First rule of the Internet: Do not read the comments," she said softly. "Look, this place can **bring out** the worst in some people. But you gotta **ignore** all this. This isn't about you. It's about them."

"It's fine," said Ralph. "People always hated me for being a Bad Guy. I didn't have a single friend for the first twenty-seven years of my life. So all this—all these 'hearts' I've been getting? Good **reminder** that this is the only heart that matters." He pulled out his medal. "As long as Vanellope likes me, I don't need anybody else. And I sure as heck don't need the Internet."

"Okay, well, **hold on**, now," said Yesss. "It's not all

bad. The Internet can also be a place where you find a steering wheel at one website and make enough money to buy it at another one. **Congratulation**s, Ralph," she said, **grin**ning. "You did it."

"Wait, really?" said Ralph, **brighten**ing.

Yesss told him to check his **account**, and he pulled out his Buzzzy **device**. "You needed twenty-seven thousand and one," she said. "You got over thirty **grand**."

"All right!" cheered Ralph. "Oh my gosh, this is great! Thank you, Yesss. I couldn't have done it without you."

"That's really true," she said.

"Hey, eBoy!" Ralph called out. "Can you give me a ride?!"

The eBoy appeared and said happily, "You got it, **ace**!"

On the way, Ralph couldn't wait to tell Vanellope the good news. He reached for his Buzzzy device.

Vanellope sat on an Internet street corner, staring at a **puddle intense**ly, trying to **figure out** what she really wanted. "C'mon, song," she said to herself. "C'mon, c'mon. What is your dream?" But nothing came to her.

"Well, ladies. I tried. No song for this princess."

Suddenly, her Buzzzy device rang, **interrupt**ing her thoughts. Vanellope opened her phone, and Ralph's face appeared as a hologram.

"We did it, kid! We got the money!" he said.

"**No way**. Ralph, that's great," Vanellope said with mixed feelings.

"I'm on my way to eBay with the eBoy now. Meet me out front in five minutes?"

"Okay, I'll see you soon," said Vanellope.

"We're going home, kid! Our lives can finally go back to normal! Woo-hoo!" Ralph said, and **hung up**.

"Wow. I can't believe it. I get to go . . . home?" Vanellope said quietly. "I guess I do just want a steering wheel." Her excitement suddenly faded as the **reality** of going back to *Sugar Rush* set in. She knew she was supposed to feel happy, but for some reason, she didn't. After all they had been through, why wasn't she **thrill**ed to know she would be going back home? Vanellope looked at the puddle again and noticed something strange in its **reflect**ion. . . .

Chapter 15

In the **reflect**ion of the **puddle**, Vanellope could see . . . *Slaughter Race!* She **gasp**ed—and was suddenly **transport**ed into the game!

Then something even stranger happened. She began to sing! The song **pour**ed out of her, **rhyme**s **and all**, as she **stroll**ed through the high-octane[1] racing game, **exploring** and **admiring** its every crazy corner.

The dirty **pigeon**s, smelly rats, fallen **wire**s, and

---

1 octane 옥탄. 탄소 수가 8개이고 주로 석유 속에 있는 무색의 액체 포화 탄화수소이다.

burning tires Vanellope saw all **made** perfect **sense** to her. Shank and her **crew**—even the hungry shark, the **appliance thieves**, and a **creepy clown**—joined in and sang along. **Odd** as it was, they all seemed to **coordinate** their actions in a ballad² that Vanellope somehow loved with all her heart.

Through her song, Vanellope came to realize what she really wanted. Her princess friends had been right! Her heart's true desire was *not* to get the **steer**ing **wheel** and go back home to *Sugar Rush*. It was to stay in *Slaughter Race* and make it her new home! She sang and danced through the game, **overjoyed** at the **revelation**, until . . .

The full moon shining above **remind**ed her of Ralph's big head, and her **jubilance** turned to worry. If she followed her dream, she'd have to leave her best friend behind. Vanellope sat down and sighed. She knew Ralph would be absolutely **crush**ed if he found out she wanted to stay in *Slaughter Race*. But now that she knew her heart's true desire, how could she **ignore** it?

---

2 ballad 발라드. 사랑을 주제로 한 감상적인 노래.

Ralph, meanwhile, was still focused on his goal. After the eBoy **drop**ped Ralph **off** at eBay, he **slap**ped his BuzzzyBuxxx card on Elaine's **checkout counter**. "You'll find more than enough dollars in my **account** now," he said proudly. "So let's **get this show on the road**."

"Nothing would make me happier," Elaine said dryly. "Your *Sugar Rush* steering wheel will ship to Litwak's Family Fun Center today. **Congratulation**s."

"Woo-hoo, yes! That's how you do it, eBoy!" Ralph **high-five**d him on his way out the door.

"**Way to go, champ**!" the eBoy said. "That's what I call **cook**in' **with gas**."

Ralph waited outside for Vanellope and noticed Spamley **nearby**, trying to get new customers. When he spotted Ralph, he smiled and said hello.

"What's the good word, brother?" asked Spamley.

Ralph told him that he and Vanellope had made enough money to return home. Spamley was happy, but

Ralph **barely** noticed. He was **distract**ed, wondering where Vanellope was. He asked Spamley if he had seen her.

"Your little **chum**? No, sir, I have not," replied Spamley.

Ralph pulled out his phone and **dial**ed Vanellope on his BuzzzFace app.

Vanellope and Shank were sitting on the **hood** of Shank's car in *Slaughter Race*. Vanellope's Buzzzy device began **vibrating** on the **dashboard** inside the car, and with each **buzz**, it **crept** closer and closer to the edge, until it finally fell onto the floor. As the device hit the seat, the call was answered without Vanellope knowing. Ralph's **holographic** image appeared behind her.

"See over there—over that mountain?" said Shank, pointing. "That's the Sequoia[3] **Speedway**. It's gonna be **unlock**ed next month. My favorite coming up is Kawaii[4] **Rival**s. It's **adorable** and tough. Kinda like you."

Ralph was shocked to see Vanellope sitting with Shank.

---

3 Sequoia 세쿼이아. 미국과 뉴질랜드가 원산이며 세계에서 가장 큰 나무이다.
4 kawaii '사랑스럽다' 또는 '귀엽다'라는 뜻의 일본어.

"What are you doing in that **awful** game with her?" he said. But because the device was **mute**d, Vanellope didn't hear him. She continued to **chat** with Shank.

"The race will end right over there," Shank said. "It's gonna be so tight."

"Wow. I love it," said Vanellope.

Ralph realized they didn't notice his hologram and **pause**d to **eavesdrop**.

"Hey, can I tell you something that I don't think I could ever tell Ralph?" asked Vanellope.

"Of course. What is it?" said Shank.

"I know it sounds crazy . . . but the second I walked into this game, it felt, well, it felt like home. I mean, more than *Sugar Rush* ever did."

"Oh, yeah? How so?" asked Shank.

"Cause it's like my dream world," Vanellope admitted. "It's full of **weirdo**s, and the racing is super dangerous, and you never know what's going to happen next. I mean, back home I know exactly what's gonna happen next, cause Ralph's dream is to do the same thing every day."

"There's no law saying best friends have to have the

same dreams," Shank said.

"Whoa, yeah," said Vanellope, **taking in** her words. "You are a very wise person, Shank. And a good friend, too. Thank you."

"You can just say 'Shank you' if you want," she said with a **smirk**.

Vanellope laughed and **gaze**d out at *Slaughter Race.*

"You know," said Shank, "you can always come visit any time you want after you get your life back to normal."

"I don't want my life to be normal," Vanellope said. "I want *this* to be my life. I want to stay here. I can't go home. I just can't."

Unable to **bear** hearing another word, Ralph ended the call. He felt like someone had **punch**ed him in the heart.

"Well, that right there is a **kick in the teeth**, friend," said Spamley, who had been watching the whole thing over Ralph's shoulder.

"I can't believe it," said Ralph. "I thought she was supposed to be my best friend."

"A straight-up **donkey** kick," Spamley added, shaking

his head.

"She's been **brainwash**ed," said Ralph. "That's what this is. Cause the Vanellope I know would never **abandon** me. I gotta get her outta there right away."

"Easy, now, tiger," said Spamley. "I admire the **impulse**, but you **charge** in there like some kinda white **knight**, she's **liable** to **hold** it **against** you."

"So, what—I'm supposed to let her stay in a game that's **obvious**ly bad for her?" said Ralph.

"Course not," said Spamley.

"Then how do I make her leave, huh? She thinks it's so great and exciting in there. I mean, unless there's a way to slow down the game and make it boring, I dunno what to do," said Ralph.

Spamley **tap**ped a finger against his nose and checked to make sure no one was watching. With **the coast clear**, he **whisper**ed, "There's ways." He **gesture**d to Ralph to follow and said, "Come with me."

Chapter 16

Ralph followed Spamley down a dark **alley** where **creepy** characters spoke in **hush**ed voices to each other in the shadows. Ralph **overhear**d one say "I got mother's **maiden names**, social **security** numbers . . .[1]" before he returned his attention to his **companion**.

"Now, this area down here is what's called the Dark Net,[2]" explained Spamley. "Lotta **shady** characters **hang**

---

1 social security number 사회 보장 번호. 미국에서 출생과 함께 부여되는 개인 신원 번호.
2 Dark Net 접속을 위해서는 특정 프로그램을 사용해야 하는 네트워크를 가리킨다. 일반적인 방법으로 접속자나 서버를 확인할 수 없기 때문에 사이버상에서 저작권이 있는 디지털 파일을 불법 공유하는 등의 범죄에 활용된다.

out down here, so try to keep a low **profile**. GORD!"

At Spamley's call, Gord instantly appeared beside them.

"Oh, there you are," said Spamley. He turned to Ralph. "Now, Gord here, he has **dabble**d in **virus** making. But his **cousin**, the guy we're going to see—big ol' son of a gun who goes by the name of Double Dan—this dude is a virus-making machine." Spamley stopped at a door with **crack**ed paint around its **edge**s. "Here we go." He slowly turned the **knob**.

Ralph paused and **whisper**ed, "Are you sure this is safe?"

"Oh, of course it is. Just whatever you do—do *not* look at his little brother," warned Spamley.

"His little brother?" asked Ralph, **confuse**d.

The door **creak**ed as Spamley pushed it open and entered. Ralph and Gord followed him into the **rundown site**.

A huge **worm**, Double Dan, worked at a **lab** table, **stir**ring strange-looking **liquid**s inside glass beakers.[3]

---

3 beaker 비커. 원통 모양의 화학 실험용 유리그릇.

"Double Dan!" said Spamley. "Long time no see. How ya doing, **chum**?"

Double Dan looked up, **annoy**ed. "Who are you?"

"JP Spamley. We met one time over at Friendster,[4] which tells you it's been a little bit. . . ."

Even though he tried to avoid it, Spamley's eyes **drift**ed toward Double Dan's neck, where a small, **squishy** face stuck out and **utter**ed a **squeak**. It was **none other than** his brother, Little Dan. Double Dan reached out and **grab**bed Spamley by the **throat**. "What are you looking at?"

"Nothing," Spamley said quickly.

"You looking at my brother?" Double Dan asked in a **threatening tone**.

"No, sir," answered Spamley.

"I saw you," said Double Dan.

"Never."

"Don't you look at my little brother," ordered Double Dan.

---

4 Friendster 프랜스터. 초창기 소셜 네트워크 서비스로, 페이스북의 등장으로 붕괴되었다.

"I wasn't," said Spamley, working extra hard to keep his eyes away from Double Dan's neck.

"He's very **self-conscious**." Double Dan **hurl**ed Spamley at the wall and turned to Ralph. "Now," he said, taking a step closer. "What are *you* doing here?"

Ralph tried his best not to **stare** at Little Dan, but when Double Dan started to make an **odd** noise, Ralph couldn't help looking. "The reason I came to your neck of the face . . . ," Ralph began, **stumbling** over his words. "I mean, there's a face in your neck. I mean woods. **Neck of the woods** . . . The reason I'm here is because I heard a **tumor**—a *rumor*—that you could give me a **harmless** virus to slow down the *Slaughter Race* game?"

"Mmm, yes," said Double Dan. "My cousin Gordon told me that you want to **crash** it." Gord **pop**ped out from behind Spamley and **wave**d hello to Double Dan.

"Crash it?" said Ralph. "No, no, no. I don't want anyone getting hurt." He watched nervously as Double Dan **grunt**ed and went to work, searching through various **drawer**s and removing a variety of **chemical**s. "If there's a way to just, I dunno, make the cars go slow or something, just so the game is boring and my friend comes back home to me. That's all."

Double Dan **bent** down and picked up a **wooden container**.

"Allow me to introduce you to Arthur," he said. He opened the box and **reveal**ed a **terrify**ing virus that made both Ralph and Spamley **shriek**. "Arthur's what I call an **insecurity** virus. Means he looks for little **flaws** and **glitch**es that make a program insecure. You **release** him into that *Slaughter Race* game, and Arthur will find some **defect** in the **code**. Then what he'll do is he'll make millions of copies of said defect and he'll **distribute** the copies all over the game. And that is **guarantee**d to slow everything down in there and make the game **quote/**unquote 'boring,' just like you want." Double Dan placed the virus back in the box and closed it before handing it to Ralph.

"Okay, and just to be super clear here . . . no one gets hurt, right?" asked Ralph.

"Are you stupid?" asked Double Dan.

"Um—I . . . ," Ralph **stutter**ed.

"Because the only way anyone gets hurt is if you are stupid. All you have to do is make sure the virus stays in *Slaughter Race*."

"Don't be stupid and let the virus out of *Slaughter Race*," repeated Ralph. "Goiter[5] it. Er—*got it,* got it."

"GET OUT!" shouted Double Dan.

"Thank you, you're a **cyst** face," Ralph said, **inch**ing toward the door. "I mean, ***assistance***. Thank you for you're a cyst face. Assistance. You know what I mean. Goodbye!" He **clutch**ed the box and hurried out, more ready than ever to get his best friend back for good.

5　goiter 갑상선종. 갑상선이 커져서 목 부위가 부풀어 오르는 증상.

Chapter 17

Vanellope was having a wonderful time playing basketball with the **crew** in *Slaughter Race*. She **impress**ed everyone by **sink**ing a behind-the-back free throw[1] to win the game.

"Oh, fiddlesticks.[2] That's game," **groan**ed Pyro.

"Beginner's luck," said Vanellope with a **shrug**.

"Aw, come on, kid. I know a **hustle** when I see one," said Debbie, laughing.

---

1 free throw 자유투. 농구에서, 상대편이 반칙을 범하였을 때 일정한 지점에서 아무런 방해 없이 공을 던지는 일.
2 fiddlesticks '말도 안 돼'라는 뜻의 감탄사.

A **courier zip**ped by on a moped[3] and **announce**d that a player was on the way. Everyone headed toward their cars, **gear**ing **up** for the race.

"**Showtime**," said Shank, walking **alongside** Vanellope. "You ready for your first race?"

"I think so," said Vanellope. But then she began to **glitch**.

Shank told Vanellope not to be nervous. She tried to **encourage** her, but Vanellope continued glitching.

"You didn't tell Ralph yet, did you?" asked Shank.

"Not exactly," replied Vanellope.

"Come on, V. He's your best friend. You gotta let him know you're planning on staying here for a while."

"He's gonna get so **upset**," said Vanellope.

Shank stopped and turned to Vanellope. "Yeah, he might. But you guys will **work** it **out**."

"What if we don't?" asked Vanellope. "What if his feelings get hurt so bad that he doesn't want to be my friend anymore?"

---

3 moped 모페드. 보조기관을 장치한 자전거 또는 배기량 50cc 이하의 초경량 오토바이.

"Look, all **friendships** change," Shank told her. "And the good ones—they get stronger because of it."

A **horn honk**ed and Butcher Boy **yell**ed to them from his car, "I don't wanna **bother** you, Shank, but the player is waiting."

Shank turned her attention back to Vanellope. "I'm not gonna tell you what to do, kid. It's your call," she said.

"Okay . . . ," replied Vanellope, still unsure what to do. But she had no time to think—the race **was about to** begin.

"Let's race!" said Shank, jumping into her car and **peel**ing **out**.

While Vanellope was busy climbing into her own car, Ralph had managed to **release** the **virus** into *Slaughter Race*. **Immediate**ly, it began **scan**ning the area for insecurities.

The race started and a player quickly **caught up** to Shank, managing to **force** her into a wall. Shank **struggle**d as she tried to **break free, spin**ning her wheels. Vanellope appeared and **mimic**ked the move she had seen Shank do when they met. She **sped** up a **ramp** and **launch**ed herself into the air, **land**ing directly in front of the **startle**d player. He crashed, and Shank escaped!

"Power drift into a drift jump!" Shank said, **cheer**ing. "You're **amazing**!"

Vanellope **giggle**d. "Thank you!"

Meanwhile, the **worm** continued searching **every inch** of the game for insecurities, climbing up buildings and scanning different players' cars.

"Looks like we're not finished. C'mon, V. Let's take this guy!" said Shank as the player **regenerate**d from his crash in the near **distance**.

But Vanellope was **distract**ed. Something had **caught her eye** on top of a building. It **resemble**d Ralph. Vanellope spun out and slowed to a stop to take another look. She **realize**d it wasn't Ralph, but an **inflatable gorilla**! The thought of Ralph made Vanellope glitch, and she began to **panic**. "Okay. Relax. Relax," she said, trying to calm herself. "Just call him after the race. It'll be okay."

The worm **squirm**ing nearby **detect**ed Vanellope's glitch and **recognize**d it as an insecurity. It quickly copied the glitch and **distribute**d it throughout the entire game!

Suddenly, some of the buildings around her began to **flash**. She looked around, confused and shocked to see more and more parts of the game **breaking down** . . . and then everything was glitching! Not knowing what else to do, she raced off to find Shank.

Watching from outside the game, Ralph and Spamley could see that things weren't right.

"What's going on, Spamley?" asked Ralph. "The whole website's going crazy. I thought that virus was only supposed to slow down the game."

"It was!" **sputter**ed Spamley. "It must have found something real un**stable** in there."

Ralph knew right away. "It's her glitch," he said. "Oh, man. I gotta get her out of there. Spamley, you better go tell Double Dan."

"You got it," said Spamley. As Ralph **bolt**ed toward the **entrance** of *Slaughter Race,* Spamley shouted back to him, "Remember not to let the virus get outta that game!"

"Come on, kid!" yelled Shank. "The game is crashing! We gotta get you out of here."

"I think it's my glitch," said Vanellope. "I don't know how this is happening!"

"It doesn't matter. We'll be fine! But we have to get you out of here before the game re**boot**s! Follow me to the **exit**!" **urge**d Shank.

Vanellope and the other racers followed Shank out as the game began to fall apart. Clouds of **dust** filled the air as buildings **crumble**d to the ground and **smash**ed to bits. A **tower**ing **skyscraper** fell down, **separating** Vanellope from the group. She tried to **swerve** out of the way, but a **beam** fell on her car, **trap**ping her.

Ralph searched through the **rubble**. "Kid! Kid! Where are you?" he shouted.

"The **server** is rebooting, Ralph!" Shank said. "Both of you have to get out of here *now!*"

Finally, Ralph **spot**ted Vanellope and pulled her out of the **wreckage**. "There you are. Come on, stay with me!" he said. But Vanellope didn't respond. He threw her over his shoulder and bolted out of the game, **dodging** falling **debris** along the way.

Outside *Slaughter Race,* the firewalls[4] started to

close. Ralph **punch**ed a hole in one of the walls and **dove** through. He and Vanellope **spill**ed onto the ground outside the game.

"C'mon, Vanellope, wake up," Ralph **beg**ged **desperate**ly. "Come on. I can't live without you."

Vanellope's eyes **flutter**ed open. "Ralph," she said weakly.

"Oh, **thank goodness**," he said, **relieve**d.

"I **mess**ed up so bad, Ralph," said Vanellope sadly.

"No, kid," said Ralph. "It's not your fault."

"Yes, it is!" Vanellope shouted. "This is all because of me and my glitch. What was I thinking? You were right." She looked at Ralph. "This was a **dumb** idea, a stupid dream. . . ."

She started to cry, and Ralph put his arms around her. "Hey, it's okay," he said. Ralph searched his mind, trying to find the right words to cheer her up. "There's . . . there's no law saying friends have to have the same dreams," he added.

---

4 firewall 방화벽. 컴퓨터의 정보 보안을 위해 외부에서 내부, 내부에서 외부의 정보통신망에 불법으로 접근하는 것을 차단하는 시스템.

Vanellope stopped **sob**bing and looked up at him. "What did you say?" she asked.

"What did I say?" said Ralph.

She pulled away from him, **sniffling**. "'There's no law saying friends have to have the same dreams'—where did you hear that?" she asked.

"Um, where did I hear that?" Ralph **fumble**d, wishing he had kept his mouth shut.

"Hey, how did you know to **rescue** me in *Slaughter Race?*" asked Vanellope, now **suspicious** that there was something Ralph wasn't telling her.

Ralph **sigh**ed. He knew he was **busted**. "Look, the **attach**ment was just supposed to slow down the game. . . ."

"Attachment?" Vanellope asked, confused.

Ralph explained that the virus he let **loose** was supposed to be **harmless**, but Vanellope couldn't believe what she was hearing.

"*You* did this?" asked Vanellope, her voice rising in anger.

"Well, I wouldn't have done anything if I hadn't heard you tell Shank that you wanted to live in *Slaughter Race* forever," Ralph said **defensively**.

"Ah, so you *spied* on me," said Vanellope. "This just gets better by the minute."

"Hey, you're not exactly **innocent** here. You were gonna **ditch** everybody and **abandon** *Sugar Rush*," said Ralph.

"Come on, I'm one of eleven racers. They'd never miss me."

"Well, what about me?" asked Ralph.

"You?" said Vanellope, now **fuming**. "Why would I ever spend another second with you after what you did?" She grabbed Ralph's medal and threw it.

"No!" Ralph **gasp**ed as the medal fell to the ground. He looked to see Vanellope running away.

"I'm going back to find Shank. Don't even think about following me!" she said, disappearing.

Ralph had never felt so low. Even though Vanellope was gone, he spoke out loud as if she were there. "Vanellope, what am I supposed to do? What do I do?"

While he sat alone, the virus worm squirmed through the firewall hole and exited *Slaughter Race*. It quickly

picked **up on** Ralph, finding him to be one hundred percent insecure. Without anyone **noticing**, it copied Ralph's insecurity . . . and began to distribute it all over the Internet.

Ralph **made his way** down to the Older Net—the part of the Internet where spam mail[5] and **expire**d websites were **discard**ed—to **retrieve** his medal. When he finally found it, he discovered it had **split** in two. He sighed and sat on a **mound** of **garbage**. "You are such an **idiot**," he said.

Just then, he noticed something coming toward him. Something that looked an **awful** lot like . . . himself.

---

5 spam mail 스팸 메일. 인터넷 ID를 가진 사람에게 일방적으로 전달되는 전자우편으로, 정크 메일이라고도 한다.

Chapter 18

As Vanellope walked away from Ralph, she headed toward the Internet's **hub**,[1] where she and Ralph first arrived. She was on a **mission** to get as far away from him as possible when suddenly, she saw Ralph coming around the corner. She couldn't believe her eyes.

"What is your problem, Ralph? I told you not to follow me!" Vanellope shouted.

But something was off. He didn't say anything.

---

1 hub 허브. 컴퓨터나 프린터와 네트워크 연결, 근거리의 다른 네트워크와 연결, 라우터 등의 네트워크 장비와 연결, 네트워크 상태 점검, 신호 증폭 기능 등의 역할을 한다.

Instead, he started to run toward her. Vanellope screamed and ran away!

Vanellope quickly realized it wasn't Ralph **chasing** her at all. It was a **clone**! Soon a **horde** of similar clones started to follow.

Vanellope stopped and turned around to see that she was in far more trouble than she'd thought. She looked up and saw an **astonish**ing **sight**. She wasn't being chased by just one Ralph clone—but millions! The **army** of Ralph clones was **taking over** the Internet, climbing every website, and destroying everything in its path!

"Sweet mother of Ralph," said Vanellope as the clones **wreak**ed **havoc**.

An **announce**ment played on a website. "In breaking news,[2]" the news **anchor** said, "the Internet is under **assault** as a **massive** service attack crashes websites and **clog**s **server**s across the web. The **so-called** '**Wreck**-It Ralph' virus is fast-moving and **destructive. Expert**s are still trying to understand who or what the virus's intended

---

2 breaking news 긴급 보도. 뉴스 속보를 말한다.

target may be."

Vanellope didn't have time to think. As the news ended, several of the clones **spot**ted her and she was back to running away as fast as she could.

At his Search Bar, KnowsMore was helping answer a user's question. "I found one hundred and thirty results for 'Where does my high school girlfriend live now?'" he said.

"Mr. KnowsMore!" Vanellope shouted as she reached him.

He was absolutely **thrill**ed to see Vanellope. He'd been so busy answering questions for users that he had no **clue** what was happening around him. "Oh, **delightful**! You're that **courteous** little **cherub** who says 'please' and 'thank you.' What can KnowsMore help you find today?"

Vanellope tried to tell him what was wrong, but she was **out of breath**. "There's . . . a . . . whole . . ."

"A Whole Foods,[3] a hole in the ozone,[4] *Whole Lotta*

---

3 Whole Foods 홀푸드. 인공 보존제, 인공 색소 등 유해 첨가물을 넣지 않은 유기농 식품을 판매하는 미국의 슈퍼마켓 체인.
4 ozone 오존층. 지상에서 20~25킬로미터 상공에 위치하며 인체나 생물에 해로운 태양의 자외선을 잘 흡수하는 성질이 있다. 그러나 환경오염에 의해 오존층에 구멍이 생겨 파괴되고 있다.

Love by British rockers Led Zeppelin,[5]" said KnowsMore. His **autofill** was still **rapid**ly trying to guess her question.

"A whole **bunch** of Ralphs chasing me!" she **blurt**ed.

KnowsMore looked behind Vanellope and saw the clones making their way toward them. "Well, isn't that interesting?" he said. "This would probably be an **appropriate** time to **shutter** my site."

Vanellope helped KnowsMore close the shutters. They were safe for now, but it wouldn't **last** long. They could hear the Ralph clones **bang**ing against the shutters and doors outside, trying hard to get in. Vanellope and KnowsMore **stack**ed and **pile**d as many books as they could against the door to create a **barrier**.

"How long do you think we can **hold** them **back**, KnowsMore?" asked Vanellope.

"For **precise**ly one second," he answered.

Just then, the door **blast**ed open and a Ralph clone **lunge**d for Vanellope. She reached for a lamp and used it to hit him over the head.

---

5 Led Zeppelin 레드 제플린. 영국의 록 밴드로 1970년대에 블루스를 기반으로 한 하드 록과 헤비메탈의 대중화에 앞장섰다.

"Ow! It's me! It's me!" the clone shouted.

But Vanellope hadn't heard the clones actually speak before. "Ralph?"

"I'm so glad you're okay. I followed those things here. I think they're looking for you, kid," he said. It was the real Ralph after all!

Vanellope was relieved, but still **furious**. "Yeah, ya think?" she shot back.

More loud noises **erupt**ed as the clones tried to **break through** the **barricade**s. They weren't slowing down. Ralph and Vanellope needed a plan—and fast!

"What did you do?" Vanellope asked Ralph.

"I don't know," he replied. "I'm so sorry. I don't know how this happened."

Luckily, they were with someone who did. "It happened because an insecurity virus cloned all of your **needy**, **clingy**, self-destructive behavior," KnowsMore said. "The very behavior which, left **unchecked**, can destroy friendships and, in this particular case, may also destroy the entire Internet. Isn't that interesting?"

"So wrecking *Slaughter Race* wasn't enough for you,

huh?" Vanellope asked Ralph.

"I didn't mean to do it. I know I **screw**ed **up** bad. I know I did," Ralph started to say. But at this point, he wasn't sure what would make Vanellope forgive him. **Desperate**, he turned to KnowsMore. "You got all the answers. Whadda we do here? How do we get rid of these things?"

The question **trigger**ed KnowsMore's search mode and he **immediate**ly came back with an answer. "I found two results for your **query**. Either you put all of the clones in **therapy**, or," he said as he grabbed a book from his shelves, "**alternative**ly, there's an **archway** in the Anti-Virus **District** made out of **security** software. If Vanellope could somehow lead the clones through that **arch**, the security software would delete them all **at once**. It's sort of a **codependent** Pied Piper[6] situation."

"Wait," Vanellope said. "We know a Pied Piper."

"We do?" Ralph asked.

---

6 Pied Piper 독일 옛 이야기 속에 나오는 '하멜른의 피리 부는 사나이(the Pied Piper of Hamelin)' 를 말한다. 마법 피리를 불어 마을의 쥐를 퇴치하였으나 약속한 보수를 받지 못하자 마을 어린 이들을 피리 소리로 꾀어내 산 속에 숨겨 버렸다고 한다.

"Yesss," Vanellope said.

"Who is it?"

"Yesss!"

"Yes what? Oh," Ralph said, finally getting it. "You mean Yesss!"

"Yes!" Vanellope **exclaim**ed.

Just then, a **limo** flew in and **pull**ed **up** beside Ralph and Vanellope. It was Yesss! Ralph and Vanellope **hop**ped into the limo and escaped with her.

"Thanks for your help, KnowsMore!" Ralph shouted back to their friend.

KnowsMore looked around his site and saw how badly **damage**d it was. "Bit of an empty **gesture** at this point, wouldn't you say?" he said.

But the Ralph clones weren't done yet. Until they had Vanellope, they were **willing** to **demolish** everything in their path.

Chapter 19

Moments later, Ralph and Vanellope sat in Yesss's **limo**. Vanellope sat next to Yesss, still **fuming** over Ralph.

"I can't believe he did this," she said to Yesss.

"I've seen it a lot, actually," said Yesss. "Not to this **extent**, of course. But **I'm telling you**, reading the **comment**s, listening to the hate those trolls[1] **spew**—it can make a person do some crazy, **horrible** things."

"Whaddaya mean? What comments?"

---

1 troll 트롤. 남들의 화를 부추기기 위해 부정적이거나 선동적인 글 및 댓글을 인터넷에 게재하는 사람.

"Oh, he didn't tell you? Ralph got trolled hard for those videos he made for you. **Bunch** of **anonymous bullies** calling him **fat** and ugly and useless, saying 'I hate you.'"

"Oh, no," Vanellope said, feeling bad.

"Yeah, and I thought he was **handling** it. Cause he said as long as he had you, he was okay," said Yesss.

But Vanellope wasn't listening to Yesss anymore. She **hung her head**, **ashamed** of the way she had **treat**ed Ralph and **conflict**ed about her feelings.

Yesss continued. "I mean, **dude obvious**ly made some real bad choices here. But he also made a bee **pun** video to help his best friend, so . . . life's **complicated**, isn't it?"

Vanellope **nod**ded. Yesss was right. Life really was complicated, and in that moment, she had an idea that could possibly save all of them—and the Internet.

The limo flew close to the **clone**s and Vanellope called to them, "Yoo-hoo! Up here! It's me, your bestest friend in the whole wide world, who you can't live without!"

One of the clones **instant**ly stopped **wreck**ing things and began **chasing** her. Soon a hundred more clones appeared, following behind. Vanellope couldn't believe it! She turned back to see thousands of clones following the limo, trying to get to her. The plan was working!

"Wow," said Ralph. "From this view, I can see how I do look pretty **needy** and **clingy** and self-**destructive**. I don't **blame** you for not wanting to be my friend anymore."

"I never said I don't want to be your friend. I said you were *acting* like a bad friend, which you were," said Vanellope. "But no matter where I live or what I do, I will always be your friend, Ralph. And that will never change."

"How do you know that?" he asked.

"I don't know. I just do," she said.

"Hey, guys," Yesss said, **break**ing **in**. "That's the Anti-**Virus District** straight ahead. We're gonna **make it**!"

The limo **made its way** to the Anti-Virus **arch** even though the Ralph clones were hot on their **trail**.

"We're gonna make it!" **cheer**ed Ralph.

But as they **celebrate**d, the millions of clones **cluster**ed together and climbed on top of each other to form a giant,

rippling wave. The wave rose, then came down hard, **crash**ing right into the limo, causing it to fly out of control and straight through a Pinterest[2] window!

Ralph, Vanellope, and Yesss **crawl**ed out of the car, carefully stepping away from the broken glass. "You guys okay?" asked Ralph.

"I'm fine," said Vanellope, **dust**ing herself off.

"All good. We can still do this," said Yesss. "Come on, big man, help me turn this thing over." Yesss and Ralph worked to lift the limo.

Vanellope noticed a sudden quiet. She looked around **curious**ly, wondering where all the clones had gone. Then she saw them.

"Um, guys?" she said, her **jaw** nearly hitting the ground. Ralph and Yesss turned to see what Vanellope was **gawk**ing at: the millions of clones had **gather**ed again, but this time they formed an **enormous** and **terrify**ing giant Ralph! The **massive** clone focused on them, its huge eyes **peer**ing over a **rooftop**.

---

2 Pinterest 핀터레스트. 자신이 좋아하는 이미지나 사진을 공유, 검색, 스크랩하는 이미지 중심의 소셜 네트워크 서비스이다.

"That is **unsettling**," said Ralph. "Get Vanellope outta here now," he added as Giant Ralph began to climb up the side of a tall building. Vanellope was worried about him, but Ralph **insist**ed she go. Then he **grab**bed a huge one-hundred-foot-long[3] **pushpin** from a website and stepped toward the **beast**. "Hey, you! You keep away from her!" he **yell**ed, **wield**ing the pin like a **club**. "I'm gonna wreck it!" He ran, jumped, and **swung** with all his **might**. "She's not your friend. She's *my* friend!" he yelled.

As Ralph battled the beast, Yesss led Vanellope toward an **exit**. Vanellope **paus**ed, looking back at Ralph, but Yesss **forced** her toward a website, trying to help her escape.

With a **flick** of its giant finger, the **colossal** clone **hurl**ed Ralph and threw the pin at him. Ralph **winced** as it **blaze**d by, missing him **by a hair**. He quickly grabbed the pin and **chuck**ed it at Giant Ralph, **knock**ing him **off-balance**. Giant Ralph **stagger**ed into the website that Vanellope and Yesss were running through, causing it to

---

3 foot/feet 길이의 단위 피트. 1피트는 약 30.48센티미터이다. (복수형은 feet이지만 뒤에 tall이나 long이 붙는 경우 feet 대신에 foot을 사용한다.)

sway. Vanellope was thrown clear off the **site**, and she **clung** to the side of a **nearby** building. She screamed as she began to lose her **grip**, **dangling** off the **edge**.

"Kid! **Hang on**! Hang on!" Ralph called.

The building **tremble**d and Vanellope fell. Surprisingly, Giant Ralph reached over and caught her in its giant hand!

"Let go of me!" shouted Vanellope. But the beast held her in its **clutch**es and **took off** running.

"Kid! Kid!" said Ralph, chasing them. "Hey, hey, get back here! You put her down! Vanellope!" Ralph jumped up onto another website, but the massive Ralph knocked it over. Ralph **dove** into an email truck just **in time** and managed to avoid being **crush**ed, but he could only watch **helpless**ly as Giant Ralph, still holding Vanellope, began to **scale** the **tower**ing Google site. At the very top, Giant Ralph paused and looked at Vanellope.

"You know, you're acting like a real Bad Guy here!" she shouted.

The clones **grunt**ed angrily. They didn't like hearing her say that.

Meanwhile, Ralph **snag**ged a flying email truck, which he used to get to the top of the website.

"Sheesh, so **sensitive**," Vanellope said to the clones, not backing down. Suddenly, she came up with an escape plan. "Hey! Wanna play I **spy**?"

Giant Ralph grunted and nodded.

"That's right," she said. "I spy with my little eye . . . something that's big and yellow and is right behind you!"

Giant Ralph looked around and didn't see anything, which gave Vanellope a chance to run.

Meanwhile, the real Ralph had been scaling the website. He saw Vanellope jump and safely caught her. "I gotcha, kid!" he said.

"What are you doing?" Vanellope asked.

"I'm saving you!" he replied.

"I was handling it, Ralph. I **was** just **about to** get away!"

"Well, how was I supposed to know that?"

"Where do you think you're even going?" Vanellope asked.

"I don't know," Ralph answered honestly. "I didn't

think that far ahead."

They finally reached the top of the highest **construction block** they could find. But Giant Ralph **caught up**—and grabbed Vanellope and Ralph! It held Vanellope in its left hand while it **squeeze**d Ralph in its right hand with all its might.

"Stop it!" shouted Vanellope. "You're **squish**ing him! You're gonna kill him!" Giant Ralph wouldn't stop squeezing. "Take me! You can have me all to yourself! Just put him down. I'll be your only friend."

"No, kid," Ralph **plead**ed.

"**That's it**," Vanellope said **reassuring**ly to Giant Ralph. "Put him down and take me. I know that's what you want."

"No! That is not what *I* want!" Ralph said. "It's not right to **hold** a friend **back** from her dreams. You don't own her. That's not how **friendship** works. You need to let her go."

Suddenly, Giant Ralph stopped to listen to what Ralph was saying.

"You need to let her go. I know it's gonna hurt a little

bit when you do. Heck, who am I **kid**ding? It's gonna hurt *a lot*. But you're gonna be okay," Ralph said. Then he said to Vanellope, "And we're gonna be okay—right, kid?"

"Of course we are," Vanellope said. "Always."

Giant Ralph **blink**ed as the words **settle**d in. It lowered its huge hand and gently set Vanellope on top of a nearby website.

"Thanks, **buddy**," Vanellope said.

"I feel good about this," Ralph said.

One by one, the clones began to disappear. "Ralph, look!" said Vanellope. "I think you fixed your **insecurity**!"

Relieved, Ralph cheered, "Woo-hoo!" But once they'd all disappeared, he had nothing left to hold on to—and he was a thousand feet above the ground! "Oh, no!" he screamed as he began to fall.

"Ralph! No!" Vanellope shouted.

Just before Ralph crashed into the ground, the Oh My Disney princesses **swoop**ed in and **rescue**d him.

"Look! Up there!" Belle **exclaim**ed. "It's a big strong man in need of rescuing!"

All the princesses **sprang** into action. They worked

together to help, each one using her own special skill. Moana made a wave that Elsa **froze** so Ralph could **slide** down it before **launch**ing into the air again. With a variety of objects, **including** dresses, a **poison** apple, and a rope made out of hair, they had built a "haira**chute**" to slow Ralph's fall.

"The hairachute is working, you guys!" Ariel said.

Pocahontas used her wind power to push Ralph's chute toward a **mattress** website, causing him to **land** on top of a **plush**, **comfy** bed.

Tiana brought a frog over to kiss him, and when he awoke, he looked around, **confuse**d.

"Who are you guys?" he asked.

"Oh, we're with Vanellope," Pocahontas explained.

"Yeah, any friend of Vanellope's is a friend of ours," added Elsa.

Moana looked at Ralph and smiled. "You're welcome."

It wasn't long before **journalist**s reported the good news:

"Internet users are breathing a **collective sigh** of relief. Just as **mysterious**ly as it had appeared, the Wreck-It Ralph virus has now **vanish**ed."

Ralph and Vanellope sat on a **bench** at a bus stop in the Internet.

"Y'know what I just **realize**d?" said Ralph. "The sun never rises or sets here. Cause everything's always on."

"Well, now, isn't that an **astute observation**," said Vanellope.

"I know," said Ralph with a **grin**. "Other than KnowsMore, I'm probably the smartest guy in the Internet."

Vanellope agreed and **giggle**d.

Shank called out from the **entrance** to *Slaughter Race* across the street. "Hey, V. We're about to come back online. You ready?"

"Be right there!" shouted Vanellope.

"Don't be a stranger, Ralph!" said Shank.

"I can't be much stranger than you," replied Ralph.

"Ooh, that's a good dad **joke**," Shank laughed as she entered *Slaughter Race*.

Vanellope turned to Ralph, trying to **figure out** what to say next. "Hey, don't forget—Shank added my **code** and everything, so I'll be able to **regenerate**. I'll be totally safe."

"No, I know. It's gonna be great. You'll be fine. You found your dream game."

"Yeah, I did. I did. So, I should probably . . . head in there now, you know. . . ."

"Oh, before you go, I wanted to give you this." Ralph reached into his pocket and handed her half of his broken heart medal.

"Oh, gosh. I'm so sorry I broke it," said Vanellope.

"No, no, it's okay. Now we can both have a half. See?" Ralph showed her his half, hanging around his neck.

Vanellope jumped into his arms and hugged him tightly. Their medals came together to form a complete heart.

"I love you so much," she said. "I'm really gonna miss you."

"I'm gonna miss you, too," said Ralph. "All right, okay. Getting a little clingy on me. Get outta here. The world's waiting for ya, kid."

She sprang out of his arms and ran toward *Slaughter Race*. Just before she reached the entrance, she looked back to see Ralph standing there with a hand up, smiling through his tears. A car **sped** by between them, and when it had passed, Vanellope was gone. Ralph turned and walked away alone.

Chapter 20

A few months later, Ralph sat in Game Central **Station** at Litwak's Family Fun Center and **Arcade**, talking on the phone with Vanellope.

"I'll be honest," Ralph said, "it still feels kinda **weird** around here. I mean, a lot has changed. Even though we got the **wheel** and saved *Sugar Rush,* it's never really gonna be the same. **For starters**, the **race**rs aren't even that **obnoxious** anymore. Raising ten kids has changed Felix and Calhoun, too." He **went on** to **mention** that even **Surge** Protector had **notice**d and **compliment**ed

Felix and Calhoun on a job well done.

"I'm also keeping busy," Ralph said, and told her about a book club he'd joined.

"Oh, and we got this new thing we do every Friday night where we all go **hang out** in a different game. I actually **host**ed this week," explained Ralph. He'd **set up** picnic tables and games out by his **brick pile** and everyone had a great time. He even brought **burn**ed pie—a recipe he'd found on the Internet. "We really do have a lot of fun." Ralph was **grateful**. "I guess that's pretty much all the news I got for you."

Vanellope smiled, her hologram **hover**ing above Ralph's Buzzzy **device** as the two **chat**ted. "Well, your stories never **disappoint**," she said. "I just wish we could hang out sooner."

"When'd you say you were getting those days off?" Ralph asked.

"Like, three months from now," Vanellope said.

"It'll go by in a **flash**," Ralph said. "Hey, you want me to bring you anything from home when I visit?"

"You know what's impossible to find on the Internet?"

said Vanellope. "A **halfway decent** burger." She missed the ones she and Ralph used to eat together in the arcade.

"I'll bring you guys a **truckload**," Ralph said. Just then, he noticed some characters heading toward their games as **daylight** began to break. "Well, the sun's coming up already. Guess I better get to it."

"Yup. Me too," Vanellope said. "Talk next week?"

"I shall await your call," he said.

"Then **adieu**," Vanellope said to her friend. "**Fart**ing[1] is such sweet **sorrow**. **So long**, **Stink** Brain!"

"Bye, kid," Ralph said.

Vanellope's hologram disappeared, and Ralph closed his eyes for a moment, **taking in** the rising sun.

Felix approached. "You doing okay, Ralph?" he asked.

Ralph smiled. "Actually, I'm doing great," he replied. "Let's go to work, **pal**."

As he rose from the **bench**, Ralph looked down at the half medal hanging around his neck and smiled. He knew that no matter how great the **distance** was between them, Vanellope would always be his best friend.

1　farting 방귀. 'parting(이별)'과 발음이 비슷한 단어를 사용해서 농담을 하고 있다.

CONTENTS

오락실 게임 세계를 넘어, 이제는 인터넷 속으로!
인터넷 세상에서 펼쳐지는 주먹왕 랄프와 바넬로피의 환상적인 모험!

디즈니의 〈주먹왕 랄프 2: 인터넷 속으로〉는 오락실 게임 캐릭터들이 오락실 영업 시간이 지난 다음에는 우리와 같은 일상을 산다는 이야기를 담아 2012년 개봉 당시 전 세계적으로 엄청난 흥행을 기록한 애니메이션 〈주먹왕 랄프〉의 속편입니다.

전작에서 게임 세계를 발칵 뒤집어 놓았던 주먹왕 랄프와 바넬로피는 절친한 사이가 되어 6년 동안 즐겁게 지냅니다. 그러던 어느 날, 변화 없는 삶에 지루해하는 바넬로피를 위해서 랄프는 그녀의 게임 '슈가 러시(Sugar Rush)'에 경주로를 직접 만들어 줍니다. 바넬로피는 매우 기뻐하며 새 경주로를 즐기며 실제 오락실에서 게임을 하고 있는 아이의 조종을 따르지 않고 마음대로 움직였고, 그 와중에 게임기의 조종 핸들이 뽑히는 사고가 일어납니다. 설상가상으로 오락실의 주인 리트왁 씨가 떨어진 핸들을 다시 끼우려고 하다가 핸들이 완전히 부서집니다. 리트왁 씨는 이베이(eBay)라는 인터넷 사이트에서 조종 핸들을 팔고 있다는 정보를 알게 되지만, 너무 비싼 가격 때문에 슈가 러시를 금요일에 고물상에 팔겠다고 하고 게임 기계의 플러그를 뽑아 버립니다. 가까스로 게임 밖으로 탈출한 바넬로피와 '슈가 러시' 캐릭터들은 졸지에 게임과 집을 잃은 신세가 됩니다.

게임을 잃어 상심한 바넬로피를 위해 랄프는 이베이로 가서 조종 핸들을 가져오겠다고 결심합니다. 그렇게 바넬로피와 랄프는 조종 핸들을 찾아 와이파이를 타고 인터넷으로 접속합니다. 하지만 인터넷 세상은 그들이 이제까지 경험했던 것과 너무 달라서 두 친구들을 혼란스럽게 합니다.

오락실 게임 캐릭터에 불과한 바넬로피와 랄프는 정신없이 복잡한 인터넷 속에서 무사히 슈가 러시의 조종 핸들을 찾아낼 수 있을까요? 사랑할 수밖에 없는 오락실 게임 캐릭터들이 일으키는 좌충우돌 모험을 담은 〈주먹왕 랄프 2: 인터넷 속으로〉를 지금 영어 원서로 읽어 보세요!

한국인을 위한 맞춤형 영어원서!

원서 읽기는 모두가 인정하는 최고의 영어 공부법입니다. 하지만 영어 구사력이 뛰어나지 않은 보통 영어 학습자들에게는 원서 읽기를 선뜻 시작하기가 부담되는 것도 사실이지요.

이 책은 영어 초보자들도 쉽게 원서 읽기를 시작하고, 꾸준한 읽기를 통해 '영어원서 읽기 습관'을 형성할 수 있도록 만들어진 책입니다. 남녀노소 누구나 좋아할 만한 내용의 원서를 기반으로 내용 이해와 영어 실력 향상을 위한 다양한 콘텐츠를 덧붙였고, 리스닝과 낭독 훈련에 활용할 수 있는 오디오북까지 함께 제공하여, 원서를 부담 없이 읽으면서 자연스럽게 영어 실력이 향상되도록 도와줍니다.

특히 원서와 워크북을 분권하여 휴대와 학습이 효과적으로 이루어지도록 배려했습니다. 일반 원서에서 찾아볼 수 없는 특장점으로, 워크북과 오디오북을 적절히 활용하면 더욱 쉽고 재미있게 영어 실력을 향상시킬 수 있습니다. ('원서'와 '워크북' 및 '오디오북 MP3 CD'의 3가지 패키지가 이상 없이 갖추어져 있는지 다시 한 번 확인해보세요!)

이런 분들께 강력 추천합니다!

- 영어원서 읽기를 처음 시작하는 독자
- 쉽고 재미있는 원서를 찾고 있는 영어 학습자
- 영화 『주먹왕 랄프 2』를 재미있게 보신 분
- 특목고 입시를 준비하는 초·중학생
- 토익 600~750점, 고등학교 상위권 수준의 영어 학습자
- 엄마표 영어를 위한 교재를 찾고 있는 부모님

본문 텍스트

내용이 담긴 본문입니다.
원어민이 읽는 일반 원서와 같은 텍스트지만, 암기해야 할 중요 어휘들은 볼드체로 표시되어 있습니다. 이 어휘들은 지금 들고 계신 워크북에 챕터별로 정리되어 있습니다.

학습 심리학 연구 결과에 따르면, 한 단어씩 따로 외우는 단어 암기는 거의 효과가 없다고 합니다. 대신 단어를 제대로 외우기 위해서는 문맥(Context) 속에서 단어를 암기해야 하며, 한 단어 당 문맥 속에서 15번 이상 마주칠 때 완벽하게 암기할 수 있다고 합니다.

이 책의 본문은 중요 어휘를 볼드로 강조하여, 문맥 속의 단어들을 더 확실히 인지(Word Cognition in Context)하도록 돕고 있습니다. 또한 대부분의 중요한 단어들은 다른 챕터에서도 반복해서 등장하기 때문에 이 책을 읽는 것만으로도 자연스럽게 어휘력을 향상시킬 수 있습니다.

또한 본문에는 내용 이해를 돕기 위해 '각주'가 첨가되어 있습니다. 각주는 굳이 암기할 필요는 없지만, 알아두면 내용을 더 깊이 있게 이해할 수 있어 원서를 읽는 재미가 배가됩니다.

워크북(Workbook)의 구성

Check Your Reading Speed
해당 챕터의 단어 수가 기록되어 있어, 리딩 속도를 측정할 수 있습니다. 특히 리딩 속도를 중시하는 독자들이 유용하게 사용할 수 있습니다.

Build Your Vocabulary
본문에 볼드 표시되어 있는 단어들이 정리되어 있습니다. 리딩 전, 후에 반복해서 보면 원서를 더욱 쉽게 읽을 수 있고, 어휘력도 빠르게 향상됩니다.

단어는 〈빈도 – 스펠링 – 발음기호 – 품사 – 한글 뜻 – 영문 뜻〉 순서로 표기되어 있으며 빈도 표시(★)가 많을수록 필수 어휘입니다. 반복 등장하는 단어는 빈도 대신 '복습'으로 표기되어 있습니다. 품사는 아래와 같이 표기했습니다.

n. 명사 │ a. 형용사 │ ad. 부사 │ v. 동사
conj. 접속사 │ prep. 전치사 │ int. 감탄사 │idiom 숙어 및 관용구

Comprehension Quiz
간단한 퀴즈를 통해 읽은 내용에 대한 이해력을 점검해 볼 수 있습니다.

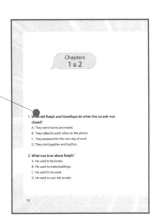

영어원서 읽기, 이렇게 시작해보세요!!

아래와 같이 프리뷰(Preview) → 리딩(Reading) → 리뷰(Review) 세 단계를 거치면서 원서를 읽으면, 더욱 효과적으로 영어실력을 향상할 수 있습니다!

1. 프리뷰(Preview) : 오늘 읽을 내용을 먼저 점검한다!

- 워크북을 통해 오늘 읽을 Chapter에 나와 있는 단어들을 쭉 훑어봅니다. 어떤 단어들이 나오는지, 내가 아는 단어와 모르는 단어가 어떤 것들이 있는지 가벼운 마음으로 살펴봅니다.

- 평소처럼 하나하나 쓰면서 암기하려고 하지는 마세요! 그렇게 해서는 원서를 읽기도 전에 지쳐 쓰러져버릴 것입니다. 익숙하지 않은 단어들을 주의 깊게 보되, 어차피 리딩을 하면서 점차 익숙해질 단어라는 것을 잊지 말고 빠르게 훑어봅니다.

- 뒤 Chapter로 갈수록 '복습'이라고 표시된 단어들이 늘어나는 것을 알 수 있습니다. '복습' 단어인데도 여전히 익숙하지 않다면 더욱 신경을 써서 봐야겠죠? 매일매일 꾸준히 읽는다면, 익숙한 단어들이 점점 많아진다는 것을 몸으로 느낄 수 있습니다.

2. 리딩(Reading) : 내용에 집중하며 빠르게 읽어가자!

- 프리뷰를 마친 후 바로 리딩을 시작합니다. 방금 살펴봤던 어휘들을 문장 속에서 다시 만나게 되는데 이 과정에서 단어의 쓰임새와 어감을 자연스럽게 익히게 됩니다.

- 모르는 단어, 이해 가지 않는 문장이 나오더라도 멈추지 말고 전체적인 맥락을 잡아가면서 스피디하게 읽어가세요. 특히 영화를 먼저 보고 책을 읽으면 맥락을 통해 읽을 수 있어 훨씬 수월합니다.

- 이해 가지 않는 문장들은 따로 표시를 하되, 일단 넘어가서 계속 읽는 것이 좋습니다. 뒷부분을 읽다 보면 자연히 이해가 되는 경우도 있고, 정 이해가 되지 않는 부분은 리딩을 마친 이후에 따로 리뷰하는 시간을 가지면 됩니다. 문제집을 풀듯이 모든 문장을 분석하면서 원서를 읽는 것이 아니라, 리딩할 때는 리딩에만, 리뷰할 때는 리뷰에만 집중하는 것이 필요합니다.

- 볼드 처리된 단어의 의미가 궁금하더라도, 워크북을 바로 펼치지 마세요. 정 궁금하다면 한 번씩 참고하는 것도 나쁘진 않지만, 워크북과 원서를 번갈아

보면서 읽는 것은 리딩의 흐름을 끊고 단어 하나하나에 집착하는 좋지 않은 리딩 습관을 만들 수 있습니다.

- 초보자라면 분당 150단어의 리딩 속도를 목표로 잡아서 리딩을 합니다. 분당 150단어는 원어민이 말하는 속도로, 영어 학습자들이 리스닝과 스피킹으로 넘어가기 위해 가장 기초적으로 달성해야 하는 단계입니다. 분당 50~80단어 정도의 낮은 리딩 속도를 가지고 있는 경우는 대부분 영어 실력이 부족해서라 기보다 '잘못된 리딩 습관'을 가지고 있어서 그렇습니다. 이해력이 조금 떨어진 다고 하더라도 분당 150단어까지는 속도에 대한 긴장감을 놓치지 말고 스피디 하게 읽어나가도록 하세요.

- 이미 150단어 이상의 리딩 속도에 도달한 상태라면, 각자의 상황에 맞게 원서를 보다 다양한 방식으로 활용해보세요. 이에 대한 자세한 조언이 워크북 말미에 실려 있습니다.

3. 리뷰(Review) : 이해력을 점검하고 꼼꼼하게 다시 살펴보자!

- 해당 Chapter의 Comprehension Quiz를 통해 이해력을 점검해봅니다.

- 오늘 만난 어휘도 다시 한 번 복습합니다. 읽으면서 중요하다고 생각했던 단어를 연습장에 써보면서 꼼꼼하게 외우는 것도 좋습니다.

- 이해가 되지 않는다고 표시해뒀던 부분도 주의 깊게 분석해봅니다. 다시 한 번 문장을 꼼꼼히 읽고, 어떤 이유에서 이해가 되질 않았는지 생각해봅니다. 따로 메모를 남기거나 노트를 작성하는 것도 좋은 방법입니다.

- 사실 꼼꼼히 리뷰하는 것은 매우 고된 과정입니다. 원서를 읽고 리뷰하는 시간을 가지는 것은 영어 실력 향상에 많은 도움이 되긴 하나, 이 과정을 철저히 지키려다가 원서 읽기의 재미를 반감시키는 것은 바람직하지 않습니다. 그럴 때는 차라리 리뷰를 가볍게 하는 것이 좋을 수 있습니다. '내용에 빠져서 재미있게', 문제집에서는 상상도 못할 '많은 양'을 읽으면서, 매일매일 조금씩 꾸준히 실력을 향상하는 것이 원서를 활용하는 기본적인 방법이며, 영어 공부의 왕도입니다. 문제집 풀듯이 원서 읽기를 시도하고 접근해서는 실패할 수밖에 없습니다.

1. **What did Ralph and Vanellope do when the arcade was closed?**
   A. They went home and rested.
   B. They talked to each other on the phone.
   C. They prepared for the next day of work.
   D. They met together and had fun.

2. **What was true about Ralph?**
   A. He used to be lonely.
   B. He used to make buildings.
   C. He used to be weak.
   D. He used to own the arcade.

3. How did Ralph feel about his current life?

   A. He felt confused about it.

   B. He felt satisfied with it.

   C. He felt disappointed with it.

   D. He felt ashamed of it.

4. What did Surge Protector think of Wi-Fi?

   A. He thought it was cool because it was new.

   B. He thought it was a magical place to shop.

   C. He thought it was hard for humans to use.

   D. He thought it was a threat because it was different.

5. Why was Vanellope unhappy with her game?

   A. She never won first place.

   B. There were no bonus levels.

   C. The game was no longer challenging.

   D. The tracks were too difficult.

CHAPTER 1

Check Your Reading Speed

1분에 몇 단어를 읽는지 리딩 속도를 측정해보세요.

$$\frac{765 \text{ words}}{\text{reading time ( ) sec}} \times 60 = (\quad) \text{ WPM}$$

Build Your Vocabulary

* **wreck** [rek] v. 파괴하다; 엉망으로 만들다; n. 충돌; 사고 잔해
  To wreck something means to completely destroy or ruin it.

arcade [ɑ:rkéid] n. 게임 센터, 오락실
  An arcade is a place where you can play games on machines which work when you put money in them.

‡ **race** [reis] v. 경주하다; 쏜살같이 가다; (머리·심장 등이) 바쁘게 돌아가다; n. 경주; 인종, 종족
  If you race, you take part in a race.

‡ **station** [stéiʃən] n. 역; 본부, 장소; 부서; 위치; v. 배치하다
  A station is a building by a railway line where trains stop so that people can get on or off.

hang out idiom 많은 시간을 보내다
  If you hang out in a place or with a person or a group of people, you spend a lot of time in there or with them.

goof [gu:f] v. 빈둥거리다; 바보 같은 실수를 하다; n. 바보, 멍청이
  If you goof around, you spend your time doing silly or stupid things.

‡ **bench** [benʧ] n. 벤치; 판사(석)
  A bench is a long seat of wood or metal that two or more people can sit on.

* **spy** [spai] v. (갑자기) 보다, 알아채다; 염탐하다; n. 스파이, 정보원
  If you spy someone or something, you notice them.

* **dot** [dat] n. 점; v. 여기저기 흩어져 있다, 산재하다; 점을 찍다
  A dot is a very small round mark, for example one that is used as the top part of the letter 'i,' as a full stop, or as a decimal point.

refer [rifɔ́:r] v. 지시하다, 나타내다; 언급하다, 입 밖에 내다; 참조하게 하다
If you refer to a particular subject or person, you talk about them or mention them.

obvious [ábviəs] a. 분명한, 확실한; 명백한
If something is obvious, it is easy to see or understand.

amaze [əméiz] v. (대단히) 놀라게 하다; 경악하게 하다 (amazed a. 놀란)
If something amazes you, it surprises you very much.

process [práses] n. (특정 결과를 달성하기 위한) 과정; v. 처리하다
A process is a series of actions which are carried out in order to achieve a particular result.

hop [hap] v. 급히 움직이다; 깡충깡충 뛰다; n. 깡충깡충 뛰기
If you hop somewhere, you move there quickly or suddenly.

make one's way idiom 나아가다, 가다
When you make your way somewhere, you walk or travel there.

guzzle [gʌzl] v. 마구 마셔 대다; 마구 먹어 대다
If you guzzle something, you drink it or eat it quickly and greedily.

counter [káuntər] n. (식당·바 등의) 카운터; 계산대; 반작용; v. 대응하다; 반박하다
In a place such as a shop or café a counter is a long narrow table or flat surface at which customers are served.

chat [tʃæt] v. 이야기를 나누다, 수다를 떨다; n. 이야기, 대화
When people chat, they talk to each other in an informal and friendly way.

sign [sain] n. 몸짓, 신호; 표지판; 기색, 흔적; v. 서명하다; 신호를 보내다
A sign is a movement of your arms, hands, or head which is intended to have a particular meaning.

pinky [píŋki] n. 새끼손가락
Your pinky is the smallest finger on your hand.

fire [faiər] v. 발사하다; (엔진이) 점화되다; 해고하다; n. 화재, 불; 발사, 총격
If someone fires a gun or a bullet, or if they fire, a bullet is sent from a gun that they are using.

imaginary [imǽdʒənèri] a. 상상에만 존재하는, 가상적인
An imaginary person, place, or thing exists only in your mind or in a story, and not in real life.

loser [lúːzər] n. (경쟁에서) 패자; 실패자, 패배자
The losers of a game, contest, or struggle are the people who are defeated or beaten.

joke [dʒouk] v. 농담하다; 농담 삼아 말하다; n. 농담; 웃음거리
If you joke, you tell someone something that is not true in order to amuse yourself.

declare [diklɛ́ər] v. 분명히 말하다; 선언하다, 공표하다
If you declare that something is true, you say that it is true in a firm, deliberate way.

swamp [swamp] n. 늪, 습지; v. 쇄도하다
A swamp is an area of very wet land with wild plants growing in it.

log [lɔːg] n. 통나무
A log is a piece of a thick branch or of the trunk of a tree that has been cut so that it can be used for fuel or for making things.

abandon [əbǽndən] v. 버리다; 버리고 떠나다; 그만두다
If you abandon a place, thing, or person, you leave the place, thing, or person permanently or for a long time, especially when you should not do so.

overboard [óuvərbɔːrd] ad. 배 밖으로, (배 밖의) 물속으로
If you fall overboard, you fall over the side of a boat into the water.

nearby [nìərbái] a. 인근의, 가까운 곳의; ad. 가까운 곳에
If something is nearby, it is only a short distance away.

flail [fleil] v. 마구 움직이다; (팔다리를) 마구 흔들다
If your arms or legs flail or if you flail them about, they wave about in an energetic but uncontrolled way.

plunge [plʌndʒ] v. (갑자기) 거꾸러지다; 급락하다; n. (갑자기) 떨어져 내림; 급락
If something or someone plunges in a particular direction, especially into water, they fall, rush, or throw themselves in that direction.

realize [ríːəlàiz] v. 깨닫다, 알아차리다; 실현하다, 달성하다
If you realize that something is true, you become aware of that fact or understand it.

basically [béisikəli] ad. 근본적으로, 원래
You use basically for emphasis when you are stating an opinion, or when you are making an important statement about something.

float [flout] v. (물 위나 공중에서) 떠가다; (물에) 뜨다; n. 부표
Something that floats in or through the air hangs in it or moves slowly and gently through it.

universe [júːnəvəːrs] n. 우주; 은하계; (특정한 유형의) 경험 세계
The universe is the whole of space and all the stars, planets, and other forms of matter and energy in it.

tiny [táini] a. 아주 작은
Something or someone that is tiny is extremely small.

speck [spek] n. 작은 얼룩, 반점
A speck is a very small stain, mark, or shape.

dust [dʌst] n. 먼지, 티끌; v. 먼지를 털다; (고운 가루를) 뿌리다
Dust is very small dry particles of earth or sand.

toss [tɔːs] v. (가볍게) 던지다; (고개를) 홱 쳐들다; n. 던지기
If you toss something somewhere, you throw it there lightly, often in a rather careless way.

back and forth idiom 여기저기에, 왔다갔다; 좌우로; 앞뒤로
If someone moves back and forth, they repeatedly move in one direction and then in the opposite direction.

nature [néiʧər] n. 본질; 천성, 본성; 자연
The nature of something is its basic quality or character.

existence [igzístəns] n. 존재, 실재, 현존
The existence of something is the fact that it is present in the world as a real thing.

bum [bʌm] n. 게으름뱅이, 쓸모없는 사람; v. ~를 화나게 하다
If someone refers to another person as a bum, they think that person is worthless or irresponsible.

pal [pæl] n. 친구; 이봐
Your pals are your friends.

punch [pʌnʧ] v. 주먹으로 치다; (자판·번호판 등을) 치다; n. 주먹으로 한 대 침
If you punch someone or something, you hit them hard with your fist.

fist [fist] n. 주먹
Your hand is referred to as your fist when you have bent your fingers in toward the palm in order to hit someone, to make an angry gesture, or to hold something.

goalpost [góulpoust] n. 골대, 골포스트
A goalpost is one of the two upright wooden posts that are connected by a crossbar and form the goal in games such as football and rugby.

cheer [ʧiər] v. 환호성을 지르다, 환호하다; n. 환호(성), 응원
When people cheer, they shout loudly to show their approval or to encourage someone who is doing something such as taking part in a game.

peek [piːk] v. 살짝 보이다; (재빨리) 훔쳐보다; n. 엿보기
If someone or something peeks from somewhere, they stick out slightly and are partly seen.

horizon [həráizn] n. 지평선, 수평선
The horizon is the line in the far distance where the sky seems to meet the land or the sea.

socket [sákit] n. 콘센트; 푹 들어간 곳, 구멍
A socket is a device or point in a wall where you can connect electrical equipment to the power supply.

solitary [sáləteri] a. 단 하나의; 혼자 하는; 홀로 있는, 외딴
Solitary can be used for emphasizing that there is not even one person or thing.

flawless [flɔ́ːlis] a. 흠 없는, 나무랄 데 없는, 완전한
If you say that something or someone is flawless, you mean that they are extremely good and that there are no faults or problems with them.

scenario [sinéəriòu] n. 예정된 계획; (사건의) 예상된 전개; (영화 등의) 각본
If you talk about a likely or possible scenario, you are talking about the way in which a situation may develop.

beep [biːp] n. 삑 (하는 소리); v. 삐 소리를 내다; (경적을) 울리다
A beep is a short, loud sound like that made by a car horn or a telephone answering machine.

alarm [əláːrm] n. 경보 장치; 불안, 공포; v. 불안하게 하다; 경보장치를 달다
An alarm is an automatic device that warns you of danger, for example by ringing a bell.

blare [blɛər] v. (소리를) 요란하게 울리다; n. 요란한 소리
If something such as a siren or radio blares or if you blare it, it makes a loud, unpleasant noise.

* **plug** [plʌg] v. ~을 밀어 넣다, 꽂다; (구멍을) 막다; n. (전기) 플러그; 마개
If you plug something into something else, you connect a piece of equipment to an electricity supply or to another piece of equipment.

* **outlet** [áutlet] n. 콘센트; (액체·기체의) 배출구
An outlet is a place, usually in a wall, where you can connect electrical devices to the electricity supply.

* **strip** [strip] n. 가느다란 조각; v. (물건을) 다 뜯어내다; 옷을 벗다 (power strip n. 멀티탭)
A power strip is a block of electrical sockets that attaches to the end of a flexible cable and allows multiple electrical devices to be plugged in.

* **gasp** [gæsp] v. 헉 하고 숨을 쉬다; 숨을 제대로 못 쉬다; n. 헉 하는 소리를 냄
When you gasp, you take a short quick breath through your mouth, especially when you are surprised, shocked, or in pain.

* **alert** [əlɔ́:rt] n. 경계경보; v. (위험 등을) 알리다; a. 경계하는; 기민한
An alert is a situation in which people prepare themselves for something dangerous that might happen soon.

CHAPTER 2

Check Your Reading Speed

1분에 몇 단어를 읽는지 리딩 속도를 측정해보세요.

$$\frac{487 \text{ words}}{\text{reading time ( ) sec}} \times 60 = (\quad) \text{ WPM}$$

Build Your Vocabulary

arcade [aːrkéid] n. 게임 센터, 오락실
An arcade is a place where you can play games on machines which work when you put money in them.

stretch [stretʃ] v. (팔다리를) 뻗다; 뻗어 있다; (길이·폭 등을) 늘이다; n. 뻗기, 펴기; (길게) 뻗은 구간
When you stretch, you put your arms or legs out straight and tighten your muscles.

awkward [ɔ́ːkwərd] a. 어색한; (처리하기) 곤란한; 불편한 (awkwardly ad. 어색하게)
An awkward movement or position is uncomfortable or clumsy.

bend [bend] v. (bent-bent) (몸·머리를) 굽히다, 숙이다; 구부리다; n. (도로·강의) 굽이, 굽은 곳
When you bend, you move the top part of your body downward and forward.

plug [plʌg] v. ~을 밀어 넣다, 꽂다; (구멍을) 막다; n. (전기) 플러그; 마개
If you plug something into something else, you connect a piece of equipment to an electricity supply or to another piece of equipment.

cord [kɔːrd] n. 전선; 끈, 줄
Cord is wire covered in rubber or plastic which connects electrical equipment to an electricity supply.

strip [strip] n. 가느다란 조각; v. (물건을) 다 뜯어내다; 옷을 벗다 (power strip n. 멀티탭)
A power strip is a block of electrical sockets that attaches to the end of a flexible cable and allows multiple electrical devices to be plugged in.

burst [bəːrst] n. (갑자기) ~을 함; 파열, 폭발; v. 터지다, 파열하다; 불쑥 움직이다
A burst of something is a sudden short period of it.

rush [rʌʃ] v. 급히 움직이다; 서두르다; n. (감정이 갑자기) 치밀어 오름; 혼잡; 기쁨, 흥분
If you rush somewhere, you go there quickly.

station [stéiʃən] n. 역; 본부, 장소; 부서; 위치; v. 배치하다
A station is a building by a railway line where trains stop so that people can get on or off.

chatter [tʃǽtər] v. 수다를 떨다, 재잘거리다; n. 수다, 재잘거림; 딱딱거리는 소리
If you chatter, you talk quickly and continuously, usually about things which are not important.

dash [dæʃ] v. (급히) 서둘러 가다; 내동댕이치다; n. (승용차의) 계기판; 돌진, 질주
If you dash somewhere, you run or go there quickly and suddenly.

glimpse [glimps] n. 잠깐 봄; 짧은 경험; v. 언뜻 보다; 깨닫다, 이해하다
If you get a glimpse of someone or something, you see them very briefly and not very well.

bet [bet] v. (내기 등에) 돈을 걸다; (~이) 틀림없다; n. 짐작, 추측; 내기
If someone is betting that something will happen, they are hoping or expecting that it will happen.

booth [buːθ] n. (칸막이를 한) 작은 공간; (임시로 만든) 점포
(photo booth n. 즉석 사진 촬영 부스)
A booth is a small area separated from a larger public area by screens or thin walls where, for example, people can make a telephone call or vote in private.

race [reis] v. 경주하다; 쏜살같이 가다; (머리·심장 등이) 바쁘게 돌아가다; n. 경주; 인종, 종족
If you race, you take part in a race.

chant [tʃænt] v. 되풀이하여 말하다; 구호를 외치다, 연호하다; n. (연이어 외치는) 구호
If you chant something or if you chant, you repeat the same words over and over again.

marquee [maːrkíː] n. (극장 출입구의) 차양; (서커스 등의) 큰 천막
A marquee is a cover over the entrance of a building, for example a hotel or a theater.

hedgehog [hédʒhɔːg] n. [동물] 고슴도치
A hedgehog is a small brown animal with sharp spikes covering its back.

pronounce [prənáuns] v. 발음하다; 표명하다, 선언하다
To pronounce a word means to say it using particular sounds.

defensive [difénsiv] a. 방어적인; 방어의 (defensively ad. 방어적으로)
Someone who is defensive is behaving in a way that shows they feel unsure or threatened.

socialize [sóuʃəlàiz] v. (사람들과) 사귀다, 어울리다; 사회화시키다
If you socialize, you meet other people socially, for example at parties.

wondrous [wʌ́ndrəs] a. 경이로운, 경탄스러운
If you describe something as wondrous, you mean it is strange and beautiful or impressive.

miraculous [mirǽkjuləs] a. 기적적인
If you describe a good event as miraculous, you mean that it is very surprising and unexpected.

* **surge** [sə:rdʒ] n. 서지(전압·전류의 급증); (갑자기) 밀려듦;
v. (재빨리) 밀려들다; (강한 감정이) 휩싸다
A surge is a sudden increase in electrical power that can damage equipment connected to it.

* **stern** [stə:rn] a. 엄중한, 근엄한; 심각한
Stern words or actions are very severe.

* **capture** [kǽpʧər] v. 사로잡다; 붙잡다; 포로로 잡다; n. 생포; 구금, 억류
If something captures your attention or imagination, you begin to be interested or excited by it.

sign [sain] n. 표지판; 몸짓, 신호; 기색, 흔적; v. 서명하다; 신호를 보내다
A sign is a piece of wood, metal, or plastic with words or pictures on it. Signs give you information about something, or give you a warning or an instruction.

pause [pɔ:z] v. (말·일을 하다가) 잠시 멈추다; 정지시키다; n. (말·행동 등의) 멈춤
If you pause while you are doing something, you stop for a short period and then continue.

crowd [kraud] n. 사람들, 군중; v. 가득 메우다; 바싹 붙어 서다
A crowd is a large group of people who have gathered together, for example to watch or listen to something interesting, or to protest about something.

joke [dʒouk] n. 농담; 웃음거리; v. 농담하다; 농담 삼아 말하다
A joke is something that is said or done to make you laugh, for example a funny story.

laugh at idiom ~을 비웃다
If you laugh at someone or something, you say unkind things about them that are intended to make them seem silly.

RALPH BREAKS THE INTERNET

keep out idiom 들어가지 않다
If you keep out of a place or you keep someone or something out, you do not go in that place, you stop them from going into that place.

be about to idiom 막 ~하려는 참이다
If you are about to do something, you are going to do it immediately.

. **linger** [líŋgər] v. 더 오래 머물다; 계속되다
If you linger somewhere, you stay there for a longer time than is necessary, for example because you are enjoying yourself.

disperse [dispə́:rs] v. 해산하다; 흩어지다
When a group of people disperses or when someone disperses them, the group splits up and the people leave in different directions.

‡ **figure** [fígjər] v. 생각하다; 중요하다; n. (멀리서 흐릿하게 보이는) 사람; 수치; (중요한) 인물
If you say 'That figures' or 'It figures', you mean that the fact referred to is not surprising.

. **sigh** [sai] n. 한숨; v. 한숨을 쉬다, 한숨짓다; 탄식하듯 말하다
A sigh is a slow breath out that makes a long soft sound, especially because you are disappointed, tired, annoyed, or relaxed.

‡ **fair** [fɛər] a. 타당한; 공정한; 아름다운; ad. 공정하게, 타당하게; n. 축제; 박람회
Something or someone that is fair is reasonable, right, and just.

. **shrug** [ʃrʌg] n. 어깨를 으쓱하기; v. (어깨를) 으쓱하다
A shrug is the action of raising and lowering your shoulders to express something.

. **bonus** [bóunəs] n. 뜻밖의 즐거움; 보너스, 상여금
A bonus is something good that you get in addition to something else, and which you would not usually expect.

‡ **lock** [lak] v. (자물쇠로) 잠그다; 고정시키다; n. 잠금장치 (unlock v. (비밀 등을) 드러내다)
If you unlock the potential or the secrets of something or someone, you release them.

shortcut [ʃɔ́:rtkʌ̀t] n. 지름길; 손쉬운 방법
A shortcut is a quicker way of getting somewhere than the usual route.

would kill for idiom 간절하게 ~을 갖고 싶다
If you would kill for something, you want it so much that you will do almost anything to get it or do it.

track [træk] n. 경주로, 트랙; (기차) 선로; 자국; v. 추적하다, 뒤쫓다
A track is a piece of ground, often oval-shaped, that is used for races involving athletes, cars, bicycles, horses, or dogs.

immediate [imíːdiət] a. 즉각적인; 당면한; 아주 가까이에 있는 (immediately ad. 즉시, 즉각)
If something happens immediately, it happens without any delay.

agree to disagree idiom 서로의 의견 차이를 인정하고 싸우지 않기로 하다
If two people who are arguing about something agree to disagree or agree to differ, they decide to stop arguing because neither of them is going to change their opinion.

Chapters 3 & 4

1. How did the *Sugar Rush* steering wheel break?

A. Swati pulled it off when she was trying to control Vanellope.

B. Swati yanked it too hard when she got angry at Nafisa.

C. Swati knocked it over when she tripped over a cord.

D. Swati and Nafisa broke it when they were fighting over the game.

2. What did the kids in the arcade do after the wheel broke?

A. They told Swati she should pay for the damage.

B. They convinced Mr. Litwak to sell the game.

C. They looked online for a new wheel.

D. They started playing other arcade games.

3. Why did Mr. Litwak decide to unplug *Sugar Rush?*

    A. He wanted to teach Vanellope a lesson.

    B. He planned to take the whole machine apart and repair it.

    C. He thought he had no choice but to get rid of the game.

    D. He was worried that other parts of the machine might break.

4. Why did the *Sugar Rush* characters gather in Felix and Calhoun's apartment?

    A. To watch a movie

    B. To talk about their problems

    C. To apply for new jobs

    D. To find new homes

5. How did Ralph plan to make Vanellope feel better?

    A. By helping her move to the Internet

    B. By getting a new wheel from the Internet

    C. By building a *Sugar Rush* website

    D. By selling *Sugar Rush* on eBay

CHAPTER 3

Check Your Reading Speed

1분에 몇 단어를 읽는지 리딩 속도를 측정해보세요.

$$\frac{1,355 \text{ words}}{\text{reading time } (\quad) \text{ sec}} \times 60 = (\quad) \text{ WPM}$$

Build Your Vocabulary

glitch [glitʃ] n. 작은 문제, 결함; v. 갑자기 고장 나다
A glitch is a problem which stops something from working properly or being successful.

* **plaster** [plǽstər] v. 딱 들러붙게 하다; 회반죽을 바르다; n. 회반죽
If you plaster a surface or a place with posters or pictures, you stick a lot of them all over it.

‡ **announcer** [ənáunsər] n. (프로그램) 방송 진행자
An announcer is someone who introduces programs on radio or television or who reads the text of a radio or television advertisement.

‡ **compete** [kəmpíːt] v. 겨루다, (시합 등에) 참가하다; 경쟁하다
If you compete in a contest or a game, you take part in it.

* **nasty** [nǽsti] a. 못된, 심술궂은; 끔찍한, 형편없는
If you describe a person or their behavior as nasty, you mean that they behave in an unkind and unpleasant way.

technically [téknikəli] ad. 엄밀히 따지면; 기술적으로
If something is technically the case, it is the case according to a strict interpretation of facts, laws, or rules, but may not be important or relevant in a particular situation.

복습 **be about to** idiom 막 ~하려는 참이다
If you are about to do something, you are going to do it immediately.

butt [bʌt] n. 엉덩이; v. (머리로) 들이받다 (kick one's butt idiom 쳐부수다)
To kick someone's butt means to punish or defeat them.

* **pedal** [pedl] n. 페달, 발판; v. 페달을 밟다; (자전거를) 타고 가다
A pedal in a car or on a machine is a lever that you press with your foot in order to control the car or machine.

‡ traffic [trǽfik] n. 차량들, 교통; 수송
Traffic refers to all the vehicles that are moving along the roads in a particular area.

＊ pack [pæk] n. 무리, 집단; 묶음; v. (짐을) 싸다; 가득 채우다
You can refer to a group of people who go around together as a pack, especially when it is a large group that you feel threatened by.

‡ challenge [ʧǽlindʒ] n. 도전; 저항; v. 도전하다; 도전 의식을 북돋우다
A challenge is something new and difficult which requires great effort and determination.

＊ steep [stiːp] a. 가파른, 비탈진; 급격한; 터무니없는
A steep slope rises at a very sharp angle and is difficult to go up.

know inside and out idiom ~을 (자기 손바닥 들여다보듯이) 환하게 알다
If you say that you know something or someone inside and out, you are emphasizing that you know them extremely well.

복습 track [træk] n. 경주로, 트랙; (기차) 선로; 자국; v. 추적하다, 뒤쫓다
A track is a piece of ground, often oval-shaped, that is used for races involving athletes, cars, bicycles, horses, or dogs.

effortless [éfərtlis] a. 힘이 들지 않는; 수월해 보이는 (effortlessly ad. 쉽게)
Something that is effortless is done easily and well.

복습 make one's way idiom 나아가다, 가다
When you make your way somewhere, you walk or travel there.

catch up idiom 따라잡다, 따라가다; (소식 등을) 듣다
If you catch someone or something up, you go faster so that you reach them in front of you.

‡ spot [spat] v. 발견하다, 찾다, 알아채다; n. (특정한) 곳; (작은) 점
If you spot something or someone, you notice them.

‡ lean [liːn] v. 기울이다, (몸을) 숙이다; ~에 기대다; a. 군살이 없는, 호리호리한
When you lean in a particular direction, you bend your body in that direction.

＊ snore [snɔːr] v. 코를 골다; n. 코 고는 소리
When someone who is asleep snores, they make a loud noise each time they breathe.

perk [pə:rk] v. 기운을 회복하다, 생기가 나다; (귀·꼬리 등이) 쫑긋 서다
If something perks you up or if you perk up, you become cheerful and lively, after feeling tired, bored, or depressed.

grin [grin] n. 활짝 웃음; v. 활짝 웃다
A grin is a broad smile.

blast [blæst] v. 빠르게 가다; 쾅쾅 울리다; 폭발시키다; n. 폭발; (한 줄기의) 강한 바람
If you blast in a specified direction, you move very quickly and loudly in that direction.

wail [weil] v. 울부짖다, 통곡하다; (길고 높은) 소리를 내다; n. 울부짖음, 통곡
If someone wails, they make long, loud, high-pitched cries which express sorrow or pain.

meantime [mí:ntàim] ad. 그 사이에
In the meantime means in the period of time between two events.

distance [dístəns] n. 먼 곳; 거리; v. (~에) 관여하지 않다 (in the distance idiom 저 멀리)
If you can see something in the distance, you can see it, far away from you.

on time idiom 시간을 어기지 않고, 정각에
If you are on time, you are there at the expected time.

notice [nóutis] v. 알아채다, 인지하다; 주의하다; n. 신경 씀, 알아챔; 통지, 예고
If you notice something or someone, you become aware of them.

handiwork [hǽndiwə̀:rk] n. (솜씨를 발휘한) 일, 작품; (특정인의) 소행, 짓
You can refer to something that you have done or made yourself as your handiwork.

gleeful [glí:fəl] a. 신이 난; 고소해하는 (gleefully ad. 유쾌하게)
Someone who is gleeful is happy and excited, often because of someone else's bad luck.

detour [dí:tuər] n. 둘러 가는 길, 우회로; v. 둘러 가다, 우회하다
If you make a detour on a journey, you go by a route which is not the shortest way, because you want to avoid something such as a traffic jam, or because there is something you want to do on the way.

steer [stiər] v. (보트·자동차 등을) 조종하다; (특정 방향으로) 움직이다
When you steer a car, boat, or plane, you control it so that it goes in the direction that you want.

lock [lak] v. (자물쇠로) 잠그다; 고정시키다; n. 잠금장치 (unlock v. (비밀 등을) 드러내다)
If you unlock the potential or the secrets of something or someone, you release them.

off-road [ɔ́ːf-ròud] ad. 일반 도로에서 벗어난; 공공 도로가 아닌
If you go off-road, you go on rough ground, away from normal roads.

bumpy [bʌ́mpi] a. (길이) 울퉁불퉁한; 평탄치 않은
A bumpy road or path has a lot of bumps on it.

homemade [houmméid] a. 집에서 만든, 손수 만든
Something that is homemade has been made in someone's home, rather than in a shop or factory.

obstacle [ábstəkl] n. 장애물; 장애
An obstacle is an object that makes it difficult for you to go where you want to go, because it is in your way.

unexpected [ʌ̀nikspéktid] a. 예기치 않은, 예상 밖의
If an event or someone's behavior is unexpected, it surprises you because you did not think that it was likely to happen.

howl [haul] v. 크게 웃다; (크고 시끄럽게) 울부짖다; n. (개·늑대 등의) 길게 짖는 소리
If you howl with laughter, you laugh very loudly.

delight [diláit] n. (큰) 기쁨; 즐거움을 주는 것; v. 많은 기쁨을 주다, 아주 즐겁게 하다
Delight is a feeling of very great pleasure.

yell [jel] v. 고함치다, 소리 지르다; n. 고함, 외침
If you yell, you shout loudly, usually because you are excited, angry, or in pain.

thrill [θril] v. 열광시키다, 정말 신나게 하다; n. 흥분, 설렘; 전율
(thrilled a. 황홀해하는, 아주 흥분한)
If someone is thrilled, they are extremely pleased about something.

urge [əːrdʒ] v. 재촉하다; 충고하다, 설득하려 하다; n. (강한) 욕구, 충동
If you urge someone to do something, you try hard to persuade them to do it.

yank [jæŋk] v. 홱 잡아당기다; n. 홱 잡아당기기
If you yank someone or something somewhere, you pull them there suddenly and with a lot of force.

wheel [hwiːl] n. (자동차 등의) 핸들; 바퀴; v. (바퀴 달린 것을) 밀다
The wheel of a car or other vehicle is the circular object that is used to steer it.

⁑ struggle [strʌgl] v. 애쓰다; 몸부림치다, 허우적거리다; 힘겹게 나아가다; n. 투쟁, 분투; 몸부림
If you struggle to do something, you try hard to do it, even though other people or things may be making it difficult for you to succeed.

⁎ rocket [rákit] v. 로켓처럼 가다, 돌진하다; 급증하다; n. 로켓; 로켓 추진 미사일
If something such as a vehicle rockets somewhere, it moves there very quickly.

hoot [huːt] v. 폭소를 터뜨리다; (경적을) 빵빵거리다; n. (차량의) 경적 소리; 비웃음, 콧방귀
If you hoot, you make a loud high-pitched noise when you are laughing or showing disapproval.

have the time of one's life idiom 마음껏 즐거운 시간을 보내다
If you have the time of your life, you enjoy yourself very much indeed.

⁎ bump [bʌmp] n. (도로의) 튀어나온 부분; 부딪치기; 쿵, 탁 (하는 소리); v. (~에) 부딪치다; 덜컹거리며 가다
A bump on a road is a raised, uneven part.

⁑ crash [kræʃ] v. 충돌하다; 부딪치다; (컴퓨터를) 고장 내다; n. 요란한 소리; (자동차·항공기) 사고
If a moving vehicle crashes or if the driver crashes it, it hits something and is damaged or destroyed.

⁎ tumble [tʌmbl] v. 굴러떨어지다; 폭삭 무너지다; n. (갑자기) 굴러떨어짐; 폭락
If someone or something tumbles somewhere, they fall there with a rolling or bouncing movement.

⁎ ditch [ditʃ] n. (들판·도로가의) 배수로; v. 버리다
A ditch is a long narrow channel cut into the ground at the side of a road or field.

⁑ land [lænd] v. 떨어지다; (땅·표면에) 내려앉다; 놓다, 두다; n. 육지, 땅; 지역
When someone or something lands, they come down to the ground after moving through the air or falling.

puddle [pʌdl] n. (빗물 등의) 물웅덩이
A puddle is a small, shallow pool of liquid that has spread on the ground.

amaze [əméiz] v. (대단히) 놀라게 하다; 경악하게 하다 (amazing a. 놀라운)
You say that something is amazing when it is very surprising and makes you feel pleasure, approval, or wonder.

exhilarate [igzílərèit] v. 아주 기쁘게 하다 (exhilarated a. 기분이 좋은, 들떠 있는)
If you are exhilarated by something, it makes you feel very happy and excited.

hip [hip] n. 둔부, 엉덩이
Your hips are the two areas at the sides of your body between the tops of your legs and your waist.

tone [toun] n. 어조, 말투; (글 등의) 분위기; 음색
Someone's tone is a quality in their voice which shows what they are feeling or thinking.

apologetic [əpàlədʒétik] a. 미안해하는, 사과하는 (apologetically ad. 사과하듯이)
If you are apologetic, you show or say that you are sorry for causing trouble for someone, for hurting them, or for disappointing them.

nearby [niərbái] ad. 가까운 곳에; a. 인근의, 가까운 곳의
If something is nearby, it is only a short distance away.

poke [pouk] v. 쑥 내밀다; (손가락 등으로) 쿡 찌르다; n. (손가락 등으로) 찌르기
If you poke your head through an opening or if it pokes through an opening, you push it through, often so that you can see something more easily.

force [fɔːrs] v. 억지로 ~하다; ~를 강요하다; n. 작용력; 힘; 영향력
If you force something into a particular position, you use a lot of strength to make it move there.

obvious [ábviəs] a. 분명한, 확실한; 명백한 (obviously ad. 분명히)
You use obviously to indicate that something is easily noticed, seen, or recognized.

one's face falls idiom 실망한 표정을 짓다; 낙담한 얼굴이 되다
If someone's face falls, they suddenly look very disappointed or upset.

crowd [kraud] n. 사람들, 군중; v. 가득 메우다; 바싹 붙어 서다
A crowd is a large group of people who have gathered together, for example to watch or listen to something interesting, or to protest about something.

gather [gǽðər] v. (사람들이) 모이다; (여기저기 있는 것을) 모으다
If people gather somewhere or if someone gathers people somewhere, they come together in a group.

go out of business idiom 폐업하다
If a shop or company goes out of business or is put out of business, it has to stop trading because it is not making enough money.

aghast [əgǽst] a. 경악한, 겁에 질린
If you are aghast, you are filled with horror and surprise.

needle [níːdl] n. 바늘; 침; v. (사람을) 갉다, 신경을 건드리다
(find a needle in a haystack idiom 찾을 가망이 없는 것을 찾다)
If you are trying to find something and say that it is like looking for a needle in a haystack, you mean that you are very unlikely indeed to find it.

cheerful [ʧíərfəl] a. 발랄한, 쾌활한 (cheerfully ad. 쾌활하게, 명랑하게)
Someone who is cheerful is happy and shows this in their behavior.

adjust [ədʒʌ́st] v. (매무새 등을) 바로잡다; 조정하다; 적응하다
If you adjust something such as your clothing or a machine, you correct or alter its position or setting.

kid [kid] v. 놀리다, 장난치다; 속이다
You can say 'you've got to be kidding' or 'you must be kidding' to someone if they have said something that you think is ridiculous or completely untrue.

scoff [skɔːf] v. 비웃다, 조롱하다; n. 비웃음, 조롱
If you scoff at something, you speak about it in a way that shows you think it is ridiculous or inadequate.

sigh [sai] v. 한숨을 쉬다, 한숨짓다; 탄식하듯 말하다; n. 한숨
When you sigh, you let out a deep breath, as a way of expressing feelings such as disappointment, tiredness, or pleasure.

salvage [sǽlvidʒ] n. 폐품 회수; 구조; (침몰선의) 인양; v. 구조하다; 인양하다
A salvage refers to the act of saving goods from damage or destruction, especially from a ship that has sunk or been damaged or a building that has been damaged by fire or a flood.

groan [groun] v. (고통·짜증으로) 신음 소리를 내다; 끙끙거리다; n. 신음, 끙 하는 소리
If you groan, you make a long, low sound because you are in pain, or because you are upset or unhappy about something.

pop [pap] v. 눈이 휘둥그레지다; 불쑥 나타나다; 펑 하는 소리가 나다; n. 펑 (하는 소리)
If your eyes pop, you look very surprised or excited when you see something.

chaos [kéias] n. 혼돈; 혼란
Chaos is a state of complete disorder and confusion.

surge [səːrdʒ] n. 서지(전압·전류의 급증); (갑자기) 밀려듦; v. (재빨리) 밀려들다; (강한 감정이) 휩싸다
A surge is a sudden increase in electrical power that can damage equipment connected to it.

‡ **whistle** [hwisl] v. 휘파람을 불다; 기적을 울리다; n. 휘파람 (소리); (기차·배 등의) 기적, 경적
When you whistle or when you whistle a tune, you make a series of musical notes by forcing your breath out between your lips, or your teeth.

stampede [stæmpíːd] n. (한쪽으로) 우르르 몰림; v. (동물·사람들이) 우르르 몰리다; 재촉하다
If there is a stampede, a group of people or animals run in a wild, uncontrolled way.

‡ **flash** [flæʃ] n. 순간; (잠깐) 반짝임; v. (잠깐) 번쩍이다; 휙 나타나다 (in a flash idiom 순식간에)
If you say that something happens in a flash, you mean that it happens suddenly and lasts only a very short time.

gangway [gǽŋwei] int. 길을 내라, 비켜라!; n. (극장·비행기 등의 좌석 사이) 통로
If you shout 'gangway,' you want people to move so that you can get someone or something through a crowd quickly.

* **cop** [kap] n. 경찰관
A cop is a policeman or policewoman.

* **trample** [træmpl] v. 짓밟다, 밟아 뭉개다; (남의 감정·권리를) 짓밟다
If someone is trampled, they are injured or killed by being stepped on by animals or by other people.

* **sake** [seik] n. 목적; 원인, 이유 (for Peter's sake idiom 도대체, 제발)
Some people use expressions such as for God's sake, for heaven's sake, for goodness sake, or for Peter's sake in order to express annoyance or impatience, or to add force to a question or request.

‡ **confuse** [kənfjúːz] v. (사람을) 혼란시키다; 혼동하다 (confused a. 혼란스러워하는)
If you are confused, you do not know exactly what is happening or what to do.

‡ **citizen** [sítəzən] n. 시민; 주민
The citizens of a town or city are the people who live there.

jiggle [dʒigl] v. (빠르게) 움직이다, 흔들다
If you jiggle something, you move it quickly up and down or from side to side.

socket [sákit] n. 콘센트; 푹 들어간 곳, 구멍
A socket is a device or point in a wall where you can connect electrical equipment to the power supply.

* **homeless** [hóumlis] a. 노숙자의; n. (pl.) 노숙자들
Homeless people have nowhere to live.

collect oneself idiom 마음을 가라앉히다
If you collect yourself, you get control of your feelings and thoughts, especially after shock, surprise, or laughter.

freak [fri:k] v. 기겁을 하다; a. 아주 기이한; n. 괴짜, 괴물 (freak out idiom 기겁하다)
If someone freaks out, or if something freaks them out, they suddenly feel extremely surprised, upset, angry, or confused.

* **panic** [pǽnik] v. 어쩔 줄 모르다, 공황 상태에 빠지다; n. 극심한 공포, 공황; 허둥지둥함
If you panic or if someone panics you, you suddenly feel anxious or afraid, and act quickly and without thinking carefully.

deadpan [dédpæn] a. 진지한 표정의, 무표정한
Deadpan humor is when you appear to be serious and are hiding the fact that you are joking or teasing someone.

figure out idiom ~을 이해하다, 알아내다; 계산하다, 산출하다
If you figure out someone or something, you come to understand them by thinking carefully.

* **rapid** [rǽpid] a. (속도가) 빠른; (행동이) 민첩한 (rapidly ad. 빠르게, 신속히)
A rapid movement is one that is very fast.

CHAPTER 4

Check Your Reading Speed
1분에 몇 단어를 읽는지 리딩 속도를 측정해보세요.

$$\frac{1,397 \text{ words}}{\text{reading time ( ) sec}} \times 60 = (\quad) \text{ WPM}$$

Build Your Vocabulary

rooftop [rúːftap] n. (건물의) 옥상
A rooftop is the outside part of the roof of a building.

chin [ʧin] n. 턱
Your chin is the part of your face that is below your mouth and above your neck.

stare [stɛər] v. 빤히 쳐다보다, 응시하다; n. 빤히 쳐다보기, 응시
If you stare at someone or something, you look at them for a long time.

depress [diprés] v. 우울하게 하다; (사업·거래 등을) 침체시키다
(depressing a. 우울하게 하는, 우울한)
Something that is depressing makes you feel sad and disappointed.

console [kánsoul] ① n. 콘솔, 제어반, 계기반 ② v. 위로하다, 위안을 주다
A console is a panel with a number of switches or knobs that is used to operate a machine.

salvage [sǽlvidʒ] n. 폐품 회수; 구조; (침몰선의) 인양; v. 구조하다; 인양하다
A salvage refers to the act of saving goods from damage or destruction, especially from a ship that has sunk or been damaged or a building that has been damaged by fire or a flood.

bumble [bʌmbl] v. 비틀거리다
If you bumble, you move or act in an awkward or confused manner.

roof [ruːf] n. 지붕; (터널·동굴 등의) 천장; v. 지붕을 씌우다
The roof of a building is the covering on top of it that protects the people and things inside from the weather.

supply [səplái] n. (pl.) 용품, 비품; 비축(량); 공급; v. 공급하다, 제공하다
You can use supplies to refer to food, equipment, and other essential things that people need, especially when these are provided in large quantities.

cheerful [ʧíərfəl] a. 발랄한, 쾌활한 (cheerfully ad. 쾌활하게, 명랑하게)
Someone who is cheerful is happy and shows this in their behavior.

raid [reid] v. 침입하다; 수색하다; 불시 단속을 벌이다; n. 습격, 급습
If someone raids a building or place, they enter it by force in order to steal
something.

fridge [frid3] n. (= refrigerator) 냉장고
A fridge is a large metal container which is kept cool, usually by electricity, so
that food that is put in it stays fresh.

bunch [bʌnʧ] n. (양·수가) 많음; 다발, 묶음
A bunch of things is a number of things, especially a large number.

pillow [pílou] n. 베개
A pillow is a rectangular cushion which you rest your head on when you are in
bed.

junk [dʒʌŋk] n. 쓸모없는 물건, 폐물, 쓰레기; v. 폐물로 처분하다
Junk is old and used goods that have little value and that you do not want any
more.

fort [fɔːrt] n. 보루, 요새
A fort is a strong building or a place with a wall or fence around it where soldiers
can stay and be safe from the enemy.

stack [stæk] v. (깔끔하게 정돈하여) 쌓다; n. 무더기, 더미
If you stack a number of things, you arrange them in neat piles.

lost in thought idiom 생각에 빠진; 사색에 잠긴
If you are lost in thought, you are not aware of what is happening around you
because you are thinking about something else.

kid [kid] v. 놀리다, 장난치다; 속이다
You can say 'you've got to be kidding' or 'you must be kidding' to someone if they
have said something that you think is ridiculous or completely untrue.

sleep in idiom (자기가 평소 일어나는 시간보다) 늦잠을 자다
If you sleep in, you sleep until later in the morning than you usually do.

hang out idiom 많은 시간을 보내다
If you hang out in a place or with a person or a group of people, you spend a lot
of time in there or with them.

* **literal** [lítərəl] a. 문자 그대로의; (번역이) 직역의 (literally ad. 그야말로; 말 그대로)
You use literally to emphasize that what you are saying is true, even though it seems exaggerated or surprising.

* **paradise** [pǽrədàis] n. 낙원; 천국
You can refer to a place or situation that seems beautiful or perfect as paradise or a paradise.

bellyache [bélieik] v. 투덜거리다, 불평을 해대다; n. 복통, 배앓이
If you say that someone is bellyaching, you mean they complain loudly and frequently about something and you think this is unreasonable or unjustified.

predictable [pridíktəbl] a. 예상할 수 있는; 너무 뻔한
If you say that an event is predictable, you mean that it is obvious in advance that it will happen.

* **stuff** [stʌf] n. 일, 것, 물건; v. 쑤셔 넣다; 채워 넣다
You can use stuff to refer to things such as a substance, a collection of things, events, or ideas, or the contents of something in a general way without mentioning the thing itself by name.

‡ **wound** [wu:nd] v. 감정을 상하게 하다; 상처를 입히다; n. 상처, 부상; (정신적) 상처
(wounded a. (마음을) 상한)
If you are wounded by what someone says or does, your feelings are deeply hurt.

복습 **glitch** [gliʧ] v. 갑자기 고장 나다; n. 작은 문제, 결함
To glitch means to suffer a sudden malfunction or fault.

‡ **concern** [kənsə́:rn] v. 걱정스럽게 하다; 관련되다; n. 우려, 걱정; 관심사
(concerned a. 걱정하는, 염려하는)
If something concerns you, it worries you.

* **weird** [wiərd] a. 기이한, 기묘한; 기괴한, 섬뜩한
If you describe something or someone as weird, you mean that they are strange.

hang one's head idiom 낙담하다; 부끄러워 고개를 숙이다
If you hang your head, you are ashamed and discouraged.

* **helpless** [hélplis] a. 무력한, 속수무책인 (helplessly ad. 어찌해 볼 수도 없이)
If you are helpless, you do not have the strength or power to do anything useful or to control or protect yourself.

복습 **pack** [pæk] v. 가득 채우다; (짐을) 싸다; n. 무리, 집단; 묶음
If people or things pack into a place or if they pack a place, there are so many of them that the place is full.

address [ədrés] v. 연설하다; 말을 걸다; 주소를 쓰다; n. 주소; 연설
If you address a group of people, you give a speech to them.

chum [ʧʌm] n. 친구
Your chum is your friend.

stir [stə:r] v. 젓다; 약간 움직이다; 자극하다; n. 동요, 충격; 젓기
If you stir a liquid or other substance, you move it around or mix it in a container using something such as a spoon.

décor [deikɔ́:r] n. 실내장식, 인테리어
The décor of a house or room is its style of furnishing and decoration.

blunt [blʌnt] a. 직설적인; 무딘, 뭉툭한; v. 약화시키다; 뭉툭하게 만들다
(bluntly ad. 직설적으로)
If you are blunt, you say exactly what you think without trying to be polite.

beg [beg] v. 구걸하다; 간청하다, 애원하다 (beggar n. 거지)
A beggar is someone who lives by asking people for money or food.

condiment [kándəmənt] n. 조미료, 양념
A condiment is a substance such as salt, pepper, or mustard that you add to food when you eat it in order to improve the flavor.

gesture [dʒésʧər] v. (손·머리 등으로) 가리키다; 몸짓을 하다; n. 몸짓; (감정·의도의) 표시
If you gesture, you use movements of your hands or head in order to tell someone something or draw their attention to something.

marvelous [má:rvələs] a. 기막히게 좋은, 경탄할 만한
If you describe someone or something as marvelous, you are emphasizing that they are very good.

spirited [spíritid] a. 기백이 넘치는, 활발한
A spirited person is very active, lively, and confident.

youngster [jʌ́ŋstər] n. 청소년, 아이
Young people, especially children, are sometimes referred to as youngsters.

adorable [ədɔ́:rəbl] a. 사랑스러운
If you say that someone or something is adorable, you are emphasizing that they are very attractive and you feel great affection for them.

convincing [kənvínsiŋ] a. 설득력 있는, 납득이 가는 (unconvincing a. 설득력이 없는)
If you describe something such as an argument or explanation as unconvincing, you find it difficult to believe because it does not seem real.

avert [əvə́:rt] v. (눈·얼굴 등을) 돌리다, 외면하다; 피하다
If you avert your eyes or gaze from someone or something, you look away from them.

willing [wíliŋ] a. 기꺼이 ~하는; 자발적인
If someone is willing to do something, they are fairly happy about doing it and will do it if they are asked or required to do it.

grab [græb] v. (와락·단단히) 붙잡다; 급히 ~하다; n. 와락 잡아채려고 함
If you grab something, you take it or pick it up suddenly and roughly.

jump into with both feet idiom 열심히 참가하다, 기세 좋게 착수하다
To jump into with both feet means to become involved in a situation too quickly without thinking about it first.

nary [nɛ́əri] a. 하나도 ~없는; ~가 아닌
Nary a means 'not a single one.'

announce [ənáuns] v. 발표하다, 알리다; 선언하다
If you announce something, you tell people about it publicly or officially.

sanctuary [sǽŋkʧuèri] n. 피난처, 안식처; 안식, 보호; 성역
A sanctuary is a place where people who are in danger from other people can go to be safe.

spit [spit] v. (spit/spat-spit/spat) (~을) 뱉다; ~에서 나오다; n. 침; (침 등을) 뱉기
If you spit liquid or food somewhere, you force a small amount of it out of your mouth.

blind [blaind] n. (창문에 치는) 블라인드; v. (잠시) 안 보이게 하다; a. 눈이 먼; 눈치 채지 못하는
A blind is a roll of cloth or paper which you can pull down over a window as a covering.

dramatic [drəmǽtik] a. 과장된; 극적인; 감격적인, 인상적인 (dramatically ad. 극적으로)
A dramatic action, event, or situation is exciting and impressive.

spice [spais] v. 묘미를 더하다; 양념을 치다; n. 양념, 향신료; 흥취
If you spice something that you say or do, you add excitement or interest to it.

basically [béisikəli] ad. 근본적으로, 원래
You use basically for emphasis when you are stating an opinion, or when you are making an important statement about something.

feral [fíərəl] a. 야생의; 야만적인; 흉포한
Feral animals are wild animals that are not owned or controlled by anyone, especially ones that belong to species which are normally owned and kept by people.

lamb [læm] n. 어린 양
A lamb is a young sheep.

shepherd [ʃépərd] n. 양치기; v. (길을) 안내하다
A shepherd is a person, especially a man, whose job is to look after sheep.

parenting [péərəntiŋ] n. 육아
Parenting is the activity of bringing up and looking after your child.

treat [triːt] v. (특정한 태도로) 대하다; 여기다, 치부하다; n. 특별한 것, 대접, 한턱
If you treat someone or something in a particular way, you behave toward them or deal with them in that way.

one's socks off idiom 열렬히, 완전히
If you do something your socks off, you do it with great energy and enthusiasm.

take over idiom 장악하다, 탈취하다; (~을) 인계받다
If you take over a place, you fill it or use the whole of it so that other people cannot use it.

knock [nak] v. 치다, 부딪치다; (문 등을) 두드리다; n. 문 두드리는 소리; 부딪침
If you knock something, you touch or hit it roughly, especially so that it falls or moves.

bounce [bauns] v. 깡충깡충 뛰다; (공 등이) 튀다; n. 탄력
If you bounce on a soft surface, you jump up and down on it repeatedly.

irritate [írətèit] v. 짜증나게 하다, 거슬리다; 자극하다 (irritated a. 짜증이 난)
If something irritates you, it keeps annoying you.

remote [rimóut] n. (= remote control) 리모컨; 원격 조종; a. 먼; 외진, 외딴; 원격의
The remote control for a television or video recorder is the device that you use to control the machine from a distance, by pressing the buttons on it.

dumb [dʌm] a. 멍청한, 바보 같은; 말을 못 하는
If you say that something is dumb, you think that it is silly and annoying.

uneasy [ʌníːzi] a. (마음이) 불안한, 우려되는; 불안한; 어색한
If you are uneasy, you feel anxious, afraid, or embarrassed, because you think that something is wrong or that there is danger.

pop [pap] v. 불쑥 나타나다; 눈이 휘둥그레지다; 펑 하는 소리가 나다; n. 펑 (하는 소리)
If something pops up, it appears or happens when you do not expect it.

trophy [tróufi] n. 트로피, 우승컵; 전리품
A trophy is a prize, for example a silver cup, that is given to the winner of a competition or race.

strike [straik] v. (struck-struck/stricken) (세게) 치다, 부딪치다; 공격하다;
n. 공격; 치기, 때리기
If you strike someone or something, you deliberately hit them.

forehead [fɔ́ːrhèd] n. 이마
Your forehead is the area at the front of your head between your eyebrows and your hair.

realize [ríːəlàiz] v. 깨닫다, 알아차리다; 실현하다, 달성하다
If you realize that something is true, you become aware of that fact or understand it.

counter [káuntər] n. (식당·바 등의) 카운터; 계산대; 반작용; v. 대응하다; 반박하다
In a place such as a shop or café a counter is a long narrow table or flat surface at which customers are served.

stool [stuːl] n. (등받이와 팔걸이가 없는) 의자, 스툴
A stool is a seat with legs but no support for your arms or back.

interrupt [intərʌ́pt] v. (말·행동을) 방해하다; 중단시키다; 차단하다
If you interrupt someone who is speaking, you say or do something that causes them to stop.

insecure [insikjúər] a. 자신이 없는; 불안정한, 안전하지 못한
If you are insecure, you lack confidence because you think that you are not good enough or are not loved.

give a break idiom ~를 너그럽게 봐주다
To give someone a break means to stop criticizing or being angry with them.

nod [nad] v. (고개를) 끄덕이다, 까딱하다; n. (고개를) 끄덕임
If you nod, you move your head downward and upward to show that you are answering 'yes' to a question, or to show agreement, understanding, or approval.

sip [sip] n. 한 모금; v. (음료를) 홀짝거리다, 조금씩 마시다
A sip is a small amount of drink that you take into your mouth.

wince [wins] v. (통증·당혹감으로) 움찔하고 놀라다
If you wince, the muscles of your face tighten suddenly because you have felt a pain or because you have just seen, heard, or remembered something unpleasant.

choke [ʧouk] v. 숨이 막히다; (목소리가) 잠기다; 채우다; n. 숨이 막힘
When you choke or when something chokes you, you cannot breathe properly or get enough air into your lungs.

smooth [smu:ð] a. (맛이) 부드러운; 순조로운; 매끈한; v. 매끈하게 하다
If you describe a drink such as wine, whisky, or coffee as smooth, you mean that it is not bitter and is pleasant to drink.

screw up idiom ~을 엉망으로 하다, 망치다
If you screw up, you make a serious mistake, or spoil something, especially a situation.

figure [fígjər] v. 생각하다; 중요하다; n. (멀리서 흐릿하게 보이는) 사람; 수치; (중요한) 인물
If you say 'That figures' or 'It figures', you mean that the fact referred to is not surprising.

bless [bles] v. (신의) 축복을 빌다; 신성하게 하다 (blessing n. 좋은 점; 축복)
A blessing is something good that you are grateful for.

swing [swiŋ] v. (swung-swung) 휙 움직이다; (전후·좌우로) 흔들다; 방향을 바꾸다; n. 흔들기; 휘두르기
If something swings in a particular direction or if you swing it in that direction, it moves in that direction with a smooth, curving movement.

chug [ʧʌg] v. (음료를) 단숨에 들이켜다; 칙칙폭폭 소리를 내며 나아가다; n. 칙칙 (하는 소리)
If you chug something, especially beer, you drink all of it without stopping.

cough [kɔ:f] v. 기침하다; (기침을 하여 무엇을) 토하다; n. 기침
When you cough, you force air out of your throat with a sudden, harsh noise.

croak [krouk] v. 목이 쉰 듯 말하다; (개구리나 까마귀가) 까악까악 울다; n. 꺽꺽하는 소리
If someone croaks something, they say it in a low, rough voice.

slam [slæm] v. 세게 치다, 놓다; 쾅 닫다; n. 쾅 하고 닫기; 탕 하는 소리
If you slam something down, you put it there quickly and with great force.

confuse [kənfjú:z] v. (사람을) 혼란시키다; 혼동하다 (confused a. 혼란스러워하는)
If you are confused, you do not know exactly what is happening or what to do.

vigorous [vígərəs] a. 활발한; 격렬한; 건강한 (vigorously ad. 힘차게)
Vigorous physical activities involve using a lot of energy, usually to do short and repeated actions.

click [klik] v. 분명해지다; (마우스를) 클릭하다; n. (마우스를) 클릭함
When you suddenly understand something, you can say that it clicks.

steer [stiər] v. (보트·자동차 등을) 조종하다; (특정 방향으로) 움직이다
When you steer a car, boat, or plane, you control it so that it goes in the direction that you want.

wheel [hwiːl] n. (자동차 등의) 핸들; 바퀴; v. (바퀴 달린 것을) 밀다
(steering wheel n. (자동차의) 핸들)
The wheel of a car or other vehicle is the circular object that is used to steer it.

that's it idiom 바로 그거야!; 그만해라
You use that's it to express agreement with or approval of what has just been said or done.

exclaim [ikskléim] v. 소리치다, 외치다
If you exclaim, you cry out suddenly in surprise, strong emotion, or pain.

lovable [lÁvəbl] a. 사랑스러운, 매력적인
If you describe someone as lovable, you mean that they have attractive qualities, and are easy to like.

scamp [skæmp] n. 개구쟁이, 장난꾸러기
If you call a boy a scamp, you mean that he is naughty or disrespectful but you like him, so you find it difficult to be angry with him.

sane [sein] a. 제정신의, 정신이 온전한; 분별 있는 (sanity n. 온전한 정신)
A person's sanity is their ability to think and behave normally and reasonably.

mission [míʃən] n. 임무; 사명; v. 길고 험난한 여정에 나서다
A mission is an important task that people are given to do, especially one that involves traveling to another country.

noble [noubl] a. 고귀한, 숭고한; 귀족의
If you say that something is a noble idea, goal, or action, you admire it because it is based on high moral principles.

cover [kÁvər] v. (일을) 대신하다; 덮다; 씌우다, 가리다; n. 위장; 몸을 숨길 곳; 덮개
If you cover for someone who is ill or away, you do their work for them while they are not there.

pal [pæl] n. 친구; 이봐
Your pals are your friends.

exit [égzit] n. (공공건물의) 출구; (고속도로의) 출구; 퇴장; v. 나가다, 떠나다; 퇴장하다
The exit is the door through which you can leave a public building.

tab [tæb] n. 계산서, 외상 장부; 식별표
A tab is the total cost of goods or services that you have to pay, or the bill or check for those goods or services.

owe [ou] v. (돈을) 빚지고 있다; 신세를 지고 있다
If you owe money to someone, they have lent it to you and you have not yet paid it back.

cheer [ʧiər] v. 환호성을 지르다, 환호하다; n. 환호(성), 응원
When people cheer, they shout loudly to show their approval or to encourage someone who is doing something such as taking part in a game.

Chapters 5 & 6

1. Why were Ralph and Vanellope unimpressed at first when they entered the router?

A. They could not find anyone famous.

B. They did not see anything exciting.

C. They thought the place looked old.

D. They expected the place to be more organized.

2. When did Mr. Litwak's avatar appear?

A. When Mr. Litwak connected to the Wi-Fi

B. When Mr. Litwak turned off his computer screen

C. When Ralph made his voice echo

D. When Vanellope turned on a green light

3. **What did Ralph and Vanellope do to get to the Internet?**

   A. They typed in a computer address that Litwak's avatar had used.

   B. They set up a capsule that Litwak's avatar had used.

   C. They chased Litwak's avatar onto a moving walkway.

   D. They followed Litwak's avatar to a capsule launch pad.

4. **What did KnowsMore do?**

   A. He helped users create things online.

   B. He helped users spell things online.

   C. He helped users find things online.

   D. He helped users buy things online.

5. **What happened when Vanellope searched "eBay Sugar Rush steering wheel"?**

   A. Many search results came up.

   B. A photo of the steering wheel appeared.

   C. An error message popped up.

   D. The search bar froze for a moment.

CHAPTER 5

Check Your Reading Speed

1분에 몇 단어를 읽는지 리딩 속도를 측정해보세요.

$$\frac{753 \text{ words}}{\text{reading time (} \quad \text{) sec}} \times 60 = (\quad) \text{ WPM}$$

Build Your Vocabulary

brick [brik] n. 벽돌
Bricks are rectangular blocks of baked clay used for building walls, which are usually red or brown.

frustrate [frʌ́streit] v. 좌절감을 주다, 불만스럽게 하다; 방해하다
(frustration n. 불만, 좌절감)
If something frustrates you, it upsets or angers you because you are unable to do anything about the problems it creates.

boo [buː] int. 야아! (겁을 주려고 외치는 소리); 우우 (야유를 보내는 소리);
v. (우우 하고) 야유하다
You say 'Boo!' loudly and suddenly when you want to surprise someone who does not know that you are there.

startle [staːrtl] v. 깜짝 놀라게 하다; 움찔하다; n. 깜짝 놀람
If something sudden and unexpected startles you, it surprises and frightens you slightly.

churn [ʧəːrn] v. (버터를 만들기 위해) 우유를 휘젓다; (물·흙탕물 등이) 마구 휘돌다
To churn means to shake milk or cream in a machine in order to produce butter.

blast [blæst] v. 빠르게 가다; 쾅쾅 울리다; 폭발시키다; n. 폭발; (한 줄기의) 강한 바람
If you blast in a specified direction, you move very quickly and loudly in that direction.

energize [énərdʒàiz] v. 기운을 북돋우다; 열기를 돋우다
To energize someone means to give them the enthusiasm and determination to do something.

plug [plʌg] v. ~을 밀어 넣다, 꽂다; (구멍을) 막다; n. (전기) 플러그; 마개
(unplug v. (전기) 플러그를 뽑다)
If you unplug an electrical device or telephone, you pull a wire out of a socket so that it stops working.

^{복습} **station** [stéiʃən] n. 역; 본부, 장소; 부서; 위치; v. 배치하다
A station is a building by a railway line where trains stop so that people can get on or off.

stoic [stóuik] a. 태연한, 냉정한; 극기의, 금욕의; n. 금욕주의자 (stoically ad. 냉정하게)
If you say that someone behaves in a stoic way, you approve of them because they do not complain or show they are upset in bad situations.

‌* **patrol** [pətróul] v. 순찰을 돌다; (특히 위협적으로) 돌아다니다; n. 순찰; 순찰대
When soldiers, police, or guards patrol an area or building, they move around it in order to make sure that there is no trouble there.

barricade [bǽrəkèid] v. 방어벽을 치다; n. 바리케이드, 장애물
If you barricade something such as a road or an entrance, you place a barricade or barrier across it, usually to stop someone getting in.

make up idiom (이야기 등을) 만들어 내다
If you make up something such as a story or excuse, you invent it, sometimes in order to deceive people.

undesirable [ʌndizáiərəbl] n. (pl.) 바람직하지 못한 사람; a. 원하지 않는, 달갑지 않은
Undesirables are people who a particular government considers to be dangerous or a threat to society, and therefore wants to get rid of.

donnybrook [dánibrùk] n. 떠들썩한 언쟁, 난투
A donnybrook is a scene of uproar and disorder or a heated argument.

on one's watch idiom ~의 책임일 때, ~가 지켜보고 있을 때
If something happens on your watch, it is done while you are in charge.

^{복습} **appreciate** [əprí:ʃièit] v. 고마워하다; 진가를 알아보다
If you appreciate something that someone has done for you or is going to do for you, you are grateful for it.

‌* **tip** [tip] n. 조언; (뾰족한) 끝; v. 기울어지다; 살짝 건드리다
A tip is a useful piece of advice.

‌* **giggle** [gigl] v. 피식 웃다, 킥킥거리다; n. 피식 웃음, 킥킥거림
If someone giggles, they laugh in a childlike way, because they are amused, nervous, or embarrassed.

^{복습} **dash** [dæʃ] v. (급히) 서둘러 가다; 내동댕이치다; n. (승용차의) 계기판; 돌진, 질주
If you dash somewhere, you run or go there quickly and suddenly.

* **sneak** [sni:k] v. (snuck-snuck) 살금살금 가다; 몰래 하다; a. 기습적인
If you sneak somewhere, you go there very quietly on foot, trying to avoid being seen or heard.

복습 **hop** [hap] v. 급히 움직이다; 깡충깡충 뛰다; n. 깡충깡충 뛰기
If you hop somewhere, you move there quickly or suddenly.

* **sidewalk** [sáidwɔ:k] n. 보도, 인도
A sidewalk is a path with a hard surface by the side of a road.

복습 **chat** [tʃæt] v. 이야기를 나누다, 수다를 떨다; n. 이야기, 대화
When people chat, they talk to each other in an informal and friendly way.

* **upward** [ʌ́pwərd] a. 위쪽을 향한; (양·가격이) 상승하고 있는
An upward movement or look is directed towards a higher place or a higher level.

* **boom** [bu:m] n. 쾅 (하는 소리); v. 굵은 목소리로 말하다; 쾅 하는 소리를 내다
A boom is a deep loud sound that continues for some time, for example the noise of thunder or an explosion.

* **sound** [saund] a. 괜찮은; 믿을 만한; 철저한; ad. 충분히, 푹; n. 소리; v. ~처럼 들리다
If you describe someone's ideas as sound, you mean that you approve of them and think they are correct.

* **offense** [əféns] n. 모욕; 위법 행위, 범죄
(no offense idiom (내 말·행동에) 기분 나빠 하지 말아라)
Some people say 'no offense' to make it clear that they do not want to upset you, although what they are saying may seem rather rude.

walkway [wɔ́:kwei] n. 통로, 보도
A walkway is a passage or path for people to walk along. Walkways are often raised above the ground.

복습 **announce** [ənáuns] v. 발표하다, 알리다; 선언하다
If you announce something, you tell people about it publicly or officially.

* **impressive** [imprésiv] a. 인상적인, 감명 깊은
Something that is impressive impresses you, for example because it is great in size or degree, or is done with a great deal of skill.

복습 **hedgehog** [hédʒhɔ:g] n. [동물] 고슴도치
A hedgehog is a small brown animal with sharp spikes covering its back.

underwhelmed [ʌndərhwélmd] a. 전혀 감동하지 않는
If you are underwhelmed by something, you are not impressed or excited by it.

* **echo** [ékou] n. (소리의) 울림, 메아리; 반복; v. (소리가) 울리다; 그대로 따라 하다
An echo is a sound which is caused by a noise being reflected off a surface such as a wall.

* **meanwhile** [mí:nwàil] ad. (다른 일이 일어나고 있는) 그동안에
Meanwhile means while a particular thing is happening.

복습 **stare** [stɛər] v. 빤히 쳐다보다, 응시하다; n. 빤히 쳐다보기, 응시
If you stare at someone or something, you look at them for a long time.

* **pad** [pæd] n. 패드; 발사대; (메모지 등의) 묶음; v. 소리 안 나게 걷다; 완충재를 대다
A pad is a fairly thick, flat piece of a material such as cloth or rubber.

bingo [bíŋgou] int. 좋았어, 옳지; n. 빙고 게임
You can say 'bingo!' when something pleasant happens, especially in a surprising, unexpected, or sudden way.

복습 **click** [klik] v. (마우스를) 클릭하다; 분명해지다; n. (마우스를) 클릭함
If you click on an area of a computer screen, you point the cursor at that area and press one of the buttons on the mouse in order to make something happen.

squawk [skwɔːk] v. 시끄럽게 떠들다; (새가 크게) 꽥꽥 울다; n. (새 등이) 꽥꽥 우는 소리
If a person squawks, they complain loudly, often in a high-pitched, harsh tone.

복습 **mood** [muːd] n. 분위기; 기분
The mood of a place is the general impression that you get of it.

복습 **tiny** [táini] a. 아주 작은
Something or someone that is tiny is extremely small.

* **platform** [plǽtfɔ:rm] n. 승강장; (장비 등을 올려놓는) 대(臺); 연단, 강단
A platform in a railway station is the area beside the rails where you wait for or get off a train.

복습 **figure** [fígjər] n. (멀리서 흐릿하게 보이는) 사람; 수치; (중요한) 인물; v. 생각하다; 중요하다
You refer to someone that you can see as a figure when you cannot see them clearly or when you are describing them.

encase [inkéis] v. 감싸다, 둘러싸다
If a person or an object is encased in something, they are completely covered or surrounded by it.

* **capsule** [kǽpsəl] n. (우주선의) 캡슐; (약품) 캡슐; v. 캡슐에 넣다
A space capsule is the part of a spacecraft in which people travel, and which often separates from the main rocket.

* **gaze** [geiz] v. (가만히) 응시하다, 바라보다; n. 응시, (눈여겨보는) 시선
If you gaze at someone or something, you look steadily at them for a long time.

awe [ɔ:] n. 경외감, 외경심; v. 경외심을 갖게 하다
Awe is the feeling of respect and amazement that you have when you are faced with something wonderful and often rather frightening.

⁑ **tube** [tju:b] n. 관; 튜브; 통
A tube is a long hollow object that is usually round, like a pipe.

zoom [zu:m] v. 쌩 하고 가다; 급등하다; n. (빠르게) 쌩 하고 지나가는 소리
If you zoom somewhere, you go there very quickly.

* **launch** [lɔ:nʧ] n. 발사; 시작; 개시; v. 맹렬히 덤비다; 발사하다 (launch pad n. 발사대)
A launch pad or launching pad is a platform from which rockets, missiles, or satellites are launched.

⁑ **enclose** [inklóuz] v. 에워싸다; (담·울타리 등으로) 두르다
If a place or object is enclosed by something, the place or object is inside that thing or completely surrounded by it.

catapult [kǽtəpʌlt] v. (갑자기) 내던지다; n. 새총; 투석기
If someone or something catapults or is catapulted through the air, they are thrown very suddenly, quickly, and violently through it.

⁑ **trip** [trip] v. 발을 헛디디다; n. 여행; 발을 헛디딤
If you trip when you are walking, you knock your foot against something and fall or nearly fall.

encapsulate [inkǽpsjulèit] v. 캡슐에 넣다; 압축하다
If you encapsulate something, you enclose it in or as if in a capsule.

pod [pad] n. (우주선·선박의 본체에서) 분리 가능한 부분; (콩이 들어 있는) 꼬투리
A pod is a detachable or self-contained unit on an aircraft, spacecraft, vehicle, or vessel, having a particular function.

복습 **burst** [bə:rst] v. 터지다, 파열하다; 불쑥 움직이다; n. (갑자기) ~을 함; 파열, 폭발
If something bursts or if you burst it, it suddenly breaks open or splits open and the air or other substance inside it comes out.

muffle [mʌfl] v. (소리를) 죽이다; (따뜻하게) 감싸다
If something muffles a sound, it makes it quieter and more difficult to hear.

* **lightning** [láitniŋ] n. 번개, 번갯불; a. 아주 빨리; 급작스럽게
Lightning is the very bright flashes of light in the sky that happen during thunderstorms.

* **cable** [keibl] n. 전선, 케이블; 굵은 철제 밧줄
A cable is a thick wire, or a group of wires inside a rubber or plastic covering, which is used to carry electricity or electronic signals.

Check Your Reading Speed
1분에 몇 단어를 읽는지 리딩 속도를 측정해보세요.

$$\frac{852 \ words}{reading \ time \ (\qquad) \ sec} \times 60 = (\qquad) \ WPM$$

Build Your Vocabulary

* **thorough** [θə́ːrou] a. 완전한; 철저한; 빈틈없는, 철두철미한 (thoroughly ad. 완전히)
Thorough is used to emphasize the great degree or extent of something.

pod [pad] n. (우주선·선박의 본체에서) 분리 가능한 부분; (콩이 들어 있는) 꼬투리
A pod is a detachable or self-contained unit on an aircraft, spacecraft, vehicle, or vessel, having a particular function.

strangle [stræŋgl] v. 목을 조이다, 옭죄다
To strangle someone means to kill them by squeezing their throat tightly so that they cannot breathe.

* **release** [rilíːs] v. 놓아주다; 풀어 주다; (감정을) 발산하다; n. 풀어 줌; 발표, 공개
If you release someone or something, you stop holding them.

land [lænd] v. 떨어지다; (땅·표면에) 내려앉다; 놓다, 두다; n. 육지, 땅; 지역
When someone or something lands, they come down to the ground after moving through the air or falling.

* **widen** [waidn] v. 넓어지다; (정도·범위 등이) 커지다
If your eyes widen, they open more.

* **skyscraper** [skáiskrèipər] n. 고층 건물
A skyscraper is a very tall building in a city.

crowd [kraud] n. 사람들, 군중; v. 가득 메우다; 바싹 붙어 서다
A crowd is a large group of people who have gathered together, for example to watch or listen to something interesting, or to protest about something.

entrance [intræns] ① v. 도취시키다, 황홀하게 하다 ② n. 입구, 문; 입장, 등장
If something or someone entrances you, they cause you to feel delight and wonder, often so that all your attention is taken up and you cannot think about anything else.

splat [splæt] v. 철썩 하고 부딪히다; n. 철퍼덕 (하는 소리)
If someone or something splats, they land or are squashed with a splat.

dash [dæʃ] v. (급히) 서둘러 가다; 내동댕이치다; n. (승용차의) 계기판; 돌진, 질주
If you dash somewhere, you run or go there quickly and suddenly.

overlook [ouvərlúk] n. 전망이 좋은 곳, 높은 곳; v. 바라보다, 내려다보다; 눈감아주다
A overlook refers to a place from where a person can look at something, especially at an area of natural beauty.

gaze [geiz] v. (가만히) 응시하다, 바라보다; n. 응시, (눈여겨보는) 시선
If you gaze at someone or something, you look steadily at them for a long time.

awestruck [ɔ́:strʌk] a. 경이로워하는
If someone is awestruck, they are very impressed and amazed by something.

site [sait] n. (인터넷) 사이트; (사건 등의) 현장; 대지
A site is the same as a website which is a set of data and information about a particular subject which is available on the Internet.

float [flout] v. (물 위나 공중에서) 떠가다; (물에) 뜨다; n. 부표
Something that floats in or through the air hangs in it or moves slowly and gently through it.

sprawl [sprɔːl] v. 제멋대로 퍼져 나가다; 팔다리를 아무렇게나 벌리고 앉다; n. 뻗어 나간 것
If you say that a place sprawls, you mean that it covers a large area of land.

superhighway [suːpərháiwèi] n. 초고속 정보 통신망; (다차선의) 고속도로
A superhighway or an information superhighway is an extensive electronic network such as the Internet, used for the rapid transfer of information such as sound, video, and graphics.

stretch [stretʃ] v. 뻗어 있다; (팔다리를) 뻗다; (길이·폭 등을) 늘이다;
n. 뻗기, 펴기; (길게) 뻗은 구간
Something that stretches over an area or distance covers or exists in the whole of that area or distance.

roam [roum] v. (이리저리) 돌아다니다; (시선·손이) 천천히 훑다
If you roam an area or roam around it, you wander or travel around it without having a particular purpose.

futuristic [fjùːtʃərístik] a. 초현대적인; 미래를 상상하는
Something that is futuristic looks or seems very modern and unusual, like something from the future.

^복_습 **stuff** [stʌf] n. 일, 것, 물건; v. 쑤셔 넣다; 채워 넣다
You can use stuff to refer to things such as a substance, a collection of things, events, or ideas, or the contents of something in a general way without mentioning the thing itself by name.

^복_습 **notice** [nóutis] v. 알아채다, 인지하다; 주의하다; n. 신경 씀, 알아챔; 통지, 예고
If you notice something or someone, you become aware of them.

^복_습 **graduate** [grǽdʒuət] v. 졸업하다, 학위를 받다; n. 졸업자 (graduation n. 졸업식; 졸업)
A graduation is a special ceremony at university, college, or school, at which degrees and diplomas are given to students who have successfully completed their studies.

upbeat [ʌ́pbìːt] a. 긍정적인, 낙관적인
If people or their opinions are upbeat, they are cheerful and hopeful about a situation.

know-it-all [nóu-it-ɔːl] n. 아는 체하는 사람, 똑똑한 체하는 사람
If you say that someone is a know-it-all, you are critical of them because they think that they know a lot more than other people.

^복_습 **satisfactory** [sætisfǽktəri] a. 만족스러운, 더할 나위 없는
Something that is satisfactory is acceptable to you or fulfils a particular need or purpose.

tree-lined [tríː-laind] a. (양쪽에) 나무가 늘어선
A tree-lined road or street has trees on either side.

suburbia [səbə́ːrbiə] n. 교외; 교외 거주자
Journalists often use suburbia to refer to the suburbs of cities and large towns considered as a whole.

^복_습 **sip** [sip] v. (음료를) 홀짝거리다, 조금씩 마시다; n. 한 모금
If you sip a drink or sip at it, you drink by taking just a small amount at a time.

[*] **blink** [bliŋk] v. (불빛이) 깜박거리다; 눈을 깜박이다; n. 눈을 깜박거림
When a light blinks, it flashes on and off.

blurt [bləːrt] v. 불쑥 내뱉다, 말하다
If someone blurts something, they say it suddenly, after trying hard to keep quiet or to keep it secret.

^복_습 **last** [læst] v. 오래가다; (특정한 시간 동안) 계속되다; 견디다; ad. 맨 끝에, 마지막에
If an event, situation, or problem lasts for a particular length of time, it continues to exist or happen for that length of time.

* **phase** [feiz] n. (변화·발달의) 단계; v. 단계적으로 하다
A phase is a particular stage in a process or in the gradual development of
something.

split second [split sékənd] n. 아주 짧은 순간; 눈 깜짝할 사이
A split second is an extremely short period of time.

whisk [hwisk] v. 재빨리 데려가다; (달걀 등을) 휘젓다; n. 신속한 움직임
If you whisk someone or something somewhere, you take them or move them
there quickly.

: **specific** [spisífik] a. 특정한; 구체적인, 명확한
You use specific to refer to a particular fixed area, problem, or subject.

* **depart** [dipá:rt] v. 떠나다, 출발하다; 그만두다
When something or someone departs from a place, they leave it and start a
journey to another place.

: **phrase** [freiz] v. (말·글을) 표현하다; n. 구절, 관용구
If you phrase something in a particular way, you express it in words in that way.

umbrage [ámbridʒ] n. 불쾌, 분개; 나뭇잎
If you say that a person takes umbrage, you mean that they are upset or offended
by something that someone says or does to them, often without much reason.

복습 **interrupt** [intərápt] v. (말·행동을) 방해하다; 중단시키다; 차단하다
If you interrupt someone who is speaking, you say or do something that causes
them to stop.

* **rack** [ræk] n. 받침대, 선반; v. (몹시) 괴롭히다
A rack is a frame or shelf, usually with bars or hooks, that is used for holding
things or for hanging things on.

* **growl** [graul] v. 으르렁거리듯 말하다; 으르렁거리다; n. 으르렁거리는 소리
If someone growls something, they say something in a low, rough, and angry
voice.

복습 **frustrate** [frástreit] v. 좌절감을 주다, 불만스럽게 하다; 방해하다
(frustrated a. 좌절감을 느끼는)
If something frustrates you, it upsets or angers you because you are unable to do
anything about the problems it creates.

복습 **lean** [li:n] v. 기울이다, (몸을) 숙이다; ~에 기대다; a. 군살이 없는, 호리호리한
When you lean in a particular direction, you bend your body in that direction.

boil [bɔil] v. 삶다; (액체가) 끓다; n. (액체가) 끓음 (soft-boiled a. (달걀이) 반숙된)
A soft-boiled egg is one that has been boiled for only a few minutes, so that the yellow part is still liquid.

autofill [ɔ́ːtoufil] n. 자동 완성
Autofill is a feature on a computer that adds information to forms automatically.

tad [tæd] n. 조금
You can use a tad in expressions such as a tad big or a tad small when you mean that it is slightly too big or slightly too small.

aggressive [əgrésiv] a. 대단히 적극적인; 공격적인
People who are aggressive in their work or other activities behave in a forceful way because they are very eager to succeed.

embarrass [imbǽrəs] v. 당황스럽게 하다, 어색하게 하다; 곤란하게 하다
(embarrassed a. 어색한, 당황스러운)
A person who is embarrassed feels shy, ashamed, or guilty about something.

query [kwíəri] n. 문의, 의문; v. 묻다, 질문하다; 의문을 제기하다
A query is a question, especially one that you ask an organization, publication, or expert.

dumbfounded [dʌ̀mfáundid] a. (놀라서) 말문이 막힌, 어안이 벙벙한
If you are dumbfounded, you are extremely surprised by something.

intuitive [intjúːətiv] a. 이해하기 쉬운; 직감에 의한
An intuitive system, method, or piece of software is easy to use because the process of operating it is very obvious.

grin [grin] n. 활짝 웃음; v. 활짝 웃다
A grin is a broad smile.

instant [ínstənt] a. 즉각적인; n. 순간, 아주 짧은 동안 (instantly ad. 즉각, 즉시)
You use instant to describe something that happens immediately.

encase [inkéis] v. 감싸다, 둘러싸다
If a person or an object is encased in something, they are completely covered or surrounded by it.

redirect [riːdirékt] v. (다른 주소·방향으로) 다시 보내다; 돌려쓰다
If you redirect someone or something, you change their course or destination.

robotic [roubátik] a. 로봇 같은; 로봇식의
Robotic is used about someone's way of speaking or looking when it seems to show no human feeling.

* **delightful** [diláitfəl] a. 정말 기분 좋은, 마음에 드는
If you describe something or someone as delightful, you mean they are very pleasant.

* **zip** [zip] v. (어떤 방향으로) 쌩 하고 가다; 지퍼를 잠그다; n. 지퍼
If you say that something or someone zip somewhere, you mean that they move very fast.

wide-eyed [waid-áid] a. 눈이 휘둥그레진; 순진한
If you describe someone as wide-eyed, you mean that they are having their eyes wide open as a result of surprise or fear.

translucent [trænslú:snt] a. 반투명한
If a material is translucent, some light can pass through it.

* **sight** [sait] n. 광경, 모습; 보기; 시력; v. 갑자기 보다
A sight is something that you see.

* **whip** [hwip] v. 격렬하게 움직이다; 휙 빼내다; n. 채찍
If you whip in a particular direction, you move fast or suddenly in that direction.

goggle [gagl] n. (pl.) 보호 안경, 고글
Goggles are large glasses that fit closely to your face around your eyes to protect them from such things as water, wind, or dust.

* **screech** [skri:ʧ] v. 끼익 하는 소리를 내다; n. 끼익, 꽥 (하는 날카로운 소리)
When you screech something, you shout it in a loud, unpleasant, high-pitched voice.

* **sign** [sain] n. 표지판; 몸짓, 신호; 기색, 흔적; v. 서명하다; 신호를 보내다
A sign is a piece of wood, metal, or plastic with words or pictures on it. Signs give you information about something, or give you a warning or an instruction.

1. **What did Ralph and Vanellope assume about eBay auctions?**

   A. They assumed every bidder was rich.

   B. They assumed bidders only bought expensive items.

   C. They assumed the goal was to say the highest number.

   D. They assumed the purpose was to collect as many items as possible.

2. **What was happening when they reached the *Sugar Rush* steering wheel auction?**

   A. Several avatars were bidding.

   B. There was less than a minute left.

   C. The bidding had already reached twenty-seven thousand.

   D. Many pop-ups were gathering around the wheel.

3. **What would happen if they couldn't pay for the wheel within twenty-four hours?**

   A. They would not be able to receive the wheel.

   B. They would have to bid on the wheel again.

   C. They would be arrested and sent to jail.

   D. They would have to fill out extra forms.

4. **Why did they approach Spamley for help?**

   A. They wanted to distract themselves with video games.

   B. They needed to make a lot of money fast.

   C. They thought they could borrow Spamley's credit card.

   D. They wondered if Spamley could fix the *Sugar Rush* game.

5. **What was true about *Slaughter Race?***

   A. It was the newest game on the Internet.

   B. It was an easy game to win.

   C. It was the cheapest online game.

   D. It was a popular racing game.

Check Your Reading Speed

1분에 몇 단어를 읽는지 리딩 속도를 측정해보세요.

$$\frac{776 \text{ words}}{\text{reading time (\quad) sec}} \times 60 = (\qquad) \text{ WPM}$$

Build Your Vocabulary

drop off idiom 내려 주다; 데려다주다
If you drop someone off, you stop and let them get out of a car.

netizen [nétəzən] n. 네티즌, 인터넷 사용자
A netizen is a person who uses the internet.

rush [rʌʃ] v. 급히 움직이다; 서두르다; n. (감정이 갑자기) 치밀어 오름; 혼잡; 기쁨, 흥분
If you rush somewhere, you go there quickly.

make one's way idiom 나아가다, 가다
When you make your way somewhere, you walk or travel there.

entrance [éntrəns] ① n. 입구, 문; 입장, 등장 ② v. 도취시키다, 황홀하게 하다
The entrance to a place is the way into it, for example a door or gate.

pop-up [páp-ʌp] n. 팝업; a. 팝업의; 그림이 입체적으로 만들어지는
A pop-up is something such as an advertisement that appears suddenly on a computer screen when you are looking at the Internet, or when you click the mouse or press a key.

surround [səráund] v. 둘러싸다, 에워싸다; 포위하다
If a person or thing is surrounded by something, that thing is situated all around them.

distract [distrǽkt] v. (주의를) 딴 데로 돌리다, 집중이 안 되게 하다
If something distracts you or your attention from something, it takes your attention away from it.

belly [béli] n. 배, 복부; (사물의) 볼록한 부분
The belly of a person or animal is their stomach or abdomen.

‡ **fat** [fæt] n. 지방; a. 살찐, 비만인
Fat is the extra flesh that animals and humans have under their skin, which is used to store energy and to help keep them warm.

복습 **weird** [wiərd] a. 기이한, 기묘한; 기괴한, 섬뜩한
If you describe something or someone as weird, you mean that they are strange.

‡ **trick** [trik] n. 요령; 속임수; 솜씨, 재주; v. 속이다, 속임수를 쓰다
A trick is a clever way of doing something.

sassy [sǽsi] a. 멋진, 대담한
If an older person describes a younger person as sassy, they mean that they are disrespectful in a lively, confident way.

* **housewife** [háuswàif] n. (pl. housewives) (전업)주부
A housewife is a married woman who does not have a paid job, but instead looks after her home and children.

‡ **congratulate** [kəngrǽtʃulèit] v. 축하하다; 기뻐하다, 자랑스러워하다
(congratulations int. 축하해요!)
You say 'Congratulations' to someone in order to congratulate them on something nice that has happened to them or something good that they have done.

복습 **pop** [pap] v. 불쑥 나타나다; 눈이 휘둥그레지다; 펑 하는 소리가 나다; n. 펑 (하는 소리)
If something pops up, it appears or happens when you do not expect it.

‡ **prison** [prizn] n. 교도소, 감옥
A prison is a building where criminals are kept as punishment or where people accused of a crime are kept before their trial.

복습 **amaze** [əméiz] v. (대단히) 놀라게 하다; 경악하게 하다
If something amazes you, it surprises you very much.

복습 **stuff** [stʌf] n. 일, 것, 물건; v. 쑤셔 넣다; 채워 넣다
You can use stuff to refer to things such as a substance, a collection of things, events, or ideas, or the contents of something in a general way without mentioning the thing itself by name.

복습 **nearby** [niərbái] a. 인근의, 가까운 곳의; ad. 가까운 곳에
If something is nearby, it is only a short distance away.

* **drag** [dræg] v. 끌다, 끌고 가다; 힘들게 움직이다; n. 끌기, 당기기; 장애물
If someone drags you somewhere you do not want to go, they make you go there.

bazaar [bəzáːr] n. 상점가, 시장 거리
In areas such as the Middle East and India, a bazaar is a place where there are many small shops and stalls.

flea market [fliː maːrkit] n. 벼룩시장
A flea market is an outdoor market which sells cheap used goods and sometimes also very old furniture.

counter [káuntər] n. 계산대; (식당·바 등의) 카운터; 반작용; v. 대응하다; 반박하다
In a place such as a shop or café a counter is a long narrow table or flat surface at which customers are served.

bid [bid] n. 가격 제시; 입찰; v. (작별을) 고하다; 값을 부르다
A bid is an offer to pay a particular amount of money for something that is being sold.

auctioneer [ɔːkʃəníər] n. 경매인
An auctioneer is a person in charge of an auction.

rattle off idiom 줄줄 말하다; 나불나불 지껄여 대다
If you rattle something off, you say or repeat them from memory, quickly and without any effort.

sorrowful [sárəfəl] a. 슬픈
Sorrowful means very sad.

kitten [kitn] n. [동물] 새끼 고양이
A kitten is a very young cat.

fuzzy [fʌ́zi] a. 솜털이 보송보송한; 흐릿한, 어렴풋한
If something is fuzzy, it has a covering that feels soft and like fur.

feline [fíːlain] n. 고양이; 고양이과의 동물; a. 고양이 같은
A feline is an animal that belongs to the cat family.

oversized [óuvərsàizd] a. 너무 큰; 특대의
Oversize or oversized things are too big, or much bigger than usual.

announcer [ənáunsər] n. (프로그램) 방송 진행자
An announcer is someone who introduces programs on radio or television or who reads the text of a radio or television advertisement.

stuffed [stʌft] a. 박제한; (속을) 채운; 배부른
If a dead animal is stuffed, it is filled with a substance so that it can be preserved and displayed.

take in idiom ~을 눈여겨보다; 이해하다
If you take in something, you spend time looking at it.

artificial [à:rtəfíʃəl] a. 인공의; 인위적인; 거짓된, 꾸민
Artificial objects, materials, or processes do not occur naturally and are created by human beings, for example using science or technology.

hip [hip] n. 둔부, 엉덩이
Your hips are the two areas at the sides of your body between the tops of your legs and your waist.

auction [ɔ́:kʃən] n. 경매; v. 경매로 팔다
An auction is a public sale where goods are sold to the person who offers the highest price.

chip [tʃip] n. 감자칩; 조각, 부스러기; v. 이가 빠지다; (조금씩) 깎다; a. 바삭바삭한
Chips are very thin slices of fried potato that are eaten cold as a snack.

celebrity [səlébrəti] n. 유명 인사; 명성
A celebrity is someone who is famous, especially in areas of entertainment such as films, music, writing, or sport.

bark [ba:rk] v. (명령·질문 등을) 빽 내지르다; (개가) 짖다; n. 나무껍질; (개 등이) 짖는 소리
If you bark at someone, you shout at them aggressively in a loud, rough voice.

joyful [dʒɔ́ifəl] a. 아주 기뻐하는; 기쁜 (joyfully ad. 기뻐하여)
Someone who is joyful is extremely happy.

utter [ʌ́tər] a. 완전한; v. (말을) 하다; (어떤 소리를) 내다 (utterly ad. 완전히)
You use utterly to emphasize that something is very great in extent, degree, or amount.

confuse [kənfjú:z] v. (사람을) 혼란시키다; 혼동하다 (confused a. 혼란스러워하는)
If you are confused, you do not know exactly what is happening or what to do.

yell [jel] v. 고함치다, 소리 지르다; n. 고함, 외침
If you yell, you shout loudly, usually because you are excited, angry, or in pain.

glitch [gliʃ] v. 갑자기 고장 나다; n. 작은 문제, 결함
To glitch means to suffer a sudden malfunction or fault.

spot [spat] v. 발견하다, 찾다, 알아채다; n. (특정한) 곳; (작은) 점
If you spot something or someone, you notice them.

^{복습} **steer** [stiər] v. (보트·자동차 등을) 조종하다; (특정 방향으로) 움직이다
When you steer a car, boat, or plane, you control it so that it goes in the direction that you want.

^{복습} **wheel** [hwi:l] n. (자동차 등의) 핸들; 바퀴; v. (바퀴 달린 것을) 밀다
(steering wheel n. (자동차의) 핸들)
The wheel of a car or other vehicle is the circular object that is used to steer it.

^{복습} **bunch** [bʌnʧ] n. (양·수가) 많음; 다발, 묶음
A bunch of things is a number of things, especially a large number.

memorabilia [mèmərəbíliə] n. (유명인·흥미로운 장소·행사 등과 관련된) 수집품, 기념품
Memorabilia are things that you collect because they are connected with a person or organization in which you are interested.

[*] **row** [rou] n. 열, 줄; 노 젓기; v. 노를 젓다
A row of things or people is a number of them arranged in a line.

^{복습} **junk** [dʒʌŋk] n. 쓸모없는 물건, 폐물, 쓰레기; v. 폐물로 처분하다
Junk is old and used goods that have little value and that you do not want any more.

^{복습} **race** [reis] v. 쏜살같이 가다; 경주하다; (머리·심장 등이) 바쁘게 돌아가다; n. 경주; 인종, 종족
If you race somewhere, you go there as quickly as possible.

^{복습} **knock** [nak] v. 치다, 부딪치다; (문 등을) 두드리다; n. 문 두드리는 소리; 부딪침
To knock someone into a particular position or condition means to hit them very hard so that they fall over or become unconscious.

tick [tik] v. (시계 등이) 째깍거리다; n. (시계가) 똑딱이는 소리
When a clock or watch ticks, it makes a regular series of short sounds as it works.

^{복습} **blurt** [blə:rt] v. 불쑥 내뱉다, 말하다
If someone blurts something, they say it suddenly, after trying hard to keep quiet or to keep it secret.

[*] **whisper** [hwíspər] v. 속삭이다, 소곤거리다; n. 속삭임, 소곤거리는 소리
When you whisper, you say something very quietly, using your breath rather than your throat, so that only one person can hear you.

^{복습} **elbow** [élbou] v. (팔꿈치로) 밀치다; n. 팔꿈치
If you elbow people aside or elbow your way somewhere, you push people with your elbows in order to move somewhere.

^복_습 **smooth** [smuːð] a. 순조로운; (맛이) 부드러운; 매끈한; v. 매끈하게 하다
You use smooth to describe something that is going well and is free of problems
or trouble.

* **impress** [imprés] v. 깊은 인상을 주다, 감동을 주다 (impressed a. 감명을 받은)
If something impresses you, you feel great admiration for it.

check out idiom (흥미로운 것을) 살펴보다; ~을 확인하다
If you check someone or something out, you look at them to see whether you
like them.

* **shrewd** [ʃruːd] a. 상황 판단이 빠른; 날카로운 (shrewdly ad. 예민하게)
A shrewd person is able to understand and judge a situation quickly and to use
this understanding to their own advantage.

get the hang of idiom ~을 할 줄 알게 되다; 요령을 알다
If you get the hang of something such as a skill or activity, you begin to understand
or realize how to do it.

run out idiom (시간·돈 등이) 없어지다, 다 되다
If time is running out, you do not have long to do something.

barefoot [béərfùt] a. 맨발의; ad. 맨발로
Someone who is barefoot or barefooted is not wearing anything on their feet.

hobo [hóubou] n. 떠돌이 일꾼
A hobo is a person who has no home, especially one who travels from place to
place and gets money by begging.

* **overall** [óuvərɔːl] n. (pl.) 멜빵바지, 작업복; a. 총체적인, 전부의
Overalls consist of a single piece of clothing that combines trousers and a jacket.
You wear overalls over your clothes in order to protect them while you are
working.

* **beam** [biːm] v. 활짝 웃다; 비추다; n. 빛줄기; 기둥
If you say that someone is beaming, you mean that they have a big smile on their
face because they are happy, pleased, or proud about something.

^복_습 **cheer** [ʧiər] v. 환호성을 지르다, 환호하다; n. 환호(성), 응원
When people cheer, they shout loudly to show their approval or to encourage
someone who is doing something such as taking part in a game.

voucher [váuʧər] n. 증명서; 영수증; 할인권
A voucher is a ticket or piece of paper that can be used instead of money to pay
for something.

slip [slip] n. (작은 종이) 조각; 미끄러짐; v. 슬며시 가다; 미끄러지다
A slip of paper is a small piece of paper.

checkout [ʧékaut] n. 계산대; (호텔에서) 체크아웃
In a supermarket, a checkout is a counter where you pay for things you are buying.

process [práses] v. 처리하다; n. (특정 결과를 달성하기 위한) 과정
When people process information, they put it through a system or into a computer in order to deal with it.

celebratory [séləbratɔ̀:ri] a. 축하하는
A celebratory meal, drink, or other activity takes place to celebrate something such as a birthday, anniversary, or victory.

fist [fist] n. 주먹
Your hand is referred to as your fist when you have bent your fingers in toward the palm in order to hit someone, to make an angry gesture, or to hold something.

bump [bʌmp] n. 부딪치기; (도로의) 튀어나온 부분; 쿵, 탁 (하는 소리);
v. (~에) 부딪치다; 덜컹거리며 가다
A bump is the action or the dull sound of two heavy objects hitting each other.

victorious [viktɔ́:riəs] a. 의기양양한, 승리를 거둔
You use victorious to describe someone who has won a victory in a struggle, war, or competition.

Check Your Reading Speed
1분에 몇 단어를 읽는지 리딩 속도를 측정해보세요.

$$\frac{1{,}201 \text{ words}}{\text{reading time (} \quad \text{) sec}} \times 60 = (\qquad) \text{ WPM}$$

Build Your Vocabulary

checkout [ʧékaut] n. 계산대; (호텔에서) 체크아웃
In a supermarket, a checkout is a counter where you pay for things you are buying.

greet [griːt] v. 인사하다; 환영하다; 반응을 보이다
When you greet someone, you say 'Hello' or shake hands with them.

straight-faced [streit-féist] a. 무표정한 얼굴을 한
A straight-faced person appears not to be amused in a funny situation.

clerk [kləːrk] n. 직원; 점원; v. 사무원으로 일하다
A clerk is a person who works in an office, bank, or law court and whose job is to look after the records or accounts.

voucher [váuʧər] n. 증명서; 영수증; 할인권
A voucher is a ticket or piece of paper that can be used instead of money to pay for something.

expedite [ékspədàit] v. 더 신속히 처리하다
If you expedite something, you cause it to be done more quickly.

scrap [skræp] v. 폐기하다, 버리다; n. (종이·옷감 등의) 조각; 폐품
If you scrap something, you get rid of it or cancel it.

rule [ruːl] v. 최고이다; 지배하다, 통치하다; n. 규칙, 규정; 지배, 통치
If you say that someone or something rules, you mean that they are more important or successful than anyone or anything else.

credit [krédit] n. 신용 거래; 입금; 칭찬; v. 입금하다; ~의 공으로 믿다 (credit card n. 신용 카드)
A credit card is a plastic card that you use to buy goods on credit.

impatient [impéiʃənt] a. 짜증난, 안달하는; 어서 ~하고 싶어 하는
If you are impatient, you are annoyed because you have to wait too long for something.

^{복습} **tone** [toun] n. 어조, 말투; (글 등의) 분위기; 음색
Someone's tone is a quality in their voice which shows what they are feeling or thinking.

* **creep** [kri:p] v. 살금살금 움직이다; 기다; n. 너무 싫은 사람
If something creeps in or creeps back, it begins to occur or becomes part of something without people realizing or without them wanting it.

* **frown** [fraun] v. 얼굴을 찡그리다; 눈살을 찌푸리다; n. 찡그림, 찌푸림
When someone frowns, their eyebrows become drawn together, because they are annoyed, worried, or puzzled, or because they are concentrating.

‡ **ridiculous** [ridíkjuləs] a. 웃기는, 말도 안 되는, 터무니없는
If you say that something or someone is ridiculous, you mean that they are very foolish.

‡ **annoy** [ənɔ́i] v. 짜증나게 하다; 귀찮게 하다 (annoyed a. 짜증이 난, 약이 오른)
If you are annoyed, you are fairly angry about something.

‡ **narrow** [nǽrou] v. (눈을) 찌푸리다; 좁히다; a. 좁은
If your eyes narrow or if you narrow your eyes, you almost close them, for example because you are angry or because you are trying to concentrate on something.

^{복습} **owe** [ou] v. (돈을) 빚지고 있다; 신세를 지고 있다
If you owe money to someone, they have lent it to you and you have not yet paid it back.

* **stun** [stʌn] v. 깜짝 놀라게 하다; 어리벙벙하게 하다; 기절시키다 (stunned a. 깜짝 놀란)
If you are stunned by something, you are extremely shocked or surprised by it and are therefore unable to speak or do anything.

galoot [gəlúːt] n. 얼빠진 놈, 얼간이, 바보
If you call someone a galoot, you mean that they are clumsy or stupid.

go with idiom ~에 동조하다, 동의하다; (생각·계획을) 지지하다
If you go with something or someone, you accept an idea or agree with them.

^{복습} **lock** [lak] v. (자물쇠로) 잠그다; 고정시키다; n. 잠금장치
When you lock something such as a door, drawer, or case, you fasten it, usually with a key, so that other people cannot open it.

‡ **deal** [di:l] v. 처리하다; n. 거래; 일, 사항; 처리
If you deal with something, you take action in order to achieve it or in order to solve a problem.

* **violate** [váiəlèit] v. 위반하다; 침해하다; 훼손하다 (violation n. 위반, 위배)
If someone violates an agreement, law, or promise, they break it.

* **policy** [páləsi] n. 정책, 방침; 보험 증권
A policy is a set of ideas or plans that is used as a basis for making decisions, especially in politics, economics, or business.

forfeit [fɔ́:rfit] v. 박탈당하다; n. 벌금; 몰수품
If you forfeit something, you lose it or are forced to give it up because you have broken a rule or done something wrong.

복습 **bid** [bid] n. 입찰; 가격 제시; v. (작별을) 고하다; 값을 부르다
A bid is an offer to pay a particular amount of money for something that is being sold.

복습 **disappoint** [dìsəpɔ́int] v. 실망시키다, 실망을 안겨 주다; 좌절시키다
(disappointed a. 실망한, 낙담한)
If you are disappointed, you are rather sad because something has not happened or because something is not as good as you had hoped.

fume [fju:m] v. (화가 나서) 씩씩대다; 연기를 내뿜다; n. 연기; 화, 흥분
If you fume over something, you express annoyance and anger about it.

rant [rænt] v. 고함치다, 큰소리로 불평하다; n. 고함
If you say that someone rants, you mean that they talk loudly or angrily, and exaggerate or say foolish things.

* **buddy** [bʌ́di] n. 친구
A buddy is a close friend, usually a male friend of a man.

scam [skæm] n. 신용 사기
A scam is an illegal trick, usually with the purpose of getting money from people or avoiding paying tax.

복습 **punch** [pʌntʃ] v. 주먹으로 치다; (자판·번호판 등을) 치다; n. 주먹으로 한 대 침
If you punch someone or something, you hit them hard with your fist.

복습 **bargain** [bá:rgən] n. 싸게 사는 물건; 합의, 흥정; v. 협상하다
Something that is a bargain is good value for money, usually because it has been sold at a lower price than normal.

복습 **fist** [fist] n. 주먹
Your hand is referred to as your fist when you have bent your fingers in toward the palm in order to hit someone, to make an angry gesture, or to hold something.

slip [slip] v. 미끄러지다; 슬며시 가다; n. (작은 종이) 조각; 미끄러짐
If something slips, it slides out of place or out of your hand.

yank [jæŋk] v. 홱 잡아당기다; n. 홱 잡아당기기
If you yank someone or something somewhere, you pull them there suddenly and with a lot of force.

hurl [hə:rl] v. (거칠게) 던지다; (욕·비난·모욕 등을) 퍼붓다
If you hurl something, you throw it violently and with a lot of force.

crash [kræʃ] v. 부딪치다; 충돌하다; (컴퓨터를) 고장 내다; n. 요란한 소리; (자동차·항공기) 사고
If something crashes somewhere, it moves and hits something else violently, making a loud noise.

kick off idiom 쫓아내다
To kick someone off something means to force them to leave a place or activity.

whine [hwain] v. 징징거리다, 우는 소리를 하다; 낑낑거리다; n. 칭얼거리는 소리; 불평
If you say that someone is whining, you mean that they are complaining in an annoying way about something unimportant.

powerless [páuərlis] a. 힘없는, 무력한; 전혀 ~할 수 없는
Someone who is powerless is unable to control or influence events.

collapse [kəlǽps] v. 쓰러지다; 주저앉다; 붕괴되다; 무너지다; n. 실패; (건물의) 붕괴
If you collapse, you suddenly faint or fall down because you are very ill or weak.

heap [hi:p] n. 더미, 무더기; 많음; v. 수북이 담다; (아무렇게나) 쌓다
(collapse into a heap idiom 쿵 하고 쓰러져 움직이지 않다)
If someone collapses in a heap, they fall heavily and untidily and do not move.

rush [rʌʃ] v. 급히 움직이다; 서두르다; n. (감정이 갑자기) 치밀어 오름; 혼잡; 기쁨, 흥분
If you rush somewhere, you go there quickly.

blow [blou] v. (blew-blown) (기회를) 날리다; (바람·입김에) 날리다; n. 강타
If you blow a chance or attempt to do something, you make a mistake which wastes the chance or causes the attempt to fail.

confident [kánfədənt] a. 자신감 있는; 확신하는 (confidently ad. 자신 있게)
If a person or their manner is confident, they feel sure about their own abilities, qualities, or ideas.

figure out idiom ~을 이해하다, 알아내다; 계산하다, 산출하다
If you figure out someone or something, you come to understand them by thinking carefully.

RALPH BREAKS THE INTERNET

* **magical** [mǽdʒikəl] a. 마술적인, 마술에 걸린 (듯한); 황홀한, 아주 멋진
Something that is magical seems to use magic or to be able to produce magic.

pop-up [páp-ʌp] n. 팝업; a. 팝업의; 그림이 입체적으로 만들어지는
A pop-up is something such as an advertisement that appears suddenly on a computer screen when you are looking at the Internet, or when you click the mouse or press a key.

click [klik] v. (마우스를) 클릭하다; 분명해지다; n. (마우스를) 클릭함
If you click on an area of a computer screen, you point the cursor at that area and press one of the buttons on the mouse in order to make something happen.

block [blak] v. 막다, 차단하다; 방해하다; n. 구역, 블록; 사각형 덩어리
If you block something that is being arranged, you prevent it from being done.

brush [brʌʃ] v. (솔이나 손으로) 털다; 솔질을 하다; n. 붓; 솔; 비
If you brush something somewhere, you remove it with quick light movements of your hands.

thank goodness idiom 정말 다행이다!
You say 'Thank God,' 'Thank Goodness,' or 'Thank heavens' when you are very relieved about something.

bet [bet] v. (~이) 틀림없다; (내기 등에) 돈을 걸다; n. 짐작, 추측; 내기 (you bet idiom 물론이지!)
You use 'You bet' to say yes in an emphatic way or to emphasize a reply or statement.

encase [inkéis] v. 감싸다, 둘러싸다
If a person or an object is encased in something, they are completely covered or surrounded by it.

rickety [ríkiti] a. 곧 무너질 듯한; 낡아빠진, 황폐한
A rickety structure or piece of furniture is not very strong or well made, and seems likely to collapse or break.

* **ample** [ǽmpl] a. 충분한, 넉넉한; 광대한, 넓은
If there is an ample amount of something, there is enough of it and usually some extra.

carriage [kǽridʒ] n. 운반; 마차
Carriage is the cost or action of transporting or delivering goods.

buster [bʌ́stər] n. 이봐, 임마
Buster is used as a mildly disrespectful form of address to a man or boy.

drag [dræg] n. 장애물; 끌기, 당기기; v. 끌다, 끌고 가다; 힘들게 움직이다
If something is a drag on the development or progress of something, it slows it down or makes it more difficult.

superhighway [su:pərháiwèi] n. 초고속 정보 통신망; (다차선의) 고속도로
A superhighway or an information superhighway is an extensive electronic network such as the Internet, used for the rapid transfer of information such as sound, video, and graphics.

steep [sti:p] a. 가파른, 비탈진; 급격한; 터무니없는
A steep slope rises at a very sharp angle and is difficult to go up.

drop-off [drap-ɔ́:f] n. 절벽
A drop-off is a vertical or very steep descent.

panic [pǽnik] v. (panicked-panicked) 어쩔 줄 모르다, 공황 상태에 빠지다;
n. 극심한 공포, 공황; 허둥지둥함
If you panic or if someone panics you, you suddenly feel anxious or afraid, and act quickly and without thinking carefully.

edge [edʒ] n. 끝, 가장자리; 우위; v. 조금씩 움직이다; 테두리를 두르다
The edge of something is the place or line where it stops, or the part of it that is furthest from the middle.

barely [béərli] ad. 간신히, 가까스로; 거의 ~아니게
You use barely to say that something is only just true or only just the case.

afloat [əflóut] a. (물에) 뜬
If someone or something is afloat, they remain partly above the surface of water and do not sink.

site [sait] n. (인터넷) 사이트; (사건 등의) 현장; 대지
A site is the same as a website which is a set of data and information about a particular subject which is available on the Internet.

stack [stæk] n. 무더기, 더미; v. (깔끔하게 정돈하여) 쌓다
A stack of things is a pile of them.

garbage [gá:rbidʒ] n. 쓰레기
Garbage is rubbish, especially waste from a kitchen.

container [kəntéinər] n. 용기, 그릇; (화물 수송용) 컨테이너
A container is something such as a box or bottle that is used to hold or store things in.

hoard [hɔːrd] v. 저장하다, 축적하다; n. 저장, 축적
If you hoard things such as food or money, you save or store them, often in secret, because they are valuable or important to you.

professional [prəféʃənl] a. 전문적인; 능숙한; 직업상 적합한; n. 전문가
Professional means relating to a person's work, especially work that requires special training.

workplace [wɔ́ːrkplèis] n. 직장, 업무 현장
Your workplace is the place where you work.

recoil [rikɔ́il] v. 움찔하다, 흠칫 놀라다; (발사할 때) 반동이 생기다; n. 반동
If something makes you recoil, you move your body quickly away from it because it frightens, offends, or hurts you.

rotten [ratn] a. 썩은, 부패한; 형편없는, 끔찍한
If food, wood, or another substance is rotten, it has decayed and can no longer be used.

stench [stentʃ] n. 악취
A stench is a strong and very unpleasant smell.

doubtful [dáutfəl] a. 확신이 없는, 의심을 품은; 불확실한
If you are doubtful about something, you feel unsure or uncertain about it.

mess [mes] n. (지저분하고) 엉망인 상태; (많은 문제로) 엉망인 상황; v. 엉망으로 만들다
If you say that something is a mess or in a mess, you think that it is in an untidy state.

chunky [tʃʌ́ŋki] a. 두툼한; (몸이) 땅딸막한
A chunky object is large and thick.

startle [staːrtl] v. 깜짝 놀라게 하다; 움찔하다; n. 깜짝 놀람
If something sudden and unexpected startles you, it surprises and frightens you slightly.

wanted [wántid] a. (경찰의) 수배 중인, 수배를 받고 있는
If someone is wanted by the police, the police are searching for them because they are thought to have committed a crime.

poster [póustər] n. (안내·홍보용) 포스터, 벽보; v. 포스터를 붙이다
A poster is a large notice or picture that you stick on a wall or board, often in order to advertise something.

amulet [金mjulit] n. (불운 등을 막아 주는) 부적
An amulet is a small object that you wear or carry because you think it will bring you good luck and protect you from evil or injury.

⁎ **wizard** [wízərd] n. (동화 등에 나오는 남자) 마법사
In legends and fairy stories, a wizard is a man who has magic powers.

⁎ **quest** [kwest] n. 탐구, 추구; v. 탐구하다, 탐색하다
A quest is a long and difficult search for something.

⁎ **commonplace** [kámənplèis] a. 아주 흔한; n. 흔히 있는 일, 다반사
If something is commonplace, it happens often or is often found, and is therefore not surprising.

back up idiom 반복해서 말하다
If you say 'back up' to someone, you want to tell them to return to something that was said earlier.

⁑ **sheet** [ʃiːt] n. (종이) 한 장; 얇은 천
A sheet of paper is a rectangular piece of paper.

soft in the head idiom 머리가 모자라는
If someone is soft in the head, they are crazy or stupid.

⁎ **chuckle** [ʧʌkl] n. 킬킬거림; 속으로 웃기; v. 킬킬 웃다; 빙그레 웃다
A chuckle is a quiet or suppressed laugh.

buttload [bʌ́tlòud] n. 상당히 많은 양
A buttload of something is a large number or amount of it.

lucrative [lúːkrətiv] a. 수익성이 좋은
A lucrative activity, job, or business deal is very profitable.

perchance [pərʧǽns] ad. 아마 어쩌면
Perchance means perhaps.

복
습 **exclaim** [ikskléim] v. 소리치다, 외치다
If you exclaim, you cry out suddenly in surprise, strong emotion, or pain.

slaughter [slɔ́ːtər] n. 대량 학살, 살육; 도살; v. (대량) 학살하다; 도축하다
Slaughter is the violent killing of a large number of people.

disbelief [dìsbilíːf] n. 믿기지 않음, 불신감
Disbelief is not believing that something is true or real.

* **wicked** [wíkid] ad. 매우, 몹시; a. 위험한, 심한; 아주 좋은; 못된; 짓궂은
  You use wicked in front of adjectives to emphasize that the specified quality is
  present to a very great degree.

: **hopeful** [hóupfəl] a. 희망에 찬, 기대하는; 희망적인
  If you are hopeful, you are fairly confident that something that you want to
  happen will happen.

1. Why did Ralph distract Shank and her crew?

   A. So that Vanellope could sneak into Shank's car

   B. So that Jimmy and Tiffany could get revenge on Shank

   C. So that Shank and her crew would calm down and be quieter

   D. So that the Department of Noise could investigate the warehouse

2. What happened as Vanellope and Ralph tried to escape the game?

   A. They ended up driving in circles.

   B. Vanellope started randomly glitching.

   C. Pyro threatened to burn them.

   D. Shank kept chasing them.

3. **Why did Shank and her crew record a video of Ralph?**
    A. To try to cheer him up
    B. To try to embarrass him
    C. To try to help him make money
    D. To try to give him a new hobby

4. **What did Shank say about BuzzzTube?**
    A. She had a friend who worked there.
    B. She posted videos on it every day.
    C. She watched a lot of viral videos on it.
    D. She used to be its top star.

5. **Why did Vanellope like *Slaughter Race?***
    A. The track was predictable.
    B. The game was refreshing.
    C. The characters were incredibly tough.
    D. There were no winners or losers.

Check Your Reading Speed
1분에 몇 단어를 읽는지 리딩 속도를 측정해보세요.

$$\frac{1,549 \text{ words}}{\text{reading time (\quad) sec}} \times 60 = (\qquad) \text{ WPM}$$

Build Your Vocabulary

slaughter [slɔ́:tər] n. 대량 학살, 살육; 도살; v. (대량) 학살하다; 도축하다
Slaughter is the violent killing of a large number of people.

explode [iksplóud] v. 폭발하다; 갑자기 ~하다; 굉음을 내다
If an object such as a bomb explodes or if someone or something explodes it, it bursts loudly and with great force, often causing damage or injury.

giddy [gídi] a. (너무 좋아서) 들뜬; 어지러운, 아찔한
If you feel giddy with delight or excitement, you feel so happy or excited that you find it hard to think or act normally.

impressive [imprésiv] a. 인상적인, 감명 깊은
Something that is impressive impresses you, for example because it is great in size or degree, or is done with a great deal of skill.

smog [smag] n. 스모그, 연무
Smog is a mixture of fog and smoke which occurs in some busy industrial cities.

uneasy [ʌní:zi] a. (마음이) 불안한, 우려되는; 불안한; 어색한
If you are uneasy, you feel anxious, afraid, or embarrassed, because you think that something is wrong or that there is danger.

ferocious [fəróuʃəs] a. 흉포한; 맹렬한, 격렬한
A ferocious animal, person, or action is very fierce and violent.

growl [graul] v. 으르렁거리다; 으르렁거리듯 말하다; n. 으르렁거리는 소리
When a dog or other animal growls, it makes a low noise in its throat, usually because it is angry.

bare [bɛər] v. (신체의 일부를) 드러내다; a. 벌거벗은; 아무것도 안 덮인; 텅 빈
If you bare something, you uncover it and show it.

kitty [kíti] n. 고양이
Kitty is a pet name or a child's name for a kitten or cat.

lunge [lʌndʒ] v. 달려들다, 돌진하다; n. 돌진
If you lunge in a particular direction, you move in that direction suddenly and clumsily.

⁕ **emerge** [imə́:rdʒ] v. 나오다, 모습을 드러내다; (어려움 등을) 헤쳐 나오다
To emerge means to come out from an enclosed or dark space such as a room or a vehicle, or from a position where you could not be seen.

sewer [su:ər] n. 하수관, 수채통
A sewer is a large underground channel that carries waste matter and rain water away, usually to a place where it is treated and made harmless.

chomp [ʧamp] v. (음식을) 쩝쩝 먹다
If a person or animal chomps their way through food or chomps on food, they chew it noisily.

⁕ **retreat** [ritrí:t] v. 멀어져 가다, 물러가다; 빠져나가다; 후퇴하다; n. 후퇴, 철수; 휴양지
If you retreat, you move away from something or someone.

복습 **sigh** [sai] n. 한숨; v. 한숨을 쉬다, 한숨짓다; 탄식하듯 말하다
A sigh is a slow breath out that makes a long soft sound, especially because you are disappointed, tired, annoyed, or relaxed.

⁕ **relieve** [rilí:v] v. 안도하다; (불쾌감·고통 등을) 없애 주다; 완화하다 (relief n. 안도, 안심)
If you feel a sense of relief, you feel happy because something unpleasant has not happened or is no longer happening.

복습 **nod** [nad] v. (고개를) 끄덕이다, 까딱하다; n. (고개를) 끄덕임
If you nod, you move your head downward and upward to show that you are answering 'yes' to a question, or to show agreement, understanding, or approval.

⁕ **warehouse** [wɛ́ərhàus] n. 창고
A warehouse is a large building where raw materials or manufactured goods are stored until they are exported to other countries or distributed to shops to be sold.

⁕ **ledge** [ledʒ] n. (벽에서 튀어나온) 선반; 절벽에서 튀어나온 바위
A ledge is a narrow shelf along the bottom edge of a window.

복습 **sneak** [sni:k] v. (snuck-snuck) 살금살금 가다; 몰래 하다; a. 기습적인
If you sneak somewhere, you go there very quietly on foot, trying to avoid being seen or heard.

* **survey** [sərvéi] v. 둘러보다, 바라보다; 조사하다; n. 개관; 조사
If you survey something, you look at or consider the whole of it carefully.

* **admire** [ædmáiər] v. 감탄하며 바라보다; 존경하다, 칭찬하다 (admiringly ad. 감탄하여)
An admiring expression shows that you like or respect someone or something.

* **gorgeous** [gɔ́:rdʒəs] a. 아주 멋진, 아름다운; 선명한, 화려한
If you say that something is gorgeous, you mean that it gives you a lot of pleasure or is very attractive.

복습 **creep** [kri:p] v. (crept-crept) 살금살금 움직이다; 기다; n. 너무 싫은 사람
When people or animals creep somewhere, they move quietly and slowly.

* **continuous** [kəntínjuəs] a. 계속되는, 지속적인; 반복된
A continuous process or event continues for a period of time without stopping.

jack [dʒæk] v. 빼앗다
To jack something means to take it illicitly.

* **downstairs** [daunstéərz] ad. 아래층으로; n. 아래층
If you go downstairs in a building, you go down a staircase toward the ground floor.

* **horrible** [hɔ́:rəbl] a. 지긋지긋한, 끔찍한; 소름끼치는, 무시무시한
If you describe something or someone as horrible, you do not like them at all.

복습 **whisper** [hwíspər] v. 속삭이다, 소곤거리다; n. 속삭임, 소곤거리는 소리
When you whisper, you say something very quietly, using your breath rather than your throat, so that only one person can hear you.

scary [skéəri] a. 무서운, 겁나는
Something that is scary is rather frightening.

복습 **surround** [səráund] v. 둘러싸다, 에워싸다; 포위하다
If a person or thing is surrounded by something, that thing is situated all around them.

* **threatening** [θrétniŋ] a. 협박하는, 위협적인; (날씨 등이) 험악한
(threateningly ad. 위협적으로)
You can describe someone's behavior as threatening when you think that they are trying to harm you.

saunter [sɔ́:ntər] v. 느긋하게 걷다
If you saunter somewhere, you walk there in a slow, casual way.

no big deal idiom 별일 아니다
If you say that it is no big deal, you mean that something is not important or not a problem.

get got idiom 호되게 당하다
If you say that someone is going to get got, you mean that they are going to be in trouble.

nail [neil] n. 못; 손톱; 발톱; v. 못으로 박다
A nail is a thin piece of metal with one pointed end and one flat end. You hit the flat end with a hammer in order to push the nail into something such as a wall.

punk [pʌŋk] n. 불량한 남자, 불량 청소년
A punk is an aggressive and violent young criminal.

crew [kruː] n. (함께 일을 하는) 팀, 조; 승무원; v. (배의) 승무원을 하다
A crew is a group of people with special technical skills who work together on a task or project.

flamethrower [fléimθròuər] n. 화염 방사기
A flamethrower is a gun that can send out a stream of burning liquid and that is used as a weapon or for clearing plants from an area of ground.

dramatic [drəmǽtik] a. 극적인; 감격적인, 인상적인; 과장된 (dramatically ad. 극적으로)
A dramatic action, event, or situation is exciting and impressive.

ignite [ignáit] v. 불을 붙이다, 점화하다
When you ignite something or when it ignites, it starts burning or explodes.

narrow [nǽrou] v. (눈을) 찌푸리다; 좁히다; a. 좁은
If your eyes narrow or if you narrow your eyes, you almost close them, for example because you are angry or because you are trying to concentrate on something.

weapon [wépən] n. 무기, 흉기
A weapon is an object such as a gun, a knife, or a missile, which is used to kill or hurt people in a fight or a war.

instant [ínstənt] n. 순간, 아주 짧은 동안; a. 즉각적인 (in an instant idiom 곧, 즉시)
An instant is an extremely short period of time.

burn [bəːrn] v. 불에 타다; 태우다; 상기되다; n. 화상
If you burn something, you destroy or damage it with fire.

immediate [imíːdiət] a. 즉각적인; 당면한; 아주 가까이에 있는 (immediately ad. 즉시, 즉각)
If something happens immediately, it happens without any delay.

⁞ scare [skɛər] v. 무서워하다; 놀라게 하다; n. 불안(감); 놀람, 공포 (scared a. 무서워하는, 겁먹은)
If you are scared that something unpleasant might happen, you are nervous and worried because you think that it might happen.

٭ gang [gæŋ] n. 친구들 무리; 범죄 조직
The gang is a group of friends who frequently meet.

복습 hang out idiom 많은 시간을 보내다
If you hang out in a place or with a person or a group of people, you spend a lot of time in there or with them.

٭ thoughtful [θɔ́ːtfəl] a. 생각에 잠긴; 사려 깊은 (thoughtfully ad. 생각에 잠겨)
If you are thoughtful, you are quiet and serious because you are thinking about something.

٭ reckon [rékən] v. 생각하다; 여겨지다; 예상하다
If you reckon that something is true, you think that it is true.

be hard on idiom ~을 심하게 대하다; ~에게 힘들다
If you are hard on someone, you treat them severely or unkindly.

calling [kɔ́ːliŋ] n. 소명; 직업, 천직
A calling is a profession or career which someone is strongly attracted to, especially one which involves helping other people.

I hear you idiom (네가 무슨 말을 하는지) 알겠어
You say 'I hear you' to someone to tell them that you understand their opinion, especially when you disagree with it.

복습 challenge [ʧǽlindʒ] n. 도전; 저항; v. 도전하다; 도전 의식을 북돋우다
A challenge is something new and difficult which requires great effort and determination.

복습 predictable [pridíktəbl] a. 예상할 수 있는; 너무 뻔한
If you say that an event is predictable, you mean that it is obvious in advance that it will happen.

insightful [ínsàitfəl] a. 통찰력 있는
If you describe a person or their remarks as insightful, you mean that they show a very good understanding of people and situations.

٭ ultimate [ʌ́ltəmət] a. 궁극적인, 최후의; 최고의 (ultimately ad. 궁극적으로, 결국)
You use ultimately to indicate that what you are saying is the most important point in a discussion.

honor [ánər] v. 존경하다, 공경하다; ~에게 영광을 베풀다; n. 영광(스러운 것); 존경, 공경
To honor someone means to treat them or regard them with special attention and respect.

journey [dʒə́:rni] n. 여행, 여정; v. 여행하다
You can refer to a person's experience of changing or developing from one state of mind to another as a journey.

sincere [sinsíər] a. 진실된, 진정한, 진심 어린; 진심의 (sincerely ad. 진심으로)
If you say or feel something sincerely, you really mean or feel it, and are not pretending.

bang [bæŋ] v. 쾅 하고 치다; 쾅 하고 닫다; 쿵 하고 찧다; n. 쾅 (하는 소리)
If you bang on something or if you bang it, you hit it hard, making a loud noise.

snap [snæp] v. 급히 움직이다; 툭 부러지다; 날카롭게 말하다; n. 탁 하는 소리
If you snap something into a particular position, or if it snaps into that position, it moves quickly into that position, with a sharp sound.

grab [græb] v. (와락·단단히) 붙잡다; 급히 ~하다; n. 와락 잡아채려고 함
If you grab something, you take it or pick it up suddenly and roughly.

game face [géim feis] n. 결의에 찬 표정
If you put on your game face, you put on a serious or determined expression when you are going to try to win or achieve something.

reveal [rivíːl] v. (보이지 않던 것을) 드러내 보이다; (비밀 등을) 밝히다
If you reveal something that has been out of sight, you uncover it so that people can see it.

gulp [gʌlp] v. 침을 꿀떡 삼키다; (숨을) 깊이 들이마시다; n. 꿀꺽 마시기
If you gulp, you swallow air, often making a noise in your throat as you do so, because you are nervous or excited.

department [dipá:rtmənt] n. (정부·기업체·대학 등과 같은 조직의 한) 부서
A department is one of the sections in an organization such as a government, business, or university.

complaint [kəmpléint] n. 불평
A complaint is a statement in which you express your dissatisfaction with a particular situation.

distract [distrǽkt] v. (주의를) 딴 데로 돌리다, 집중이 안 되게 하다
If something distracts you or your attention from something, it takes your attention away from it.

tiptoe [típtòu] v. (발끝으로) 살금살금 걷다
If you tiptoe somewhere, you walk there very quietly without putting your heels on the floor when you walk.

hop [hap] v. 급히 움직이다; 깡충깡충 뛰다; n. 깡충깡충 뛰기
If you hop somewhere, you move there quickly or suddenly.

settle [setl] v. 편하게 앉다; 자리를 잡다; 결정하다
If you settle yourself somewhere or settle somewhere, you sit down or make yourself comfortable.

what-have-you idiom ~등의 그런 종류
You say what-have-you at the end of a list in order to refer generally to other things of the same kind.

miserable [mízərəbl] a. 비참한; 우울하게 하는; 보잘것없는 (miserably ad. 형편없이)
A miserable failure is a very great one.

stutter [stʌ́tər] v. 말을 더듬다, 더듬거리다; n. 말을 더듬기
If someone stutters, they have difficulty speaking because they find it hard to say the first sound of a word.

stomp [stamp] v. 짓밟다; 쿵쿵거리며 걷다; n. (발을) 쿵쾅거리기
If you stomp on something, you step down hard on it.

gas [gæs] n. (= gas pedal) 가속 페달; 기체, 가스; 휘발유
If you step on the gas when you are driving a vehicle, you go faster.

force [fɔːrs] v. 억지로 ~하다; ~를 강요하다; n. 작용력; 힘; 영향력
If someone forces you to do something, they make you do it even though you do not want to, for example by threatening you.

dive [daiv] v. 급히 움직이다; 급강하하다; (물속으로) 뛰어들다; n. 급강하; (물속으로) 뛰어들기
If you dive in a particular direction or into a particular place, you jump or move there quickly.

ram [ræm] v. 들이받다; (억지로) 밀어 넣다, 쑤셔 넣다; n. [동물] 숫양
If a vehicle rams something such as another vehicle, it crashes into it with a lot of force, usually deliberately.

plaster [plǽstər] v. 딱 들러붙게 하다; 회반죽을 바르다; n. 회반죽
If you plaster a surface or a place with posters or pictures, you stick a lot of them all over it.

* **hood** [hud] n. (자동차 등의) 덮개; (외투 등에 달린) 모자
The hood of a car is the metal cover over the engine at the front.

‡ **speed** [spi:d] v. (sped-sped) 빨리 가다; 더 빠르게 하다; n. 속도
If you speed somewhere, you move or travel there quickly, usually in a vehicle.

‡ **passenger** [pǽsəndʒər] n. 승객 (passenger seat n. (자동차의) 조수석)
A passenger in a vehicle such as a bus, boat, or plane is a person who is travelling in it, but who is not driving it or working on it.

work like a charm idiom 기적같이 성공하다
If you say that something worked like a charm, you mean that it was very effective or successful.

복습 **blast** [blæst] v. 빠르게 가다; 쾅쾅 울리다; 폭발시키다; n. 폭발; (한 줄기의) 강한 바람
If you blast in a specified direction, you move very quickly and loudly in that direction.

복습 **whip** [hwip] v. 격렬하게 움직이다; 휙 빼내다; n. 채찍
If you whip in a particular direction, you move fast or suddenly in that direction.

brand-new [brǽnd-njúː] a. 아주 새로운, 신상품의
A brand-new object is completely new.

* **envious** [énviəs] a. 부러워하는, 선망하는
If you are envious of someone, you want something that they have.

복습 **yank** [jæŋk] v. 홱 잡아당기다; n. 홱 잡아당기기
If you yank someone or something somewhere, you pull them there suddenly and with a lot of force.

controller [kəntróulər] n. (기계의) 조종 장치; (조직이나 부서의) 관리자
A controller is a piece of equipment that controls the operation of an electrical device.

‡ **shame** [ʃeim] n. 애석한 일; 수치심, 창피; v. 창피스럽게 하다; 망신시키다
If you say that something is a shame, you are expressing your regret about it and indicating that you wish it had happened differently.

복습 **thrill** [θril] n. 흥분, 설렘; 전율; v. 열광시키다, 정말 신나게 하다
If something gives you a thrill, it gives you a sudden feeling of great excitement, pleasure, or fear.

uncharted [ʌnʧɑ́ːrtid] a. 미지의, 잘 알지 못하는; 지도에 표시되어 있지 않은
If you describe a situation, experience, or activity as uncharted territory or waters, you mean that it is new or unfamiliar.

territory [térətɔ̀ːri] n. 영역; 지역, 영토
You can use territory to refer to an area of knowledge or experience.

interrupt [ìntərʌ́pt] v. (말·행동을) 방해하다; 중단시키다; 차단하다
If someone or something interrupts a process or activity, they stop it for a period of time.

out of nowhere idiom 어디서인지 모르게, 난데없이
If you say that something or someone appears out of nowhere, you mean that they appear suddenly and unexpectedly.

mess [mes] v. 엉망으로 만들다; n. (지저분하고) 엉망인 상태; (많은 문제로) 엉망인 상황
(mess with idiom ~에 얽혀 들다)
If you mess with someone, you get involved with someone who may react in a dangerous or violent way.

bull [bul] n. [동물] 황소
A bull is a male animal of the cow family.

horn [hɔːrn] n. (양·소 등의) 뿔; 나팔; (차량의) 경적
The horns of an animal such as a cow or deer are the hard pointed things that grow from its head.

slick [slik] a. 능란한; (겉만) 번드르르한; 교활한; v. 매끈하게 하다
A slick action is done quickly and smoothly, and without any obvious effort.

in the clear idiom 위험을 벗어난, 깨끗해진
If someone is in the clear, they are not in danger, or are not blamed or suspected of anything.

upset [ʌpsét] a. 속상한, 마음이 상한; v. 속상하게 하다; (계획·상황 등이) 잘못되게 하다
If you are upset, you are unhappy or disappointed because something unpleasant has happened to you.

curb [kəːrb] n. 도로 경계석, 연석; v. 억제하다
The curb is the raised edge of a pavement or sidewalk which separates it from the road.

basin [beisn] n. (큰 강의) 유역; 대야
The basin of a large river is the area of land around it from which streams run down into it.

commotion [kəmóuʃən] n. 소란, 소동
A commotion is a lot of noise, confusion, and excitement.

복습 **track** [træk] n. 경주로, 트랙; (기차) 선로; 자국; v. 추적하다, 뒤쫓다
A track is a piece of ground, often oval-shaped, that is used for races involving athletes, cars, bicycles, horses, or dogs.

lose one's cookies idiom 토하다
If you lose your cookies, food and drink comes back up from your stomach and out through your mouth.

복습 **gleeful** [glí:fəl] a. 신이 난; 고소해하는 (gleefully ad. 유쾌하게)
Someone who is gleeful is happy and excited, often because of someone else's bad luck.

hit the gas idiom 가속 페달을 세게 밟다
If you hit the gas, you push down on the accelerator in a vehicle in a sudden and forceful way.

＊ **tunnel** [tʌnl] n. 터널, 굴; v. 굴을 뚫다
A tunnel is a long passage which has been made under the ground, usually through a hill or under the sea.

＊ **tail** [teil] n. 끝부분; (동물의) 꼬리; v. 미행하다 (on one's tail idiom ~를 바짝 뒤따라가는)
If you are on someone's tail, you follow them closely.

taunt [tɔ:nt] v. 놀리다, 비웃다, 조롱하다; n. 놀림, 비웃음, 조롱
If someone taunts you, they say unkind or insulting things to you, especially about your weaknesses or failures.

＊ **spiral** [spáiərəl] v. 나선형으로 움직이다, 나선형을 그리다; 급증하다; n. 나선, 나선형
If something spirals or is spiraled somewhere, it grows or moves in a spiral curve.

복습 **zip** [zip] v. (어떤 방향으로) 쌩 하고 가다; 지퍼를 잠그다; n. 지퍼
If you say that something or someone zip somewhere, you mean that they move very fast.

복습 **impress** [imprés] v. 깊은 인상을 주다, 감동을 주다 (impressed a. 감명을 받은)
If something impresses you, you feel great admiration for it.

keep up idiom (~의 속도 등을) 따라가다; ~을 계속하다
If you keep up with someone or something, you move at the same speed as them.

expert [ékspəːrt] a. 숙련된; 전문가의, 전문적인; n. 전문가
(expertly ad. 훌륭하게, 전문적으로)
Someone who is expert at doing something is very skilled at it.

maneuver [mənúːvər] v. (능숙하게) 움직이다; 계책을 부리다; n. (기술적인) 동작; 묘책
If you maneuver something into or out of an awkward position, you skillfully move it there.

be about to idiom 막 ~하려는 참이다
If you are about to do something, you are going to do it immediately.

pile [pail] n. 무더기; 쌓아 놓은 것, 더미; v. 쌓다; 집어넣다; 우르르 가다
A pile of things is a mass of them that is high in the middle and has sloping sides.

sight [sait] n. 광경, 모습; 보기; 시력; v. 갑자기 보다
A sight is something that you see.

flame [fleim] n. 불길, 불꽃; 격정; v. 활활 타오르다; 시뻘게지다
A flame is a hot bright stream of burning gas that comes from something that is burning.

knuckle [nʌkl] v. 주먹을 쥐다; 주먹으로 치다; n. 손가락 관절
(white-knuckle idiom (겁이 나서) 주먹을 꼭 쥐다)
If you white-knuckle something, you hold it so tightly that your knuckles have gone white because you are frightened.

dashboard [dǽʃbɔːrd] n. (승용차의) 계기판
The dashboard in a car is the panel facing the driver's seat where most of the instruments and switches are.

dead end [ded énd] n. 막다른 길; 막다른 지경
If a street is a dead end, there is no way out at one end of it.

grin [grin] v. 활짝 웃다; n. 활짝 웃음
When you grin, you smile broadly.

confident [kánfədənt] a. 확신하는; 자신감 있는
If you are confident about something, you are certain that it will happen in the way you want it to.

exit [égzit] n. (고속도로의) 출구; (공공건물의) 출구; 퇴장; v. 나가다, 떠나다; 퇴장하다
An exit on a motorway or highway is a place where traffic can leave it.

out of the blue idiom 갑자기, 난데없이
If something happens out of the blue, it happens suddenly and unexpectedly.

rev [rev] v. (엔진의) 회전 속도를 올리다; n. (엔진의) 회전 속도
When the engine of a vehicle revs, or when you rev it, the engine speed is increased as the accelerator is pressed.

load [loud] v. (짐·사람 등을) 싣다; (데이터나 프로그램을) 로딩하다;
n. (많은 양의) 짐; (수·양이) 많음
If you load a vehicle or a container, you put a large quantity of things into it.

ramp [ræmp] n. (화물 적재·도로 연결 등을 위한) 램프, 경사로
A ramp is a sloping surface between two places that are at different levels.

launch [lɔ:ntʃ] v. 맹렬히 덤비다; 발사하다; n. 발사; 시작; 개시
If you launch yourself in a specific direction, you make a sudden energetic movement in that direction.

land [lænd] v. 떨어지다; (땅·표면에) 내려앉다; 놓다, 두다; n. 육지, 땅; 지역
When someone or something lands, they come down to the ground after moving through the air or falling.

spin [spin] v. (spun-spun) (빙빙) 돌다; 돌아서다; n. 회전
(spin out idiom (자동차가) 휙 돌면서 길을 벗어나다)
If a car spins out, the driver loses control of it and the car spins around.

collide [kəláid] v. 충돌하다, 부딪치다; (의견 등이) 상충하다
If two or more moving people or objects collide, they crash into one another.

realize [rí:əlàiz] v. 깨닫다, 알아차리다; 실현하다, 달성하다
If you realize that something is true, you become aware of that fact or understand it.

trap [træp] v. (위험한 장소에) 가두다; (함정으로) 몰아넣다; n. 함정; 덫
If you are trapped somewhere, something falls onto you or blocks your way and prevents you from moving or escaping.

Check Your Reading Speed

1분에 몇 단어를 읽는지 리딩 속도를 측정해보세요.

$$\frac{1,018 \text{ words}}{\text{reading time ( ) sec}} \times 60 = (\quad) \text{ WPM}$$

Build Your Vocabulary

stay put idiom 그대로 있다
If you stay put, you remain somewhere.

stuck [stʌk] a. 움직일 수 없는, 꼼짝 못하는; 갇힌
If something is stuck in a particular position, it is fixed tightly in this position and is unable to move.

squeeze [skwi:z] v. (좁은 곳에) 비집고 들어가다; (꼭) 쥐다; n. (손으로 꼭) 쥐기
If you squeeze a person or thing somewhere or if they squeeze there, they manage to get through or into a small space.

struggle [strʌgl] v. 몸부림치다, 허우적거리다; 애쓰다; 힘겹게 나아가다; n. 투쟁, 분투; 몸부림
If you struggle when you are being held, you twist, kick, and move violently in order to get free.

wiggle [wigl] v. 꿈틀꿈틀 움직이다; n. 꿈틀꿈틀 움직이기
If you wiggle something or if it wiggles, it moves up and down or from side to side in small quick movements.

mutter [mʌtər] v. 중얼거리다; 투덜거리다; n. 중얼거림
If you mutter, you speak very quietly so that you cannot easily be heard, often because you are complaining about something.

dust [dʌst] v. 먼지를 털다; (고운 가루를) 뿌리다; n. 먼지, 티끌
When you dust something such as furniture, you remove dust from it, usually using a cloth.

criminal [krímənl] n. 범인, 범죄자; a. 범죄의; 형사상의
A criminal is a person who regularly commits crimes.

race [reis] v. 경주하다; 쏜살같이 가다; (머리·심장 등이) 바쁘게 돌아가다; n. 경주; 인종, 종족
(racer n. 경주 참가자)
A racer is a person or animal that takes part in races.

track [træk] n. 경주로, 트랙; (기차) 선로; 자국; v. 추적하다, 뒤쫓다
A track is a piece of ground, often oval-shaped, that is used for races involving athletes, cars, bicycles, horses, or dogs.

gaze [geiz] n. 응시, (눈여겨보는) 시선; v. (가만히) 응시하다, 바라보다
You can talk about someone's gaze as a way of describing how they are looking at something, especially when they are looking steadily at it.

embarrass [imbǽrəs] v. 당황스럽게 하다, 어색하게 하다; 곤란하게 하다
If something or someone embarrasses you, they make you feel shy or ashamed.

wail [weil] v. 울부짖다, 통곡하다; (길고 높은) 소리를 내다; n. 울부짖음, 통곡
If someone wails, they make long, loud, high-pitched cries which express sorrow or pain.

uncontrollable [ʌ̀nkəntróuləbl] a. 억제할 수 없는, 걷잡을 수 없는
(uncontrollably ad. 제어하기 힘들게, 감당하기 어렵게)
If you describe a situation or series of events as uncontrollable, you believe that nothing can be done to control them or to prevent things from getting worse.

cut off idiom (말을) 중단시키다; 단절시키다
To cut off means to prevent someone from continuing what they are saying.

respect [rispékt] v. 존경하다; 존중하다; n. 존경(심); 존중
If you respect someone, you have a good opinion of their character or ideas.

outward [áutwərd] a. 겉보기의, 외형의; 밖으로 향하는
The outward features of something are the ones that you can see from the outside.

display [displéi] n. (느낌·능력 등의) 표현; 전시; v. (자질·느낌을) 드러내다; 전시하다
A display is an occasion when someone shows a particular feeling, quality, or attitude.

vulnerable [vʌ́lnərəbl] a. 취약한, 연약한 (vulnerability n. 상처받기 쉬움)
Someone who is vulnerable is weak and without protection, with the result that they are easily hurt physically or emotionally.

pull together idiom 정신 차리다; 함께 일하다, 협력하다
If you pull it together or pull yourself together, you gain control of your feelings and start to act in a calm and sensible way.

friendship [fréndʃip] n. 우정; 친선; 교우 관계
You use friendship to refer in a general way to the state of being friends, or the feelings that friends have for each other.

^복^습 **crew** [kru:] n. (함께 일을 하는) 팀, 조; 승무원; v. (배의) 승무원을 하다
A crew is a group of people with special technical skills who work together on a task or project.

^복^습 **honor** [ánər] v. 존경하다, 공경하다; ~에게 영광을 베풀다; n. 영광(스러운 것); 존경, 공경
To honor someone means to treat them or regard them with special attention and respect.

^복^습 **journey** [dʒə́:rni] n. 여행, 여정; v. 여행하다
You can refer to a person's experience of changing or developing from one state of mind to another as a journey.

^복^습 **gesture** [dʒésʧər] v. (손·머리 등으로) 가리키다; 몸짓을 하다; n. 몸짓; (감정·의도의) 표시
If you gesture, you use movements of your hands or head in order to tell someone something or draw their attention to something.

^복^습 **blow** [blou] v. (바람·입김에) 날리다; (기회를) 날리다; n. 강타
If the wind blows something somewhere or if it blows there, the wind moves it there.

⋆ **react** [riǽkt] v. 반응하다; 반응을 보이다
When you react to something that has happened to you, you behave in a particular way because of it.

⁑ **powerful** [páuərfəl] a. 강력한; 영향력 있는, 유력한
A powerful machine or substance is effective because it is very strong.

⋆ **intense** [inténs] a. 극심한, 강렬한; 치열한; 진지한
Intense is used to describe something that is very great or extreme in strength or degree.

⁑ **cheek** [ʧi:k] n. 뺨, 볼; 엉덩이
Your cheeks are the sides of your face below your eyes.

billow [bílou] v. 부풀어 오르다; (연기·구름 등이) 피어오르다; n. 자욱하게 피어오르는 것
When something made of cloth billows, it swells out and moves slowly in the wind.

^복^습 **yell** [jel] v. 고함치다, 소리 지르다; n. 고함, 외침
If you yell, you shout loudly, usually because you are excited, angry, or in pain.

^복^습 **wreck** [rek] v. 파괴하다; 엉망으로 만들다; n. 충돌; 사고 잔해
To wreck something means to completely destroy or ruin it.

account [əkáunt] n. 이용 계정; 계좌; 설명, 이야기; v. 간주하다, 여기다
An account is an arrangement you have with a company or Internet provider to use a service they provide.

post [poust] v. (웹사이트에) 게시하다; (근무 위치에) 배치하다; n. (근무) 구역; 기둥, 말뚝
If you post information on the Internet, you make the information available to other people on the Internet.

viral [váiərəl] a. 입소문이 난, 유행이 된 (go viral idiom 입소문이 나다)
If a picture, video, or joke goes viral, it spreads widely, especially on the Internet or mobile phones.

chick [ʧik] n. 젊은 여자; 병아리
Chick is an informal way of refering a young woman.

hook up idiom (전원·인터넷 등에) 연결하다
If you hook up something to a piece of electronic equipment or to a power supply, the two things are connected together.

rub [rʌb] v. (손·손수건 등을 대고) 문지르다; (두 손 등을) 맞비비다; n. 문지르기, 비비기
If you rub a part of your body, you move your hand or fingers backward and forward over it while pressing firmly.

praise [preiz] n. 칭찬, 찬사, 찬양; v. 칭찬하다
Praise is what you say or write about someone when you are expressing approval for their achievements or qualities.

talk shop idiom 전문적인 이야기를 하다
To talk shop means to talk about your work, especially in a way that is boring for other people.

burn [bəːrn] v. 불에 타다; 태우다; 상기되다; n. 화상
If you burn something, you destroy or damage it with fire.

coy [kɔi] a. 얘기를 잘 안 하는; 내숭을 떠는 (coyly ad. 부끄러운 듯이)
If someone is being coy, they are unwilling to talk about something that they feel guilty or embarrassed about.

rematch [ríːmæʧ] n. 재시합
A rematch is a second game or contest between two people or teams who have already faced each other.

butt [bʌt] n. 엉덩이; v. (머리로) 들이받다 (kick one's butt idiom 혼내주다)
To kick someone's butt means to punish or defeat them.

awe [ɔ:] n. 경외감, 외경심; v. 경외심을 갖게 하다
Awe is the feeling of respect and amazement that you have when you are faced
with something wonderful and often rather frightening.

zoom [zu:m] v. 쌩 하고 가다; 급등하다; n. (빠르게) 쌩 하고 지나가는 소리
If you zoom somewhere, you go there very quickly.

admire [ædmáiər] v. 감탄하며 바라보다; 존경하다, 칭찬하다
If you admire someone or something, you look at them with pleasure.

show-off [ʃóu-ɔ:f] n. 과시적인 사람
If you say that someone is a show-off, you are criticizing them for trying to
impress people by showing in a very obvious way what they can do or what they
own.

roll one's eyes idiom 눈을 굴리다
If you roll your eyes or if your eyes roll, they move round and upward to show you
are bored or annoyed.

linger [líŋgər] v. 더 오래 머물다; 계속되다
If you linger somewhere, you stay there for a longer time than is necessary, for
example because you are enjoying yourself.

freak [fri:k] a. 아주 기이한; n. 괴짜, 괴물; v. 기겁을 하다
A freak event or action is one that is a very unusual or extreme example of its
type.

bounce [bauns] v. 깡충깡충 뛰다; (공 등이) 튀다; n. 탄력
If someone bounces somewhere, they move there in an energetic way, because
they are feeling happy.

firm [fə:rm] a. 단호한, 확고한; 단단한 (firmly ad. 단호히)
If you describe someone as firm, you mean they behave in a way that shows that
they are not going to change their mind, or that they are the person who is in
control.

reel [ri:l] v. (마음이) 어지럽다; 비틀거리다; n. 릴, 물레
If you are reeling from a shock, you are feeling extremely surprised or upset
because of it.

rattle off idiom 줄줄 말하다; 나불나불 지껄여 대다
If you rattle something off, you say or repeat them from memory, quickly and
without any effort.

defensive [difénsiv] a. 방어적인; 방어의 (defensively ad. 방어적으로)
Someone who is defensive is behaving in a way that shows they feel unsure or threatened.

confuse [kənfjúːz] v. (사람을) 혼란시키다; 혼동하다 (confused a. 혼란스러워하는)
If you are confused, you do not know exactly what is happening or what to do.

awesome [ɔ́ːsəm] a. 기막히게 좋은, 굉장한; 어마어마한, 엄청난
An awesome person or thing is very impressive and often frightening.

intersection [intərsékʃən] n. 교차로, 교차 지점; 교차함, 가로지름
An intersection is a place where roads or other lines meet or cross.

loot [luːt] n. 돈; 전리품; v. 훔치다, 약탈하다
Loot is stolen money or valuable objects taken by soldiers from the enemy after winning a battle.

sarcastic [saːrkǽstik] a. 빈정대는, 비꼬는; 풍자적인 (sarcastically ad. 비꼬는 투로)
Someone who is sarcastic says or does the opposite of what they really mean in order to mock or insult someone.

out of nowhere idiom 어디서인지 모르게, 난데없이
If you say that something or someone appears out of nowhere, you mean that they appear suddenly and unexpectedly.

friendly [fréndli] a. (행동이) 친절한; 상냥한; n. (pl.) 우호적인 사람
If someone is friendly, they behave in a pleasant, kind way, and like to be with other people.

alert [ələ́ːrt] n. 경계경보; v. (위험 등을) 알리다; a. 경계하는; 기민한
An alert is a situation in which people prepare themselves for something dangerous that might happen soon.

expire [ikspáiər] v. (기한이) 만료되다, 만기가 되다
When something such as a contract, deadline, or visa expires, it comes to an end or is no longer valid.

gulp [gʌlp] v. 침을 꿀떡 삼키다; (숨을) 깊이 들이마시다; n. 꿀꺽 마시기
If you gulp, you swallow air, often making a noise in your throat as you do so, because you are nervous or excited.

waste [weist] v. 낭비하다; 헛되이 쓰다; n. 낭비, 허비; (pl.) 쓰레기, 폐기물
If you waste something such as time, money, or energy, you use too much of it doing something that is not important or necessary, or is unlikely to succeed.

nickel-and-dime idiom (알뜰하게 굴어서) 획득하다; 돈이 얼마 안 되는

If you accuse a person of nickel-and-diming someone or something, you are criticizing that person for weakening or exhausting them, for example, by continually taking small amounts of money away from them, or by continually making small changes or requests.

Chapters 11 & 12

1. What did Yesss first think of Ralph?

A. She thought he might be a genius.

B. She thought he had a good heart.

C. She thought he looked familiar.

D. She thought he was not worth her time.

2. What kind of videos did Ralph plan to make?

A. Videos that required professional skills

B. Videos that were educational

C. Videos with exciting music

D. Videos with trending themes

3. What did Yesss tell the pop-ups to do?

A. Steal hearts from different sites for Ralph

B. Go to various sites to get clicks for Ralph

C. Spread rumors about Ralph on entertainment sites

D. Create accounts for Ralph on social media sites

4. Why did Ralph suggest sending Vanellope to a fan site?

A. He assumed she would love it.

B. He wanted her to have a unique experience.

C. He figured she would be safe there.

D. He hoped she would make new friends there.

5. Why did Vanellope get in trouble at OhMyDisney.com?

A. She did not have permission to carry a pop-up.

B. She interfered with the princess BFF quiz.

C. She made fun of all the Disney characters.

D. She lied to avatars about her identity.

Check Your Reading Speed

1분에 몇 단어를 읽는지 리딩 속도를 측정해보세요.

$$\frac{1,094 \text{ words}}{\text{reading time ( ) sec}} \times 60 = (\qquad) \text{ WPM}$$

Build Your Vocabulary

* **clip** [klip] n. 짧은 영상; 핀, 클립; v. 핀으로 고정하다; 깎다, 자르다
  A clip from a film or a radio or television program is a short piece of it that is broadcast separately.

* **float** [flout] v. (물 위나 공중에서) 떠가다; (물에) 뜨다; n. 부표
  Something that floats in or through the air hangs in it or moves slowly and gently through it.

* **take in** idiom ~을 눈여겨보다; 이해하다
  If you take in something, you spend time looking at it.

* **netizen** [nétəzən] n. 네티즌, 인터넷 사용자
  A netizen is a person who uses the internet.

* **suck** [sʌk] v. (특정한 방향으로) 빨아들이다; 빨아 먹다; 엉망이다, 형편없다; n. 빨기, 빨아 먹기
  If something sucks a liquid, gas, or object in a particular direction, it draws it there with a powerful force.

* **hose** [houz] n. 호스; v. 호스로 물을 뿌리다
  A hose is a long, flexible pipe made of rubber or plastic. Water is directed through a hose in order to do things such as put out fires, clean cars, or water gardens.

* **measure** [méʒər] v. 측정하다; 판단하다; n. 조치, 정책; 척도
  If something measures a particular length, width, or amount, that is its size or intensity, expressed in numbers.

tick up idiom 상승하다
  To tick up means to increase slowly and by small degrees.

* **obvious** [ábviəs] a. 분명한, 확실한; 명백한 (obviously ad. 분명히)
  You use obviously to indicate that something is easily noticed, seen, or recognized.

giggle [gigl] n. 피식 웃음, 킥킥거림; v. 피식 웃다, 킥킥거리다
A giggle is a high laugh, especially a nervous or silly one.

frown [fraun] v. 얼굴을 찡그리다; 눈살을 찌푸리다; n. 찡그림, 찌푸림
When someone frowns, their eyebrows become drawn together, because they are
annoyed, worried, or puzzled, or because they are concentrating.

sift [sift] v. 면밀히 조사하다, 샅샅이 살피다; 체로 거르다
If you sift through something such as evidence, you examine it thoroughly.

stack [stæk] n. 무더기, 더미; v. (깔끔하게 정돈하여) 쌓다
A stack of things is a pile of them.

assistant [əsístənt] n. 조수, 보조원
Someone's assistant is a person who helps them in their work.

nearby [nìərbái] ad. 가까운 곳에; a. 인근의, 가까운 곳의
If something is nearby, it is only a short distance away.

inspire [inspáiər] v. 영감을 주다; 고무하다; (감정 등을) 불어넣다
(uninspired a. 독창적이지 않은)
If you describe something or someone as uninspired, you are criticizing them
because they do not seem to have any original or exciting qualities.

cliché [kli:ʃéi] n. 상투적인 문구 (clichéd a. 케케묵은, 진부한)
If you describe something as cliché, you mean that it has been said, done, or used
many times before, and is boring or untrue.

cautious [kɔ́:ʃəs] a. 조심스러운, 신중한 (cautiously ad. 조심스럽게)
If you describe someone's attitude or reaction as cautious, you mean that it is
limited or careful.

genius [dʒí:njəs] n. 천재; 천재성; 특별한 재능
A genius is a highly talented, creative, or intelligent person.

drivel [drívəl] n. 쓸데없는 짓; v. 계속 쓸데없는 말을 하다
If you describe something that is written or said as drivel, you are critical of it
because you think it is very silly.

doorway [dɔ́:rwèi] n. 출입구
A doorway is a space in a wall where a door opens and closes.

peer [piər] v. 유심히 보다, 눈여겨보다; n. 또래
If you peer at something, you look at it very hard, usually because it is difficult
to see clearly.

curate [kjúərit] v. 조직하다, 체계화하다
If an exhibition is curated by someone, they organize it.

content [kántent] ① n. 내용물; (책의) 목차 ② a. (자기가 가진 것에) 만족하는; v. ~에 자족하다
If you refer to the content or contents of something such as a book, speech, or television program, you are referring to the subject that it deals with, the story that it tells, or the ideas that it expresses.

site [sait] n. (인터넷) 사이트; (사건 등의) 현장; 대지
A site is the same as a website which is a set of data and information about a particular subject which is available on the Internet.

trifle with idiom ~을 하찮게 보다
If you trifle with someone or something, you treat them without respect as if they are not very important.

mouth-breathing [máuθ-briːðiŋ] a. 어리석은
If you describe someone as mouth-breathing, you mean that they are very stupid.

hobo [hóubou] n. 떠돌이 일꾼
A hobo is a person who has no home, especially one who travels from place to place and gets money by begging.

trundle [trʌndl] v. 터덜터덜 걷다; 굴러가다
If you say that someone is trundling somewhere, you mean that they are walking slowly, often in a tired way or with heavy steps.

security [sikjúərəti] n. 보안, 경비; 경비 담당 부서; 안도감, 안심
Security refers to all the measures that are taken to protect a place, or to ensure that only people with permission enter it or leave it.

blow [blou] v. (바람·입김에) 날리다; (기회를) 날리다; n. 강타
If the wind blows something somewhere or if it blows there, the wind moves it there.

tone [toun] n. 어조, 말투; (글 등의) 분위기; 음색
Someone's tone is a quality in their voice which shows what they are feeling or thinking.

present [préznt] ① a. 있는; 현재의; n. 현재 (presence n. 있음, 존재(함))
② v. 보여 주다; 주다, 수여하다
If you are in someone's presence, you are in the same place as that person, and are close enough to them to be seen or heard.

beverage [bévəridʒ] n. (물 외의) 음료
Beverages are drinks.

dope [doup] a. 멋진, 좋은; n. 멍청이, 얼간이; 약물; v. (선수에게) 약물을 투여하다
If you describe something as dope, you mean that it is very good in an informal way.

trend [trend] v. 인기를 얻다; n. 동향, 추세 (trending a. 유행하는)
If something is trending, it is very popular as a subject discussed on the microblogging service Twitter.

chant [ʧænt] v. 되풀이하여 말하다; 구호를 외치다, 연호하다; n. (연이어 외치는) 구호
If you chant something or if you chant, you repeat the same words over and over again.

buzzkill [bʌ́zkil] v. 기분을 망치다; n. 기분 망치는 것
A buzzkill refers to something or someone that spoils people's feelings of excitement, enjoyment, or pleasure.

fest [fest] n. 축제; 대회, 집회
Fest is used in combination with other nouns to create a word for a situation in which there is a lot of something.

viral [váiərəl] a. 입소문이 난, 유행이 된
You can use viral to describe something that quickly becomes very popular or well known by being published on the internet or sent from person to person by email or phone.

device [diváis] n. 장치, 기구; 폭발물; 방법
A device is an object that has been invented for a particular purpose, for example for recording or measuring something.

account [əkáunt] n. 이용 계정; 계좌; 설명, 이야기; v. 간주하다, 여기다
An account is an arrangement you have with a company or Internet provider to use a service they provide.

convert [kənvə́:rt] v. 전환시키다, 개조하다; (의견·습관 등을) 바꾸다
If one thing is converted or converts into another, it is changed into a different form.

nowhere [nóuhwɛər] ad. 아무데도 ~없다
(nowhere near idiom 결코 ~가 아니게, ~와는 아주 동떨어지게)
If you use nowhere near in front of a word or expression, you are emphasizing that the real situation is very different from, or has not yet reached, the state which that word or expression suggests.

emphasize [émfəsàiz] v. 강조하다; 힘주어 말하다
To emphasize something means to indicate that it is particularly important or true, or to draw special attention to it.

deadline [dédlain] n. 기한, 마감 시간
A deadline is a time or date before which a particular task must be finished or a particular thing must be done.

tap out idiom ~을 다 써 버리다; 포기하다
To tap out means to deplete the resources of someone, something, or oneself.

trench [trentʃ] v. 도랑을 파다; n. (전장의) 참호; 도랑, 해자(垓子)
To trench means to dig a long narrow channel that is cut into the ground.

desperate [déspərət] a. 간절히 원하는; 필사적인, 극단적인 (desperately ad. 간절히)
If you are desperate for something or desperate to do something, you want or need it very much indeed.

pal [pæl] n. 친구; 이봐
Your pals are your friends.

bet [bet] v. (~이) 틀림없다; (내기 등에) 돈을 걸다; n. 짐작, 추측; 내기
You use expressions such as 'I bet,' 'I'll bet,' and 'you can bet' to indicate that you are sure something is true.

bunch [bʌntʃ] n. (양·수가) 많음; 다발, 묶음
A bunch of things is a number of things, especially a large number.

saturate [sætʃərèit] v. 과잉 공급하다; 포화시키다; 흠뻑 적시다
If people or things saturate a place or object, they fill it completely so that no more can be added.

trip [trip] v. 발을 헛디디다; n. 여행; 발을 헛디딤
If you trip when you are walking, you knock your foot against something and fall or nearly fall.

frighten [fraitn] v. 겁먹게 하다, 놀라게 하다 (frightened a. 겁먹은, 무서워하는)
If you are frightened, you are anxious or afraid, often because of something that has just happened or that you think may happen.

zucchini [zuːkíːni] n. [식물] 애호박
Zucchini are long thin vegetables with a dark green skin.

goat [gout] n. [동물] 염소
A goat is an animal with horns and a coat of hair, that lives wild in mountain areas or is kept on farms for its milk or meat.

hot pepper [hát pepər] n. [식물] 고추; 고춧가루
A hot pepper is a plant bearing very hot medium-sized oblong red peppers.

challenge [ʧǽlindʒ] n. 도전; 저항; v. 도전하다; 도전 의식을 북돋우다
A challenge is something new and difficult which requires great effort and determination.

walk-through [wɔ́:k-θrù:] n. (어떤 절차에 대한) 자세한 설명; (연극·공연 등의) 연습
A walk-through is a set of instructions showing someone how to use something, for example, new software.

unbox [ʌnbáks] v. 상자에서 꺼내다
If you unbox, you take something out of a box, for example something that you have recently bought or have moved to a different place.

makeup [méikʌp] n. 분장, 메이크업; 조립, 구성
Makeup is substances that people put on their faces, including their eyes and lips, in order to look attractive or to change their appearance.

tutorial [tjuːtɔ́ːriəl] n. 사용 지침서; 개별 지도 시간; a. 개인 지도의
A tutorial is a document or website on a computer that shows you how to use a product in a series of easy stages.

pun [pʌn] n. 말장난, 말재간
A pun is a clever and amusing use of a word or phrase with two meanings, or of words with the same sound but different meanings.

animate [ǽnəmèit] v. 만화 영화로 만들다; 생기를 불어넣다
(animated a. (사진·그림 등이) 동영상으로 된)
An animated film is one in which puppets or drawings appear to move.

buzz [bʌz] v. 윙윙거리다; 부산스럽다, 활기가 넘치다; n. 윙윙거리는 소리
If something buzzes or buzzes somewhere, it makes a long continuous sound, like the noise a bee makes when it is flying.

wink [wiŋk] v. 윙크하다; (빛이) 깜박거리다; n. 윙크
When you wink at someone, you look toward them and close one eye very briefly, usually as a signal that something is a joke or a secret.

unison [júːnisn] n. 조화, 화합, 일치 (in unison idiom 일제히)
If two or more people do something in unison, they do it together at the same time.

* **retort** [ritɔ́ːt] v. 쏘아붙이다, 대꾸하다; n. 쏘아붙이기, 응수
To retort means to reply angrily to someone.

* **determine** [ditɔ́ːrmin] v. ~을 하기로 결정하다; 알아내다, 밝히다
(determined a. 단단히 결심한)
If you are determined to do something, you have made a firm decision to do it and will not let anything stop you.

‡ **invent** [invént] v. 발명하다; (사실이 아닌 것을) 지어내다
If you invent something such as a machine or process, you are the first person to think of it or make it.

복습 **exclaim** [ikskléim] v. 소리치다, 외치다
If you exclaim, you cry out suddenly in surprise, strong emotion, or pain.

cubicle [kjúːbikl] n. 칸막이한 작은 방
A cubicle is a very small enclosed area.

laid-back [leid-bǽk] a. 느긋한, 태평스러운
If you describe someone as laid-back, you mean that they behave in a calm relaxed way as if nothing will ever worry them.

‡ **employee** [implɔ́iiː] n. 직원, 종업원
An employee is a person who is paid to work for an organization or for another person.

scroll [skroul] v. 스크롤하다(컴퓨터 화면을 상하로 움직이다); n. 두루마리
If you scroll through text on a computer screen, you move the text up or down to find the information that you need.

복습 **notice** [nóutis] v. 알아채다, 인지하다; 주의하다; n. 신경 씀, 알아챔; 통지, 예고
If you notice something or someone, you become aware of them.

복습 **click** [klik] v. (마우스를) 클릭하다; 분명해지다; n. (마우스를) 클릭함
If you click on an area of a computer screen, you point the cursor at that area and press one of the buttons on the mouse in order to make something happen.

goofy [gúːfi] a. 바보 같은, 얼빠진
If you describe someone or something as goofy, you think they are rather silly or ridiculous.

RALPH BREAKS THE INTERNET

* **mate** [meit] n. 동료; 친구; v. 짝짓기를 하다
You can refer to someone's friends as their mates, especially when you are talking about a man and his male friends.

복습 **check out** idiom (흥미로운 것을) 살펴보다; ~을 확인하다
If you check someone or something out, you look at them to see whether you like them.

dude [djuːd] n. 놈, 녀석
A dude is a man.

복습 **toss** [tɔːs] v. (가볍게) 던지다; (고개를) 홱 쳐들다; n. 던지기
If you toss something somewhere, you throw it there lightly, often in a rather careless way.

* **spicy** [spáisi] a. 양념 맛이 강한
Spicy food is strongly flavored with spices.

복습 **bang** [bæŋ] v. 쾅 하고 치다; 쾅 하고 닫다; 쿵 하고 찧다; n. 쾅 (하는 소리)
If you bang on something or if you bang it, you hit it hard, making a loud noise.

복습 **ridiculous** [ridíkjuləs] a. 웃기는, 말도 안 되는, 터무니없는
If you say that something or someone is ridiculous, you mean that they are very foolish.

복습 **run out** idiom (시간·돈 등이) 없어지다, 다 되다
If time is running out, you do not have long to do something.

Check Your Reading Speed

1분에 몇 단어를 읽는지 리딩 속도를 측정해보세요.

$$\frac{925 \text{ words}}{\text{reading time (} \quad \text{) sec}} \times 60 = (\quad) \text{ WPM}$$

Build Your Vocabulary

* **pace** [peis] v. 서성거리다; (일의) 속도를 유지하다; n. 속도; 걸음
  If you pace a small area, you keep walking up and down it, because you are anxious or impatient.

address [ədrés] v. 연설하다; 말을 걸다; 주소를 쓰다; n. 주소; 연설
  If you address a group of people, you give a speech to them.

army [ɑ́ːrmi] n. 부대; 집단; 군대
  An army of people, animals, or things is a large number of them, especially when they are regarded as a force of some kind.

pop-up [pɑ́p-ʌp] n. 팝업; a. 팝업의; 그림이 입체적으로 만들어지는
  A pop-up is something such as an advertisement that appears suddenly on a computer screen when you are looking at the Internet, or when you click the mouse or press a key.

* **drill** [dril] n. (군사) 훈련; 드릴; 반복 연습; v. (드릴로) 구멍을 뚫다; 훈련시키다
  A drill is repeated training for a group of people, especially soldiers, so that they can do something quickly and efficiently.

on fire idiom 열중하여, 흥분하여
  If you say that someone is on fire, you mean that they are doing very well or they are very enthusiastic.

literal [lítərəl] a. 문자 그대로의; (번역이) 직역의
  The literal sense of a word or phrase is its most basic sense.

figurative [fígjurətiv] a. 비유적인
  If you use a word or expression in a figurative sense, you use it with a more abstract or imaginative meaning than its ordinary literal one.

genius [dʒíːnjəs] n. 천재; 천재성; 특별한 재능
  A genius is a highly talented, creative, or intelligent person.

RALPH BREAKS THE INTERNET

nod [nad] v. (고개를) 끄덕이다, 까딱하다; n. (고개를) 끄덕임
If you nod, you move your head downward and upward to show that you are answering 'yes' to a question, or to show agreement, understanding, or approval.

solemn [sáləm] a. 엄숙한, 근엄한 (solemnly ad. 장엄하게, 엄숙하게)
Someone or something that is solemn is very serious rather than cheerful or humorous.

phase [feiz] n. (변화·발달의) 단계; v. 단계적으로 하다
A phase is a particular stage in a process or in the gradual development of something.

elite [eilíːt] a. 엘리트의; 정선된; n. 엘리트 (계층)
Elite people or organizations are considered to be the best of their kind.

pop [pap] v. 불쑥 나타나다; 눈이 휘둥그레지다; 펑 하는 소리가 나다; n. 펑 (하는 소리)
If something pops up, it appears or happens when you do not expect it.

click [klik] n. (마우스를) 클릭함; v. (마우스를) 클릭하다; 분명해지다
A click is the act of pressing a button on the mouse of a computer to operate it.

entertain [èntərtéin] v. 즐겁게 해 주다; (집에서 손님을) 접대하다
(entertainment n. (영화·음악 등의) 오락(물))
Entertainment consists of performances of plays and films, and activities such as reading and watching television, that give people pleasure.

campaign [kæmpéin] n. 캠페인, (조직적인) 운동
A campaign is a planned set of activities that people carry out over a period of time in order to achieve something such as social or political change.

all-out [ɔ́ːl-áut] a. 총력을 기울인, 전면적인
You use all-out to describe actions that are carried out in a very energetic and determined way, using all the resources available.

viral [váiərəl] a. 입소문이 난, 유행이 된
You can use viral to describe something that quickly becomes very popular or well known by being published on the internet or sent from person to person by email or phone.

assault [əsɔ́ːlt] n. 도전; 공격; 폭행(죄); v. 폭행하다; (청각·후각 등을) 괴롭히다
An assault is a determined or serious attempt to do something difficult.

march [maːrʧ] v. 행진하다; (단호한 태도로 급히) 걸어가다; n. 행군, 행진; 3월
If you say that someone marches somewhere, you mean that they walk there quickly and in a determined way, for example because they are angry.

hangar [hǽŋər] n. 격납고
A hangar is a large building in which aircraft are kept.

annoy [ənɔ́i] v. 짜증나게 하다; 귀찮게 하다 (annoyingly ad. 성가시게, 귀찮게)
Someone or something that is annoying makes you feel fairly angry and impatient.

aggressive [əgrésiv] a. 대단히 적극적인; 공격적인
People who are aggressive in their work or other activities behave in a forceful
way because they are very eager to succeed.

poke [pouk] v. (손가락 등으로) 쿡 찌르다; 쑥 내밀다; n. (손가락 등으로) 찌르기
If you poke someone or something, you quickly push them with your finger or
with a sharp object.

nonstop [nanstáp] ad. 연속적으로; 도중에서 정거하지 않고
Something that is nonstop continues without any pauses or interruptions.

sign [sain] n. 표지판; 몸짓, 신호; 기색, 흔적; v. 서명하다; 신호를 보내다
A sign is a piece of wood, metal, or plastic with words or pictures on it. Signs give
you information about something, or give you a warning or an instruction.

judge [dʒʌdʒ] v. 판단하다; 심판을 보다; 짐작하다; n. 판사; 심판 (judgment n. 판단)
Judgment is the ability to make sensible guesses about a situation or sensible
decisions about what to do.

tend [tend] v. (~하는) 경향이 있다, (~을) 하기 쉽다; 돌보다, 보살피다
If something tends to happen, it usually happens or it often happens.

taste [teist] n. 감식력, 감각; 기호, 취향; 맛; v. 맛이 나다
A person's taste is their choice in the things that they like or buy, for example
their clothes, possessions, or music. If you say that they have poor taste, you
disapprove of their choices.

pause [pɔːz] v. (말·일을 하다가) 잠시 멈추다; 정지시키다; n. (말·행동 등의) 멈춤
If you pause while you are doing something, you stop for a short period and then
continue.

case in point idiom (논의 중인 문제·상황 등에) 딱 들어맞는 사례
If you say that something is a case in point, you mean that it is a good example of
something you have just mentioned.

browse [brauz] v. (정보를 찾아) 인터넷을 돌아다니다; 둘러보다, 훑어보다
If you browse on a computer, you search for information in computer files or on
the Internet, especially on the World Wide Web.

limo [límou] n. (= limousine) 리무진(대형 승용차)
A limo is the same as a limousine which is a large and very comfortable car. Limousines are usually driven by a chauffeur and are used by very rich or important people.

come with idiom ~이 딸려 있다
To come with something means to be provided together with it.

keep in touch idiom 연락하다
If you are, keep, or stay in touch with someone, you write, phone, or visit each other regularly.

usher [ʌ́ʃər] v. 안내하다; n. (교회·극장 등의) 좌석 안내원
If you usher someone somewhere, you show them where they should go, often by going with them.

hesitant [hézətənt] a. 주저하는, 망설이는, 머뭇거리는
If you are hesitant about doing something, you do not do it quickly or immediately, usually because you are uncertain, embarrassed, or worried.

＊ **reassure** [ri:əʃúər] v. 안심시키다
If you reassure someone, you say or do things to make them stop worrying about something.

measly [mí:zli] a. 쥐꼬리만한
If you describe an amount, quantity, or size as measly, you are critical of it because it is very small or inadequate.

복습 **wheel** [hwi:l] n. (자동차 등의) 핸들; 바퀴; v. (바퀴 달린 것을) 밀다
The wheel of a car or other vehicle is the circular object that is used to steer it.

＊ **reality** [riǽləti] n. 현실; 실제로 존재하는 것
The reality of a situation is the truth about it, especially when it is unpleasant or difficult to deal with.

복습 **hop** [hap] v. 급히 움직이다; 깡충깡충 뛰다; n. 깡충깡충 뛰기
If you hop somewhere, you move there quickly or suddenly.

＊ **celebrate** [séləbrèit] v. 기념하다, 축하하다
If you celebrate, you do something enjoyable because of a special occasion or to mark someone's success.

복습 **blast** [blæst] v. 빠르게 가다; 쾅쾅 울리다; 폭발시키다; n. 폭발; (한 줄기의) 강한 바람
If you blast in a specified direction, you move very quickly and loudly in that direction.

holographic [hàləgrǽfik] a. 홀로그램의
Holographic means relating to or produced using holograms.

globe [gloub] n. 구체; 세계; 지구
Any ball-shaped object can be referred to as a globe.

glow [glou] v. 빛나다, 타다; (얼굴이) 상기되다; n. (은은한) 불빛; 홍조
If something glows, it produces a dull, steady light.

arcade [a:rkéid] n. 게임 센터, 오락실
An arcade is a place where you can play games on machines which work when you put money in them.

district [dístrikt] n. 지구, 지역, 구역
A district is a particular area of a town or country.

widen [waidn] v. 넓어지다; (정도·범위 등이) 커지다
If your eyes widen, they open more.

slaughter [slɔ́:tər] n. 대량 학살, 살육; 도살; v. (대량) 학살하다; 도축하다
Slaughter is the violent killing of a large number of people.

spin [spin] v. (spun-spun) (빙빙) 돌다; 돌아서다; n. 회전
If something spins or if you spin it, it turns quickly around a central point.

technically [téknikəli] ad. 엄밀히 따지면; 기술적으로
If something is technically the case, it is the case according to a strict interpretation of facts, laws, or rules, but may not be important or relevant in a particular situation.

redirect [rì:dirékt] v. (다른 주소·방향으로) 다시 보내다; 돌려쓰다
If you redirect someone or something, you change their course or destination.

bonkers [báŋkərz] a. 완전히 제정신이 아닌
If you say that someone is bonkers, you mean that they are silly or act in a crazy way.

flit [flit] v. (가볍게) 돌아다니다, 휙 스치다
If you flit around or flit between one place and another, you go to lots of places without staying for very long in any of them.

joint [dʒɔint] n. 장소; 관절; 연결 부위; a. 공동의, 합동의
You can refer a place where people go for entertainment as a joint.

eventually [ivénʧuəli] ad. 결국, 마침내
Eventually means at the end of a situation or process or as the final result of it.

monotone [mánətoun] n. 단조로운 소리; a. (소리·색깔이) 단조로운
If someone speaks in a monotone, their voice does not vary at all in tone or loudness and so it is not interesting to listen to.

donkey [dáŋki] n. [동물] 당나귀
A donkey is an animal which is like a horse but which is smaller and has longer ears.

take place idiom (사건 등이) 일어나다; (행사가) 개최되다
If something takes place, it happens or occurs.

announcer [ənáunsər] n. (프로그램) 방송 진행자
An announcer is someone who introduces programs on radio or television or who reads the text of a radio or television advertisement.

applaud [əplɔ́ːd] v. 박수를 치다; 갈채를 보내다
When a group of people applaud, they clap their hands in order to show approval, for example when they have enjoyed a play or concert.

spotlight [spátlait] n. 스포트라이트, 환한 조명; 주목, 관심; v. 세간의 이목을 집중시키다
A spotlight is a powerful light, for example in a theater, which can be directed so that it lights up a small area.

friendship [fréndʃip] n. 우정; 친선; 교우 관계
You use friendship to refer in a general way to the state of being friends, or the feelings that friends have for each other.

fair [fɛər] a. 아름다운; 타당한; 공정한; ad. 공정하게, 타당하게; n. 축제; 박람회
If you describe someone or something as fair, you mean that they are beautiful.

immediate [imíːdiət] a. 즉각적인; 당면한; 아주 가까이에 있는 (immediately ad. 즉시, 즉각)
If something happens immediately, it happens without any delay.

whisk [hwisk] v. 재빨리 데려가다; (달걀 등을) 휘젓다; n. 신속한 움직임
If you whisk someone or something somewhere, you take them or move them there quickly.

pod [pad] n. (우주선·선박의 본체에서) 분리 가능한 부분; (콩이 들어 있는) 꼬투리
A pod is a detachable or self-contained unit on an aircraft, spacecraft, vehicle, or vessel, having a particular function.

crowd [kraud] n. 사람들, 군중; v. 가득 메우다; 바싹 붙어 서다
A crowd is a large group of people who have gathered together, for example to watch or listen to something interesting, or to protest about something.

security [sikjúərəti] n. 보안, 경비; 경비 담당 부서; 안도감, 안심
Security refers to all the measures that are taken to protect a place, or to ensure that only people with permission enter it or leave it.

guard [ga:rd] n. 경비 요원; 경비, 감시; v. 지키다, 보호하다 (security guard n. 보안 요원)
A security guard is someone whose job is to protect a building or to collect and deliver large amounts of money.

permit [pərmít] n. 허가증; v. 허락하다
A permit is an official document which says that you may do something.

authorize [ɔ́:θəràiz] v. 정식으로 허가하다, 권한을 부여하다 (unauthorized a. 승인되지 않은)
If something is unauthorized, it has been produced or is happening without official permission.

bait [beit] n. 미끼; v. 미끼를 놓다; (일부러) 화를 돋우다
To use something as bait means to use it to trick or persuade someone to do something.

grab [græb] v. (와락·단단히) 붙잡다; 급히 ~하다; n. 와락 잡아채려고 함
If you grab something, you take it or pick it up suddenly and roughly.

zoom [zu:m] v. 쌩 하고 가다; 급등하다; n. (빠르게) 쌩 하고 지나가는 소리
If you zoom somewhere, you go there very quickly.

bolt [boult] v. 달아나다; 빗장을 지르다; n. 번쩍하는 번개; 볼트
If a person or animal bolts, they suddenly start to run very fast, often because something has frightened them.

chase [ʧeis] n. 추적, 추격; 추구함; v. 뒤쫓다, 추적하다; 추구하다
A chase is the act of going after someone or something very quickly in order to catch them.

desperate [déspərət] a. 간절히 원하는; 필사적인, 극단적인 (desperately ad. 간절히)
If you are desperate for something or desperate to do something, you want or need it very much indeed.

route [ru:t] n. 길, 경로; 방법; v. 보내다, 전송하다
A route is a way from one place to another.

^복_습 **trap** [træp] v. (위험한 장소에) 가두다; (함정으로) 몰아넣다; n. 함정; 덫
If you are trapped somewhere, something falls onto you or blocks your way and prevents you from moving or escaping.

⋆ **corridor** [kɔ́:ridər] n. 복도; 통로
A corridor is a long passage in a building or train, with doors and rooms on one or both sides.

^복_습 **nowhere** [nóuhwɛər] ad. 아무데도 ~없다
You use nowhere when making negative statements to say that a suitable place of the specified kind does not exist.

Chapters 13 & 14

1. **Why did the Oh My Disney princesses ask Vanellope so many questions?**

   A. They wanted to know everything about her.

   B. They wanted to find out what made her a princess.

   C. They wanted to know if she had any secrets.

   D. They wanted to find out if she was related to any of them.

2. **Why did the princesses recommend staring at important water?**

   A. It could help Vanellope sing about her dream.

   B. It could make Vanellope achieve her dream.

   C. It could cause Vanellope to dream about singing.

   D. It could turn Vanellope into a talented singer.

3. What happened right after Ralph and Yesss made another video?

   A. eBoy stopped by to watch it.

   B. Ralph's Buzzzy device rang.

   C. Yesss thought of another bee pun.

   D. The video would not upload.

4. What did Yesss say to Ralph about the Internet?

   A. It contained truthful comments.

   B. It always stayed the same.

   C. It had some positive aspects.

   D. It was an unnecessary part of life.

5. How did Vanellope react when Ralph said they could go home?

   A. She was surprisingly relieved.

   B. She was not that enthusiastic.

   C. She was completely grateful.

   D. She was full of panic.

Check Your Reading Speed

1분에 몇 단어를 읽는지 리딩 속도를 측정해보세요.

$$\frac{963 \text{ words}}{\text{reading time ( ) sec}} \times 60 = (\quad) \text{ WPM}$$

Build Your Vocabulary

guard [gɑːrd] n. 경비 요원; 경비, 감시; v. 지키다, 보호하다
A guard is a specially organized group of people, such as soldiers or policemen, who protect or watch someone or something.

sight [sait] n. 광경, 모습; 보기; 시력; v. 갑자기 보다
If something is in sight or within sight, you can see it.

lock [lɑk] v. (자물쇠로) 잠그다; 고정시키다; n. 잠금장치
When you lock something such as a door, drawer, or case, you fasten it, usually with a key, so that other people cannot open it.

label [léibəl] v. (표에 정보를) 적다; 꼬리표를 붙이다; n. 표, 라벨; 꼬리표
If something is labeled, a label is attached to it giving information about it.

struggle [strʌgl] v. 애쓰다; 몸부림치다, 허우적거리다; 힘겹게 나아가다; n. 투쟁, 분투; 몸부림
If you struggle to do something, you try hard to do it, even though other people or things may be making it difficult for you to succeed.

glitch [glitʃ] v. 갑자기 고장 나다; n. 작은 문제, 결함
To glitch means to suffer a sudden malfunction or fault.

sign [sain] n. 기색, 흔적; 표지판; 몸짓, 신호; v. 서명하다; 신호를 보내다
If there is a sign of something, there is something which shows that it exists or is happening.

pavilion [pəvíljən] n. 경기장, 공연장; 파빌리온; 임시 구조물
A pavilion is a large building in which sports or entertainments take place.

set out idiom (여행을) 시작하다; ~을 진열하다
If you set out, you start a journey.

dressing room [drésiŋ ru:m] n. (극장의) 분장실; (선수들의) 탈의실
A dressing room is a room in a theater where performers can dress and get ready
for their performance.

face to face idiom ~에 직면한, 대면한
If you come face to face with someone, you meet them and can talk to them or
look at them directly.

awkward [ɔ́ːkwərd] a. 어색한; (처리하기) 곤란한; 불편한 (awkwardly ad. 어색하게)
Someone who feels awkward behaves in a shy or embarrassed way.

leap [liːp] v. (서둘러) ~하다; 뛰다, 뛰어오르다; n. 높이뛰기, 도약; 급증
If you leap somewhere, you move there suddenly and quickly.

sword [sɔːrd] n. 검(劍), 칼
A sword is a weapon with a handle and a long sharp blade.

grip [grip] v. 꽉 잡다, 움켜잡다; (마음·흥미·시선을) 끌다; n. 꽉 붙잡음; 통제, 지배
If you grip something, you take hold of it with your hand and continue to hold it
firmly.

clutch [klʌʧ] v. (꽉) 움켜잡다; n. 움켜쥠
If you clutch at something or clutch something, you hold it tightly, usually because
you are afraid or anxious.

smash [smæʃ] v. 박살내다; (세게) 부딪치다; 부서지다; n. 박살내기; 요란한 소리
If you smash something or if it smashes, it breaks into many pieces, for example
when it is hit or dropped.

slipper [slípər] n. 슬리퍼, 실내화
Slippers are light slip-on shoes, especially one used for dancing.

wave [weiv] v. (무엇을 손에 들고) 흔들다; (손·팔을) 흔들다; n. 물결; (손·팔을) 흔들기
If you wave something, you hold it up and move it rapidly from side to side.

jagged [dʒǽgid] a. 삐죽삐죽한, 들쭉날쭉한
Something that is jagged has a rough, uneven shape or edge with lots of sharp
points.

edge [edʒ] n. 끝, 가장자리; 우위; v. 조금씩 움직이다; 테두리를 두르다
The edge of something is the place or line where it stops, or the part of it that is
furthest from the middle.

in case idiom (~할) 경우에 대비해서
If you do something in case or just in case a particular thing happens, you do it because that thing might happen.

embarrass [imbǽrəs] v. 당황스럽게 하다, 어색하게 하다; 곤란하게 하다
(embarrassing a. 당혹스러운)
Something that is embarrassing makes you feel shy or ashamed.

simultaneous [sàiməltéiniəs] a. 동시에 일어나는, 동시의
(simultaneously ad. 동시에; 일제히)
Things which are simultaneous happen or exist at the same time.

poison [pɔizn] v. 독살하다; 나쁜 영향을 주다; n. 독, 독약
If someone poisons another person, they kill the person or make them ill by giving them poison.

dramatic [drəmǽtik] a. 극적인; 감격적인, 인상적인; 과장된 (dramatically ad. 극적으로)
A dramatic action, event, or situation is exciting and impressive.

curse [kə:rs] v. 저주를 내리다; 욕설을 하다; n. 저주; 욕설, 악담 (cursed a. 저주받은)
Someone or something that is cursed is suffering as the result of a curse.

kidnap [kídnæp] v. 납치하다, 유괴하다
To kidnap someone is to take them away illegally and by force, and usually to hold them prisoner in order to demand something from their family, employer, or government.

enslave [insléiv] v. (사람을) 노예로 만들다; 사로잡다
To enslave someone means to make them into a slave.

assume [əsú:m] v. (사실일 것으로) 추정하다; (특질·양상을) 띠다
If you assume that something is true, you imagine that it is true, sometimes wrongly.

deal [di:l] n. 거래; 일, 사항; 처리; v. 처리하다
If you make a deal, do a deal, or cut a deal, you complete an agreement or an arrangement with someone, especially in business.

underwater [ʌndərwɔ́:tər] a. 물속의, 수중의; ad. 수면 아래로, 물속에서
Something that exists or happens underwater exists or happens below the surface of the sea, a river, or a lake.

witch [witʃ] n. 마녀
In fairy stories, a witch is a woman, usually an old woman, who has evil magic powers.

gag [gæg] v. 토할 것 같다; (입에) 재갈을 물리다; n. 재갈; 장난
If you gag, you cannot swallow and nearly vomit.

squeal [skwi:l] v. 꽤액 소리를 지르다; 끼익 하는 소리를 내다; n. 끼익 하는 소리
If someone or something squeals, they make a long, high-pitched sound.

hesitate [hézətèit] v. 망설이다, 주저하다; 거리끼다 (hesitation n. 주저, 망설임)
Hesitation is an unwillingness to do something, or a delay in doing it, because you
are uncertain, worried, or embarrassed about it.

trill [tril] v. 떨리는 소리로 노래하다; 명랑하게 말하다; n. 떨리는 목소리; (새가) 지저귀는 소리
If you say that a woman trills, you mean that she talks or laughs in a high-pitched
voice which sounds rather musical but which also sounds rather irritating.

delight [diláit] n. (큰) 기쁨; 즐거움을 주는 것; v. 많은 기쁨을 주다, 아주 즐겁게 하다
Delight is a feeling of very great pleasure.

outfit [áutfit] n. 한 벌의 옷, 복장; 장비; v. (복장·장비를) 갖추어 주다
An outfit is a set of clothes.

gown [gaun] n. (여성의) 드레스; 가운, 학위복
A gown is a dress, usually a long dress, which women wear on formal occasions.

casual [kǽʒuəl] a. 격식을 차리지 않는; 태평스러운 (듯한), 무심한
Casual clothes are ones that you normally wear at home or on holiday, and not
on formal occasions.

shrug [ʃrʌg] n. 어깨를 으쓱하기; v. (어깨를) 으쓱하다
A shrug is the action of raising and lowering your shoulders to express something.

comfort [kʌ́mfərt] n. 안락, 편안; 위로, 위안; v. 위로하다, 위안하다
If you are doing something in comfort, you are physically relaxed and contented,
and are not feeling any pain or other unpleasant sensations.

hoodie [húdi] n. 모자 달린 옷
A hoodie is a a piece of clothing with a hood that you wear on the top part of your
body, usually made of thick cotton.

sweatpants [swétpænts] n. 운동복 바지
Sweatpants are soft, loose trousers that you wear for doing sport or exercise, or
as informal clothing.

fluff [flʌf] n. (동물이나 새의) 솜털; 보풀; v. 망치다; 부풀리다 (fluffy a. 솜털의, 솜털로 뒤덮인)
If you describe something such as a towel or a toy animal as fluffy, you mean that
it is very soft.

* **boot** [buːt] n. 목이 긴 신발, 부츠; v. 세게 차다; (컴퓨터를) 부팅하다
Boots are shoes that cover your whole foot and the lower part of your leg.

sloppy [slápi] a. 엉성한, 대충 하는; 헐렁한
If you describe someone's work or activities as sloppy, you mean they have been done in a careless and lazy way.

‡ **knot** [nat] n. 올린 머리; 매듭; (긴장·화 등으로) 뻣뻣한 느낌; v. 매듭을 묶다
A knot is a woman's hairstyle with the hair tied into a round shape.

* **hail** [heil] int. 만세, 행복하기를!; v. (사람을) 부르다; 신호를 보내다; n. 우박
All hail is used to greet or salute to someone important such as a king or queen.

comfy [kʌ́mfi] a. 편안한, 안락한
A comfy item of clothing, piece of furniture, room, or position is a comfortable one.

복습 **cheer** [ʧiər] v. 환호성을 지르다, 환호하다; n. 환호(성), 응원
When people cheer, they shout loudly to show their approval or to encourage someone who is doing something such as taking part in a game.

‡ **twist** [twist] v. 일그러뜨리다; 휘다, 구부리다; (고개·몸 등을) 돌리다;
n. (손으로) 돌리기; (고개·몸 등을) 돌리기
If you twist something, especially a part of your body, or if it twists, it moves into an unusual, uncomfortable, or bent position, for example because of being hit or pushed, or because you are upset.

복습 **confuse** [kənfjúːz] v. (사람을) 혼란시키다; 혼동하다 (confusion n. 혼란)
If there is confusion about something, it is not clear what the true situation is, especially because people believe different things.

복습 **spotlight** [spátlait] n. 스포트라이트, 환한 조명; 주목, 관심; v. 세간의 이목을 집중시키다
A spotlight is a powerful light, for example in a theater, which can be directed so that it lights up a small area.

* **assure** [əʃúər] v. 장담하다, 확언하다; 확인하다
If you assure someone that something is true or will happen, you tell them that it is definitely true or will definitely happen, often in order to make them less worried.

clear one's throat idiom 목을 가다듬다; 헛기침하다
If you clear your throat, you cough once in order to make it easier to speak or to attract people's attention.

RALPH BREAKS THE INTERNET

‡ **stiff** [stif] a. 딱딱한, 경직된; 뻣뻣한; 심한; ad. 몹시, 극심하게 (stiffly ad. 딱딱하게)
Stiff behavior is rather formal and not very friendly or relaxed.

‡ **steer** [stiər] v. (보트·자동차 등을) 조종하다; (특정 방향으로) 움직이다
(steering wheel n. (자동차의) 핸들)
When you steer a car, boat, or plane, you control it so that it goes in the direction
that you want.

‡ **wince** [wins] v. (통증·당혹감으로) 움찔하고 놀라다
If you wince, the muscles of your face tighten suddenly because you have felt a
pain or because you have just seen, heard, or remembered something unpleasant.

∗ **tune** [tju:n] n. 곡, 선율; (마음의) 상태; v. (악기의) 음을 맞추다 (out-of-tune a. 음이 맞지 않는)
A person or musical instrument that is out of tune does not produce exactly the
right notes.

unpack [ʌnpǽk] v. 분석하다; (짐을) 풀다
If you unpack an idea or problem, you analyze it and consider it in detail.

metaphor [métəfɔ̀:r] n. 은유, 비유
A metaphor is an imaginative way of describing something by referring to
something else which is the same in a particular way.

‡ **literal** [lítərəl] a. 문자 그대로의; (번역이) 직역의 (literally ad. 말 그대로; 그야말로)
If a word or expression is translated literally, its most simple or basic meaning is
translated.

lousy [láuzi] a. 형편없는; (아주) 안 좋은, 엉망인
If you describe someone as lousy, you mean that they are very bad at something
they do.

‡ **reflect** [riflékt] v. (상을) 비추다; 반사하다; 깊이 생각하다
When something is reflected in a mirror or in water, you can see its image in the
mirror or in the water.

‡ **stare** [stɛər] v. 빤히 쳐다보다, 응시하다; n. 빤히 쳐다보기, 응시
If you stare at someone or something, you look at them for a long time.

∗ **well** [wel] n. 우물; 근원; v. (액체가) 솟아 나오다, 샘솟다
A well is a hole in the ground from which a supply of water is extracted.

trough [trɔ:f] n. 구유, 여물통
A trough is a long narrow container from which farm animals drink or eat.

confess [kənfés] v. 고백하다, 인정하다; 자백하다
If someone confesses to doing something wrong, they admit that they did it.

bubble [bʌbl] n. 거품; (감정의) 약간; v. (감정이) 차오르다; 거품이 일다
Bubbles are small balls of air or gas in a liquid.

clarify [klǽrəfài] v. 명확하게 하다, 분명히 말하다
To clarify something means to make it easier to understand, usually by explaining it in more detail.

magical [mǽdʒikəl] a. 마술적인, 마술에 걸린 (듯한); 황홀한, 아주 멋진
(magically ad. 마술에 걸린 듯이, 신비하게)
Something that is magical seems to use magic or to be able to produce magic.

sink in idiom 충분히 이해되다, 인식되다
If an unpleasant or surprising fact or idea sinks in, you gradually start to believe it, understand it, or realize the effect it will have on you.

knock [nak] n. 문 두드리는 소리; 부딪침; v. 치다, 부딪치다; (문 등을) 두드리다
A knock is a sudden short noise made when someone or something hits a surface.

announce [ənáuns] v. 발표하다, 알리다; 선언하다
If you announce something, you tell people about it publicly or officially.

sigh [sai] n. 한숨; v. 한숨을 쉬다, 한숨짓다; 탄식하듯 말하다
A sigh is a slow breath out that makes a long soft sound, especially because you are disappointed, tired, annoyed, or relaxed.

teardrop [tíərdràp] n. 눈물방울
A teardrop is a large tear that comes from your eye when you are crying quietly.

lean [li:n] v. 기울이다, (몸을) 숙이다; ~에 기대다; a. 군살이 없는, 호리호리한
When you lean in a particular direction, you bend your body in that direction.

depart [dipá:rt] v. 떠나다, 출발하다; 그만두다
When something or someone departs from a place, they leave it and start a journey to another place.

Check Your Reading Speed

1분에 몇 단어를 읽는지 리딩 속도를 측정해보세요.

$$\frac{1,093 \text{ words}}{\text{reading time ( ) sec}} \times 60 = (\qquad) \text{ WPM}$$

Build Your Vocabulary

meanwhile [míːnwàil] ad. (다른 일이 일어나고 있는) 그동안에
Meanwhile means while a particular thing is happening.

wreck [rek] v. 파괴하다; 엉망으로 만들다; n. 충돌; 사고 잔해
To wreck something means to completely destroy or ruin it.

inspect [inspékt] v. 면밀하게 살피다, 점검하다; 시찰하다
If you inspect something, you look at every part of it carefully in order to find out about it or check that it is all right.

heft [heft] n. 무게, 중량; v. 들어올리다; 들어서 무게를 대중하다
A heft is the weight of something or someone.

wobble [wabl] v. (불안정하게) 흔들리다; 뒤뚱거리며 가다; n. 흔들림; (마음·자신감의) 동요
If something or someone wobbles, they make small movements from side to side, for example because they are unsteady.

swarm [swɔːrm] n. (곤충의) 떼, 무리; v. 군중; 많이 모여들다; 무리를 지어 다니다
A swarm of bees or other insects is a large group of them flying together.

buzz [bʌz] v. 윙윙거리다; 부산스럽다, 활기가 넘치다; n. 윙윙거리는 소리
If something buzzes or buzzes somewhere, it makes a long continuous sound, like the noise a bee makes when it is flying.

screech [skriːʃ] v. 끼익 하는 소리를 내다; n. 끼익, 꽥 (하는 날카로운 소리)
When you screech something, you shout it in a loud, unpleasant, high-pitched voice.

edit [édit] v. 편집하다; 수정하다
If you edit a film or a television or radio program, you choose some of what has been filmed or recorded and arrange it in a particular order.

upload [ʌ́plòud] v. 업로드하다
If you upload data, you transfer it to your computer or from your computer to another computer.

pun [pʌn] n. 말장난, 말재간
A pun is a clever and amusing use of a word or phrase with two meanings, or of words with the same sound but different meanings.

genius [dʒíːnjəs] n. 천재; 천재성; 특별한 재능
A genius is a highly talented, creative, or intelligent person.

cheerful [tʃíərfəl] a. 발랄한, 쾌활한 (cheerfully ad. 쾌활하게, 명랑하게)
Someone who is cheerful is happy and shows this in their behavior.

bid [bid] n. 입찰; 가격 제시; v. (작별을) 고하다; 값을 부르다
A bid is an offer to pay a particular amount of money for something that is being sold.

expire [ikspáiər] v. (기한이) 만료되다, 만기가 되다
When something such as a contract, deadline, or visa expires, it comes to an end or is no longer valid.

frustrate [frʌ́streit] v. 좌절감을 주다, 불만스럽게 하다; 방해하다
(frustrated a. 좌절감을 느끼는)
If something frustrates you, it upsets or angers you because you are unable to do anything about the problems it creates.

lollipop [lálipàp] n. 막대 사탕
A lollipop is a sweet consisting of a hard disc or ball of a sugary substance on the end of a stick.

load [loud] v. (데이터나 프로그램을) 로딩하다; (짐·사람 등을) 싣다;
n. (많은 양의) 짐; (수·양이) 많음
If a web page or an application loads or is loaded, it appears on a screen.

make it idiom 해내다; (힘든 경험 등을) 버텨 내다; 가다
If you make it, you are successful in achieving something difficult, or in surviving through a very difficult period.

tech [tek] a. (= technical) 기술적인; n. (= technology) (과학) 기술; 기계, 장비
Technical means involving the sorts of machines, processes, and materials that are used in industry, transport, and communications.

‡ **support** [səpɔ́ːrt] n. 지지, 지원; (정신적인) 도움; v. 지지하다; (넘어지지 않도록) 떠받치다
Technical support is a service provided by a computer company to help customers
who are having problems using their products.

∗ **wander** [wándər] v. (이리저리) 돌아다니다; (일행들로부터) 떨어져 나가다; n. (이리저리) 거닐기
If you wander in a place, you walk around there in a casual way, often without
intending to go in any particular direction.

복
습 **fluff** [flʌf] n. (동물이나 새의) 솜털; 보풀; v. 망치다; 부풀리다 (fluffy a. 솜털의, 솜털로 뒤덮인)
If you describe something such as a towel or a toy animal as fluffy, you mean that
it is very soft.

복
습 **stuck** [stʌk] a. 움직일 수 없는, 꼼짝 못하는; 갇힌
If something is stuck in a particular position, it is fixed tightly in this position and
is unable to move.

‡ **jar** [dʒɑːr] n. 병; v. 불쾌감을 주다, (신경을) 거슬리다; 부딪치다
A jar is a glass container with a lid that is used for storing food.

‡ **replace** [ripléis] v. 대신하다, 대체하다; 교체하다
If you replace one thing or person with another, you put something or someone
else in their place to do their job.

복
습 **force** [fɔːrs] v. 억지로 ~하다; ~를 강요하다; n. 작용력; 힘; 영향력
If someone forces you to do something, they make you do it even though you do
not want to, for example by threatening you.

복
습 **hose** [houz] n. 호스; v. 호스로 물을 뿌리다
A hose is a long, flexible pipe made of rubber or plastic. Water is directed through
a hose in order to do things such as put out fires, clean cars, or water gardens.

복
습 **netizen** [nétəzən] n. 네티즌, 인터넷 사용자
A netizen is a person who uses the internet.

복
습 **suck** [sʌk] v. (특정한 방향으로) 빨아들이다; 빨아 먹다; 엉망이다, 형편없다; n. 빨기, 빨아 먹기
If something sucks a liquid, gas, or object in a particular direction, it draws it
there with a powerful force.

복
습 **notice** [nóutis] v. 알아채다, 인지하다; 주의하다; n. 신경 씀, 알아챔; 통지, 예고
If you notice something or someone, you become aware of them.

복
습 **chase** [ʧeis] v. 뒤쫓다, 추적하다; 추구하다; n. 추적, 추격; 추구함
If you chase someone, or chase after them, you run after them or follow them
quickly in order to catch or reach them.

label [léibəl] v. (표에 정보를) 적다; 꼬리표를 붙이다; n. 표, 라벨; 꼬리표
If something is labeled, a label is attached to it giving information about it.

comment [kámənt] n. 논평, 언급; v. 논평하다, 견해를 밝히다
A comment is something that you say which expresses your opinion of something or which gives an explanation of it.

stumble into idiom 우연히 발견하다
If you stumble into something, you find it by chance.

spot [spat] v. 발견하다, 찾다, 알아채다; n. (특정한) 곳; (작은) 점
If you spot something or someone, you notice them.

realize [ríːəlàiz] v. 깨닫다, 알아차리다; 실현하다, 달성하다
If you realize that something is true, you become aware of that fact or understand it.

stink [stiŋk] v. 좋지 않다; (고약한) 냄새가 나다; n. 악취
If you say that something stinks, you mean that you disapprove of it because it involves ideas, feelings, or practices that you do not like.

fade [feid] v. 서서히 사라지다; (색깔이) 바래다, 희미해지다
When something that you are looking at fades, it slowly becomes less bright or clear until it disappears.

misspell [mìsspél] v. 철자를 잘못 쓰다, 철자가 틀리다
If someone misspells a word, they spell it wrongly.

laugh at idiom ~을 비웃다
If you laugh at someone or something, you say unkind things about them that are intended to make them seem silly.

cruel [kruːəl] a. 잔혹한, 잔인한; 고통스러운, 괴로운
Someone who is cruel deliberately causes pain or distress to people or animals.

spell [spel] n. 주문; 마법; v. (어떤 단어의) 철자를 쓰다; 철자를 맞게 쓰다
(break out of one's spell idiom 정신을 차리다)
If someone or something breaks you out of your spell, they make you stop paying all your attention to a thing.

dude [djuːd] n. 놈, 녀석
A dude is a man.

instant [ínstənt] a. 즉각적인; n. 순간, 아주 짧은 동안 (instantly ad. 즉각, 즉시)
You use instant to describe something that happens immediately.

bring out idiom ~을 끌어내다, 발휘되게 하다
To bring out means to make someone or something show a quality that they have.

ignore [ignɔ́ːr] v. 무시하다; (사람을) 못 본 척하다
If you ignore someone or something, you pay no attention to them.

reminder [rimáindər] n. 상기시키는 것
Something that serves as a reminder of another thing makes you think about the other thing.

hold on idiom 기다려, 멈춰
You can use 'hold on' to ask someone to wait or stop for a short time.

congratulate [kəngrǽʧulèit] v. 축하하다; 기뻐하다, 자랑스러워하다
(congratulations int. 축하해요!)
You say 'Congratulations' to someone in order to congratulate them on something nice that has happened to them or something good that they have done.

grin [grin] v. 활짝 웃다; n. 활짝 웃음
When you grin, you smile broadly.

brighten [braitn] v. (얼굴 등이) 환해지다; 반짝이다
If someone brightens or their face brightens, they suddenly look happier.

account [əkáunt] n. 이용 계정; 계좌; 설명, 이야기; v. 간주하다, 여기다
An account is an arrangement you have with a company or Internet provider to use a service they provide.

device [diváis] n. 장치, 기구; 폭발물; 방법
A device is an object that has been invented for a particular purpose, for example for recording or measuring something.

grand [grænd] n. (pl. grand) 천 달러; a. 웅장한, 장려한; 원대한
A grand is a thousand dollars or a thousand pounds.

ace [eis] n. 명수, 고수; (카드의) 에이스; a. 아주 좋은
If you describe someone such as a sports player as an ace, you mean that they are very good at what they do.

puddle [pʌdl] n. (빗물 등의) 물웅덩이
A puddle is a small, shallow pool of liquid that has spread on the ground.

intense [inténs] a. 진지한; 극심한, 강렬한; 치열한 (intensely ad. 열심히)
If you describe a person as intense, you mean that they appear to concentrate very hard on everything that they do, and they feel and show their emotions in a very extreme way.

figure out idiom ~을 이해하다, 알아내다; 계산하다, 산출하다
If you figure out someone or something, you come to understand them by thinking carefully.

interrupt [intərʌ́pt] v. (말·행동을) 방해하다; 중단시키다; 차단하다
If you interrupt someone who is speaking, you say or do something that causes them to stop.

no way idiom 말도 안 돼; 절대로 아니다; 싫어
You can say 'no way' for expressing surprise, or for telling someone that you do not believe them.

hang up idiom 전화를 끊다; ~을 중지하다
To hang up means to end a telephone conversation, often very suddenly.

reality [riǽləti] n. 현실; 실제로 존재하는 것
The reality of a situation is the truth about it, especially when it is unpleasant or difficult to deal with.

thrill [θril] v. 열광시키다, 정말 신나게 하다; n. 흥분, 설렘; 전율
(thrilled a. 황홀해하는, 아주 흥분한)
If someone is thrilled, they are extremely pleased about something.

reflect [riflékt] v. (상을) 비추다; 반사하다; 깊이 생각하다 (reflection n. (거울 등에 비친) 상)
A reflection is an image that you can see in a mirror or in glass or water.

1. **How did Ralph find out Vanellope's true feelings about**
   Slaughter Race?

   A. He called her through BuzzzFace and asked her about it.

   B. He walked into the game again and spied on her.

   C. He heard her talk about it secretly with Shank.

   D. He got a message from her about it on his Buzzzy device.

2. **What did Ralph think when he found out what Vanellope's**
   dream was?

   A. He thought Vanellope was a selfish friend.

   B. He thought Vanellope was trying to punish him.

   C. He thought there was no way to change Vanellope's mind.

   D. He thought it was not what Vanellope really wanted.

3. **What was true about Double Dan?**

    A. He was a creator of viruses.

    B. He worked for Gord.

    C. He had a large family.

    D. He liked having guests around.

4. **What kind of virus did Ralph want?**

    A. A virus that would slow down *Slaughter Race*

    B. A virus that could attack multiple characters

    C. A virus that would make *Slaughter Race* crash

    D. A virus that could not be detected or stopped

5. **What did Ralph need to do with the virus called Arthur?**

    A. He needed to make copies of it.

    B. He needed to keep it within *Slaughter Race*.

    C. He needed to fix its defect.

    D. He needed to give it directly to Shank.

Check Your Reading Speed

1분에 몇 단어를 읽는지 리딩 속도를 측정해보세요.

$$\frac{1{,}031 \text{ words}}{\text{reading time ( ) sec}} \times 60 = (\qquad) \text{ WPM}$$

Build Your Vocabulary

reflect [riflékt] v. (상을) 비추다; 반사하다; 깊이 생각하다 (reflection n. (거울 등에 비친) 상)
A reflection is an image that you can see in a mirror or in glass or water.

puddle [pʌdl] n. (빗물 등의) 물웅덩이
A puddle is a small, shallow pool of liquid that has spread on the ground.

slaughter [slɔ́ːtər] n. 대량 학살, 살육; 도살; v. (대량) 학살하다; 도축하다
Slaughter is the violent killing of a large number of people.

race [reis] n. 경주; 인종, 종족; v. 경주하다; 쏜살같이 가다; (머리·심장 등이) 바쁘게 돌아가다
A race is a competition to see who is the fastest, for example in running, swimming, or driving.

gasp [gæsp] v. 헉 하고 숨을 쉬다; 숨을 제대로 못 쉬다; n. 헉 하는 소리를 냄
When you gasp, you take a short quick breath through your mouth, especially when you are surprised, shocked, or in pain.

transport [trænspɔ́ːrt] v. 수송하다; 실어 나르다; n. 수송; 운송 수단
To transport people or goods somewhere is to take them from one place to another in a vehicle.

pour [pɔːr] v. 쏟아져 나오다; 마구 쏟아지다; 붓다, 따르다
When feelings or words pour out, or someone pours them out, they are expressed, usually after they have been kept hidden for some time.

rhyme [raim] n. (시의) 운; v. (두 단어나 음절이) 운이 맞다
A rhyme is a word which rhymes with another word, or a set of lines which rhyme.

and all idiom ~까지; ~을 포함하여
You use and all when you want to emphasize that what you are talking about includes the thing mentioned, especially when this is surprising or unusual.

* **stroll** [stroul] v. 거닐다, 산책하다; n. (한가로이) 거닐기, 산책
If you stroll somewhere, you walk there in a slow, relaxed way.

* **explore** [iksplɔ́:r] v. 탐험하다, 탐사하다; 분석하다
If you explore a place, you travel around it to find out what it is like.

복습 **admire** [ædmáiər] v. 감탄하며 바라보다; 존경하다, 칭찬하다
If you admire someone or something, you look at them with pleasure.

* **pigeon** [pídʒən] n. [동물] 비둘기
A pigeon is a bird, usually grey in color, which has a fat body.

* **wire** [waiər] n. 전선, (전화기 등의) 선; v. 전선을 연결하다; 배선 공사를 하다
A wire is a cable which carries power or signals from one place to another.

복습 **burn** [bə:rn] v. 불에 타다; 태우다; 상기되다; n. 화상
If you burn something, you destroy or damage it with fire.

make sense idiom 타당하다; 이해가 되다
If something makes sense, it is a sensible or practical thing to do.

복습 **crew** [kru:] n. (함께 일을 하는) 팀, 조; 승무원; v. (배의) 승무원을 하다
A crew is a group of people with special technical skills who work together on a task or project.

* **appliance** [əpláiəns] n. (가정용) 기기
An appliance is a device or machine in your home that you use to do a job such as cleaning or cooking.

* **thief** [θi:f] n. (pl. thieves) 도둑, 절도범
A thief is a person who steals something from another person.

creepy [krí:pi] a. 오싹하게 하는, 으스스한; (섬뜩할 정도로) 기이한
If you say that something or someone is creepy, you mean they make you feel very nervous or frightened.

* **clown** [klaun] n. 광대; 얼간이, 바보; v. 광대 짓을 하다
A clown is a performer in a circus who wears funny clothes and bright make-up, and does silly things in order to make people laugh.

* **odd** [ad] a. 이상한, 특이한; 홀수의
If you describe someone or something as odd, you think that they are strange or unusual.

* **coordinate** [kouɔ́ːrdənət] v. 조직화하다; (몸의 움직임을) 조정하다; n. 좌표
If you coordinate an activity, you organize the various people and things involved in it.

steer [stiər] v. (보트·자동차 등을) 조종하다; (특정 방향으로) 움직이다
When you steer a car, boat, or plane, you control it so that it goes in the direction that you want.

wheel [hwiːl] n. (자동차 등의) 핸들; 바퀴; v. (바퀴 달린 것을) 밀다
(steering wheel n. (자동차의) 핸들)
The wheel of a car or other vehicle is the circular object that is used to steer it.

overjoyed [òuvərdʒɔ́id] a. 매우 기뻐하는
If you are overjoyed, you are extremely pleased about something.

reveal [rivíːl] v. (비밀 등을) 밝히다; (보이지 않던 것을) 드러내 보이다
(revelation n. (비밀 등을) 드러냄, 폭로)
The revelation of something is the act of making it known.

remind [rimáind] v. 상기시키다, 다시 한 번 알려 주다
If someone reminds you of a fact or event that you already know about, they say something which makes you think about it.

jubilant [dʒúːbələnt] a. 승리감에 넘치는, 득의만면한, 의기양양한 (jubilance n. 환희)
If you are jubilant, you feel extremely happy because of a success.

crush [krʌʃ] v. 좌절시키다; 으스러뜨리다; 밀어 넣다; n. 홀딱 반함
If you are crushed by something, it upsets you a great deal.

ignore [ignɔ́ːr] v. 무시하다; (사람을) 못 본 척하다
If you ignore someone or something, you pay no attention to them.

drop off idiom 내려 주다; 데려다주다
If you drop someone off, you stop and let them get out of a car.

* **slap** [slæp] v. 털썩 놓다; (손바닥으로) 철썩 때리다; n. 철썩 때리기, 치기
If you slap something onto a surface, you put it there quickly, roughly, or carelessly.

checkout [ʧékaut] n. 계산대; (호텔에서) 체크아웃
In a supermarket, a checkout is a counter where you pay for things you are buying.

counter [káuntər] n. 계산대; (식당·바 등의) 카운터; 반작용; v. 대응하다; 반박하다
In a place such as a shop or café a counter is a long narrow table or flat surface at which customers are served.

account [əkáunt] n. 계좌; 이용 계정; 설명, 이야기; v. 간주하다, 여기다
If you have an account with a bank or a similar organization, you have an
arrangement to leave your money there and take some out when you need it.

get the show on the road idiom (활동·여정을) 시작하다
To get the show on the road means to begin an activity that has been planned.

congratulate [kəngrǽʧulèit] v. 축하하다; 기뻐하다, 자랑스러워하다
(congratulations int. 축하해요!)
You say 'Congratulations' to someone in order to congratulate them on something
nice that has happened to them or something good that they have done.

high-five [hai-fáiv] v. 하이파이브를 하다; n. 하이파이브
If you high-five someone, you greet them by slapping the palms of their raised
arms with your own.

way to go idiom 잘했어!
You can say 'way to go' to someone to tell that they have done something well, or
that you are proud of their achievement.

champ [ʧæmp] n. (= champion) 챔피언
A champ is the same as a champion who has won the first prize in a competition,
contest, or fight.

cook with gas idiom 매우 잘 하다; 잘 작동하다
If you say that someone is cooking with gas, you means that they are doing
something very well.

nearby [nìərbái] a. 인근의, 가까운 곳의; ad. 가까운 곳에
If something is nearby, it is only a short distance away.

barely [béərli] ad. 간신히, 가까스로; 거의 ~아니게
You use barely to say that something is only just true or only just the case.

distract [distrǽkt] v. (주의를) 딴 데로 돌리다, 집중이 안 되게 하다
If something distracts you or your attention from something, it takes your
attention away from it.

chum [ʧʌm] n. 친구
Your chum is your friend.

dial [dáiəl] v. 다이얼을 돌리다, 전화를 걸다; n. (시계·계기 등의) 문자반
If you dial or if you dial a number, you turn the dial or press the buttons on a
telephone in order to phone someone.

hood [hud] n. (자동차 등의) 덮개; (외투 등에 달린) 모자
The hood of a car is the metal cover over the engine at the front.

vibrate [váibreit] v. (가늘게) 떨다, 진동하다
If something vibrates or if you vibrate it, it shakes with repeated small, quick movements.

dashboard [dǽʃbɔːrd] n. (승용차의) 계기판
The dashboard in a car is the panel facing the driver's seat where most of the instruments and switches are.

buzz [bʌz] n. 윙윙거리는 소리; v. 윙윙거리다; 부산스럽다, 활기가 넘치다
You can use buzz to refer to a long continuous sound, usually caused by lots of people talking at once.

creep [kriːp] v. (crept-crept) 살금살금 움직이다; 기다; n. 너무 싫은 사람
If something creeps somewhere, it moves very slowly.

holographic [hàləgrǽfik] a. 홀로그램의
Holographic means relating to or produced using holograms.

speedway [spíːdwei] n. (자동차·오토바이의) 경주(장)
Speedway is the sport of racing motorcycles on special tracks.

lock [lak] v. (자물쇠로) 잠그다; 고정시키다; n. 잠금장치 (unlock v. (비밀 등을) 드러내다)
If you unlock the potential or the secrets of something or someone, you release them.

rival [ráivəl] n. 경쟁자, 경쟁 상대
Your rival is a person, business, or organization who you are competing or fighting against in the same area or for the same things.

adorable [ədɔ́ːrəbl] a. 사랑스러운
If you say that someone or something is adorable, you are emphasizing that they are very attractive and you feel great affection for them.

awful [ɔ́ːfəl] a. 끔찍한, 지독한; (정도가) 대단한, 아주 심한
If you say that something is awful, you mean that it is extremely unpleasant, shocking, or bad.

mute [mjuːt] v. 소리를 줄이다; 약화하다; a. 무언의, 말없는
If you mute a noise or sound, you lower its volume or make it less distinct.

chat [ʧæt] v. 이야기를 나누다, 수다를 떨다; n. 이야기, 대화
When people chat, they talk to each other in an informal and friendly way.

pause [pɔ:z] v. (말·일을 하다가) 잠시 멈추다; 정지시키다; n. (말·행동 등의) 멈춤
If you pause while you are doing something, you stop for a short period and then continue.

eavesdrop [íːvzdràp] v. 엿듣다, 도청하다
If you eavesdrop on someone, you listen secretly to what they are saying.

weirdo [wíərdou] n. 괴짜, 별난 사람
If you describe someone as a weirdo, you disapprove of them because they behave in an unusual way which you find difficult to understand or accept.

take in idiom 이해하다; ~을 눈여겨보다
If you take in something, you understand and remember something that you hear or read.

smirk [sməːrk] n. 능글맞은 웃음; v. 히죽히죽 웃다
A smirk is a smile that expresses satisfaction or pleasure about having done something or knowing something that is not known by someone else.

gaze [geiz] v. (가만히) 응시하다, 바라보다; n. 응시, (눈여겨보는) 시선
If you gaze at someone or something, you look steadily at them for a long time.

bear [bɛər] v. 참다, 견디다; (아이를) 낳다; n. [동물] 곰
If you can't bear someone or something, you dislike them very much.

punch [pʌnʧ] v. 주먹으로 치다; (자판·번호판 등을) 치다; n. 주먹으로 한 대 침
If you punch someone or something, you hit them hard with your fist.

kick in the teeth idiom 큰 실망; 감정을 상하게 하는 것
If you describe an event as a kick in the teeth, you are emphasizing that it is very disappointing and upsetting.

donkey [dáŋki] n. [동물] 당나귀
A donkey is an animal which is like a horse but which is smaller and has longer ears.

brainwash [bréinwaʃ] v. 세뇌시키다
If you brainwash someone, you force them to believe something by continually telling them that it is true, and preventing them from thinking about it properly.

abandon [əbǽndən] v. 버리다; 버리고 떠나다; 그만두다
If you abandon a place, thing, or person, you leave the place, thing, or person permanently or for a long time, especially when you should not do so.

* **impulse** [ímpʌls] n. 충동, 욕구; 충격, 자극
An impulse is a sudden desire to do something.

* **charge** [ʧaːrdʒ] v. 급히 가다; (요금·값을) 청구하다; n. 책임, 담당; 요금
If you charge toward someone or something, you move quickly and aggressively toward them.

* **knight** [nait] n. (중세의) 기사; v. 나이트 작위를 서임하다
(white knight n. 구조를 위해 나타나는 용사)
In medieval times, a knight was a man of noble birth, who served his king or lord in battle.

* **liable** [láiəbl] a. ~하기 쉬운; 법적 책임이 있는
If people or things are liable to something unpleasant, they are likely to experience it or do it.

hold against idiom ~을 거론하여 비난하다, ~때문에 원망하다
If you hold it against someone, you like someone less because they have done something wrong or behaved badly in the past.

* **obvious** [ábviəs] a. 분명한, 확실한; 명백한 (obviously ad. 분명히)
You use obviously to indicate that something is easily noticed, seen, or recognized.

* **tap** [tæp] v. (가볍게) 톡톡 두드리다; 박자를 맞추다; n. 수도꼭지; (가볍게) 두드리기
If you tap something, you hit it with a quick light blow or a series of quick light blows.

the coast is clear idiom 들킬 위험이 없다
When you say that the coast is clear, you mean that it is safe to do something because there is no one to see or catch you.

* **whisper** [hwíspər] v. 속삭이다, 소곤거리다; n. 속삭임, 소곤거리는 소리
When you whisper, you say something very quietly, using your breath rather than your throat, so that only one person can hear you.

* **gesture** [dʒésʧər] v. (손·머리 등으로) 가리키다; 몸짓을 하다; n. 몸짓; (감정·의도의) 표시
If you gesture, you use movements of your hands or head in order to tell someone something or draw their attention to something.

Check Your Reading Speed
1분에 몇 단어를 읽는지 리딩 속도를 측정해보세요.

$$\frac{827 \text{ words}}{\text{reading time ( ) sec}} \times 60 = (\quad) \text{ WPM}$$

Build Your Vocabulary

* **alley** [ǽli] n. 골목, 샛길; 통로
An alley is a narrow passage or street with buildings or walls on both sides.

복습 **creepy** [kríːpi] a. 오싹하게 하는, 으스스한; (섬뜩할 정도로) 기이한
If you say that something or someone is creepy, you mean they make you feel very nervous or frightened.

* **hush** [hʌʃ] v. ~을 조용히 시키다; 진정시키다; n. 침묵, 고요 (hushed a. 소리를 낮춘, 숨죽인)
A hushed voice or hushed conversation is very quiet.

overhear [òuvərhíər] v. (overheard-overheard) (남의 대화 등을) 우연히 듣다
If you overhear someone, you hear what they are saying when they are not talking to you and they do not know that you are listening.

maiden name [méidn neim] n. (여자의) 결혼하기 전 성(姓)
A married woman's maiden name is her parents' surname, which she used before she got married and started using her husband's surname.

복습 **security** [sikjúərəti] n. 보안, 경비; 경비 담당 부서; 안도감, 안심
Security refers to all the measures that are taken to protect a place, or to ensure that only people with permission enter it or leave it.

* **companion** [kəmpǽnjən] n. 동료; 친구; 동행
A companion is someone who shares the experiences of another, especially when these are unpleasant or unwelcome.

* **shady** [ʃéidi] a. 수상한 구석이 있는; 그늘이 드리워진
You can describe activities as shady when you think that they might be dishonest or illegal. You can also use shady to describe people who are involved in such activities.

hang out idiom 많은 시간을 보내다
If you hang out in a place or with a person or a group of people, you spend a lot of time in there or with them.

profile [próufail] n. 인지도, (대중의) 관심; 개요; v. ~의 개요를 쓰다
(keep a low profile idiom 세간의 이목을 피하다)
If you keep a low profile, you avoid doing things that will make people notice you.

dabble [dæbl] v. (오락이나 취미 삼아) 조금 해 보다
If you dabble in something, you take part in it but not very seriously.

virus [váiərəs] n. (컴퓨터) 바이러스; 바이러스
In computer technology, a virus is a program that introduces itself into a system, altering or destroying the information stored in the system.

cousin [kʌzn] n. 사촌
Your cousin is the child of your uncle or aunt.

crack [kræk] v. 갈라지다, 금이 가다; 깨지다, 부서지다; n. 날카로운 소리; 금; (좁은) 틈
If something hard cracks, or if you crack it, it becomes slightly damaged, with lines appearing on its surface.

edge [edʒ] n. 끝, 가장자리; 우위; v. 조금씩 움직이다; 테두리를 두르다
The edge of something is the place or line where it stops, or the part of it that is furthest from the middle.

knob [nab] n. (동그란) 손잡이; 혹, 마디
A knob is a round handle on a door or drawer which you use in order to open or close it.

whisper [hwíspər] v. 속삭이다, 소곤거리다; n. 속삭임, 소곤거리는 소리
When you whisper, you say something very quietly, using your breath rather than your throat, so that only one person can hear you.

confuse [kənfjúːz] v. (사람을) 혼란시키다; 혼동하다 (confused a. 혼란스러워하는)
If you are confused, you do not know exactly what is happening or what to do.

creak [kriːk] v. 삐걱거리다; n. 삐걱거리는 소리
If something creaks, it makes a short, high-pitched sound when it moves.

rundown [rʌndáun] a. 부진한, 쇠퇴한; 황폐한
A rundown place of business is not as active as it used to be or does not have many customers.

^복 **site** [sait] n. (인터넷) 사이트; (사건 등의) 현장; 대지
A site is the same as a website which is a set of data and information about a particular subject which is available on the Internet.

^복 **worm** [wə:rm] n. 벌레; 컴퓨터 파괴 프로그램; v. 꿈틀거리며 나아가다
A worm is a small animal with a long thin body, no bones and no legs.

lab [læb] n. (= laboratory) 실험실, 연구실
A lab is the same as a laboratory, which is a building or a room where scientific experiments, analyses, and research are carried out.

^복 **stir** [stə:r] v. 젓다; 약간 움직이다; 자극하다; n. 동요, 충격; 젓기
If you stir a liquid or other substance, you move it around or mix it in a container using something such as a spoon.

^복 **liquid** [líkwid] n. 액체; a. 액체의
A liquid is a substance which is not solid but which flows and can be poured, for example water.

^복 **chum** [ʧʌm] n. 친구
Your chum is your friend.

^복 **annoy** [ənɔ́i] v. 짜증나게 하다; 귀찮게 하다 (annoyed a. 짜증이 난, 약이 오른)
If you are annoyed, you are fairly angry about something.

[*] **drift** [drift] v. (서서히) 이동하다; (물·공기에) 떠가다; n. 표류; 흐름
To drift somewhere means to move there slowly or gradually.

squishy [skwíʃi] a. 질척질척한
Something that is squishy is soft and easy to squash.

^복 **utter** [ʌ́tər] v. (어떤 소리를) 내다; (말을) 하다; a. 완전한
If someone utters sounds or words, they say them.

[*] **squeak** [skwi:k] n. 찍 하는 소리; v. 꽥 소리치다; 끽 하는 소리를 내다
A squeak is a short, high-pitched sound or cry.

none other than idiom 다름 아닌 바로 ~인
You use none other than and no other than to emphasize the name of a person or thing when something about that person or thing is surprising in a particular situation.

^복 **grab** [græb] v. (와락·단단히) 붙잡다; 급히 ~하다; n. 와락 잡아채려고 함
If you grab something, you take it or pick it up suddenly and roughly.

throat [θróut] n. 목; 목구멍
Your throat is the front part of your neck.

threatening [θrétniŋ] a. 협박하는, 위협적인; (날씨 등이) 험악한
You can describe someone's behavior as threatening when you think that they are trying to harm you.

tone [toun] n. 어조, 말투; (글 등의) 분위기; 음색
Someone's tone is a quality in their voice which shows what they are feeling or thinking.

self-conscious [self-kánʃəs] a. 남의 시선을 의식하는, 자의식이 강한
Someone who is self-conscious is easily embarrassed and nervous because they feel that everyone is looking at them and judging them.

hurl [həːrl] v. (거칠게) 던지다; (욕·비난·모욕 등을) 퍼붓다
If you hurl something, you throw it violently and with a lot of force.

stare [stɛər] v. 빤히 쳐다보다, 응시하다; n. 빤히 쳐다보기, 응시
If you stare at someone or something, you look at them for a long time.

odd [ad] a. 이상한, 특이한; 홀수의
If you describe someone or something as odd, you think that they are strange or unusual.

stumble [stʌmbl] v. (말·글 읽기를 하다가) 더듬거리다; 비틀거리다; 발을 헛디디다
If you stumble while you are reading aloud or speaking, you make a mistake, and have to pause before saying the words properly.

neck of the woods idiom 근처, 지역, 일대
Your neck of the woods is the area you come from, or the area where you are.

tumor [tjúːmər] n. 종양
A tumor is a mass of diseased or abnormal cells that has grown in a person's or animal's body.

rumor [rúːmər] n. 소문, 유언비어; v. 소문내다
A rumor is a story or piece of information that may or may not be true, but that people are talking about.

harmless [háːrmlis] a. 해롭지 않은, 무해한
Something that is harmless does not have any bad effects, especially on people's health.

crash [kræʃ] v. (컴퓨터를) 고장 내다; 충돌하다; 부딪치다; n. 요란한 소리; (자동차·항공기) 사고
If a computer or a computer program crashes, it fails suddenly.

pop [pap] v. 불쑥 나타나다; 눈이 휘둥그레지다; 펑 하는 소리가 나다; n. 펑 (하는 소리)
If something pops up, it appears or happens when you do not expect it.

wave [weiv] v. (손·팔을) 흔들다; (무엇을 손에 들고) 흔들다; n. 물결; (손·팔을) 흔들기
If you wave or wave your hand, you move your hand from side to side in the air, usually in order to say hello or goodbye to someone.

grunt [grʌnt] v. 끙 앓는 소리를 내다; (돼지가) 꿀꿀거리다; n. (사람이) 끙 하는 소리
If you grunt, you make a low sound, especially because you are annoyed or not interested in something.

drawer [drɔːr] n. 서랍
A drawer is part of a desk, chest, or other piece of furniture that is shaped like a box and is designed for putting things in.

chemical [kémikəl] n. 화학 물질; a. 화학의; 화학적인
Chemicals are substances that are used in a chemical process or made by a chemical process.

bend [bend] v. (bent-bent) (몸·머리를) 굽히다, 숙이다; 구부리다; n. (도로·강의) 굽이, 굽은 곳
When you bend, you move the top part of your body downward and forward.

wooden [wudn] a. 나무로 된, 목재의; 경직된
Wooden objects are made of wood.

container [kəntéinər] n. (화물 수송용) 컨테이너; 용기, 그릇
A container is a very large metal or wooden box used for transporting goods so that they can be loaded easily onto ships and lorries.

reveal [rivíːl] v. (보이지 않던 것을) 드러내 보이다; (비밀 등을) 밝히다
If you reveal something that has been out of sight, you uncover it so that people can see it.

terrify [térəfài] v. (몹시) 무섭게 하다 (terrifying a. 무서운; 겁나게 하는)
If something is terrifying, it makes you very frightened.

shriek [ʃriːk] v. (날카롭게) 비명을 지르다; 악을 쓰며 말하다; n. (날카로운) 비명
When someone shrieks, they make a short, very loud cry, for example because they are suddenly surprised, are in pain, or are laughing.

insecure [insikjúər] a. 불안정한, 안전하지 못한; 자신이 없는 (insecurity n. 불안정, 위험)
Something that is insecure is not safe or protected.

flaw [flɔ:] n. 결함; 흠; 결점
A flaw in something such as a pattern or material is a fault in it that should not be there.

glitch [glitʃ] n. 작은 문제, 결함; v. 갑자기 고장 나다
A glitch is a problem which stops something from working properly or being successful.

release [rilíːs] v. 놓아주다; 풀어 주다; (감정을) 발산하다; n. 풀어 줌; 발표, 공개
If you release someone or something, you stop holding them.

defect [díːfekt] n. 결점, 결함
A defect is a fault or imperfection in a person or thing.

code [koud] n. (컴퓨터) 코드; 암호, 부호; v. 암호로 쓰다
Computer code is a system or language for expressing information and instructions in a form which can be understood by a computer.

distribute [distríbjuːt] v. 분포시키다; 나누어 주다, 분배하다
To distribute a substance over something means to scatter it over it.

guarantee [gærəntíː] v. 보장하다; 품질 보증을 하다; 확신하다; n. 굳은 약속, 확약; 보장
If you guarantee something, you promise that it will definitely happen, or that you will do or provide it for someone.

quote [kwout] v. 인용하다; (예를) 들다; n. 인용문 (unquote v. 인용(문)을 끝맺다)
You can say quote before and unquote after a word or phrase, or quote, unquote before or after it, to show that you are quoting someone or that you do not believe that a word or phrase used by others is accurate.

stutter [stʌtər] v. 말을 더듬다, 더듬거리다; n. 말을 더듬기
If someone stutters, they have difficulty speaking because they find it hard to say the first sound of a word.

cyst [sist] n. 낭포, 낭종
A cyst is a growth containing liquid that appears inside your body or under your skin.

inch [intʃ] v. 조금씩 움직이다; n. 조금, 약간
To inch somewhere or to inch something somewhere means to move there very slowly and carefully, or to make something do this.

assistance [əsístəns] n. 도움, 원조, 지원
If you give someone assistance, you help them do a job or task by doing part of the work for them.

^{복습} **clutch** [klʌʧ] v. (꽉) 움켜잡다; n. 움켜쥠

If you clutch at something or clutch something, you hold it tightly, usually because you are afraid or anxious.

1. **What did the virus do inside *Slaughter Race?***
   A. It replaced the glitch in Vanellope with an insecurity.
   B. It took the glitch out of Vanellope and moved it to the game.
   C. It made Vanellope's glitch stronger and more dangerous.
   D. It copied Vanellope's glitch and made the game unstable.

2. **Why was Vanellope suspicious of Ralph after they got out of the game?**
   A. She thought maybe he wanted to hurt Shank and her crew.
   B. She thought it was strange that he knew to save her.
   C. She thought he was acting more emotional than usual.
   D. She thought maybe he didn't want to be friends with her anymore.

3. What happened when the virus exited _Slaughter Race?_

   A. It detected Ralph's insecurity.

   B. It explored the Older Net.

   C. Ralph saw it leave and ran after it.

   D. Ralph screamed and threw a firewall at it.

4. What was the Ralph clones' goal?

   A. To be free

   B. To destroy the real Ralph

   C. To get Vanellope

   D. To reboot the Internet

5. How could the clones be removed from the Internet?

   A. They could be pushed off a bridge.

   B. They could be deleted by an arch.

   C. They could be led through an exit door.

   D. They could be captured by a security team.

Check Your Reading Speed

1분에 몇 단어를 읽는지 리딩 속도를 측정해보세요.

$$\frac{1,459 \text{ words}}{\text{reading time (\quad) sec}} \times 60 = (\quad) \text{ WPM}$$

Build Your Vocabulary

crew [kruː] n. (함께 일을 하는) 팀, 조; 승무원; v. (배의) 승무원을 하다
A crew is a group of people with special technical skills who work together on a task or project.

impress [imprés] v. 깊은 인상을 주다, 감동을 주다
If something impresses you, you feel great admiration for it.

sink [siŋk] v. 구멍에 넣다; 가라앉다; 주저앉다; n. 개수대
If you sink a ball in games such as golf or pool, you put the ball into a hole.

groan [groun] v. (고통·짜증으로) 신음 소리를 내다; 끙끙거리다; n. 신음, 끙 하는 소리
If you groan, you make a long, low sound because you are in pain, or because you are upset or unhappy about something.

shrug [ʃrʌg] n. 어깨를 으쓱하기; v. (어깨를) 으쓱하다
A shrug is the action of raising and lowering your shoulders to express something.

hustle [hʌsl] n. 사기; 법석, 혼잡; v. 서둘러 가다; (거칠게) 떠밀다
A hustle can refer to a dishonest way of making money.

courier [kɔ́ːriər] n. 운반원; 택배 회사
A courier is a person who is paid to take letters and parcels direct from one place to another.

zip [zip] v. (어떤 방향으로) 쌩 하고 가다; 지퍼를 잠그다; n. 지퍼
If you say that something or someone zip somewhere, you mean that they move very fast.

announce [ənáuns] v. 발표하다, 알리다; 선언하다
If you announce something, you tell people about it publicly or officially.

gear up idiom 준비를 갖추다, ~에게 준비를 갖추게 하다
If you are gearing up, you are ready and able to do something or become or make yourself ready.

showtime [ʃóutaim] n. (공연) 시작 시간
Showtime is used to signal the beginning of an event or process that is expected to be dramatic, decisive, or otherwise significant.

. **alongside** [əlɔ́ːŋsáid] prep. ~ 옆에, 나란히; ~와 함께; ~와 동시에
If one thing is alongside another thing, the first thing is next to the second.

복습 **glitch** [glitʃ] v. 갑자기 고장 나다; n. 작은 문제, 결함
To glitch means to suffer a sudden malfunction or fault.

ː **encourage** [inkə́ːridʒ] v. 격려하다, 용기를 북돋우다; 부추기다
If you encourage someone, you give them confidence, for example by letting them know that what they are doing is good and telling them that they should continue to do it.

복습 **upset** [ʌpsét] a. 속상한, 마음이 상한; v. 속상하게 하다; (계획·상황 등이) 잘못되게 하다
If you are upset, you are unhappy or disappointed because something unpleasant has happened to you.

work out idiom 해결하다; ~을 계획해 내다; (일이) 잘 풀리다
If you work something out, you deal with a problem in a satisfactory way.

복습 **friendship** [fréndʃip] n. 우정; 친선; 교우 관계
You use friendship to refer in a general way to the state of being friends, or the feelings that friends have for each other.

복습 **horn** [hɔːrn] n. (차량의) 경적; (양·소 등의) 뿔; 나팔
On a vehicle such as a car, the horn is the device that makes a loud noise as a signal or warning.

honk [haŋk] v. (자동차 경적을) 울리다; (기러기가) 울다; n. 빵빵 (자동차 경적 소리)
If you honk the horn of a vehicle or if the horn honks, you make the horn produce a short loud sound.

복습 **yell** [jel] v. 고함치다, 소리 지르다; n. 고함, 외침
If you yell, you shout loudly, usually because you are excited, angry, or in pain.

. **bother** [báðər] v. 신경 쓰이게 하다, 괴롭히다; 신경 쓰다; n. 성가심
If someone bothers you, they talk to you when you want to be left alone or interrupt you when you are busy.

be about to idiom 막 ~하려는 참이다
If you are about to do something, you are going to do it immediately.

peel out idiom 쌩 하고 떠나다
If you peel out, you suddenly make a car start moving very quickly so that it makes a lot of noise.

release [rilíːs] v. 놓아주다; 풀어 주다; (감정을) 발산하다; n. 풀어 줌; 발표, 공개
If you release someone or something, you stop holding them.

virus [váiərəs] n. (컴퓨터) 바이러스; 바이러스
In computer technology, a virus is a program that introduces itself into a system, altering or destroying the information stored in the system.

immediate [imíːdiət] a. 즉각적인; 당면한; 아주 가까이에 있는 (immediately ad. 즉시, 즉각)
If something happens immediately, it happens without any delay.

scan [skæn] v. (유심히) 살피다; 훑어보다; 정밀 촬영하다; n. 정밀 검사
When you scan a place or group of people, you look at it carefully, usually because you are looking for something or someone.

catch up idiom 따라잡다, 따라가다; (소식 등을) 듣다
If you catch someone or something up, you go faster so that you reach them in front of you.

force [fɔːrs] v. 억지로 ~하다; ~를 강요하다; n. 작용력; 힘; 영향력
If someone forces you to do something, they make you do it even though you do not want to, for example by threatening you.

struggle [strʌgl] v. 애쓰다; 몸부림치다, 허우적거리다; 힘겹게 나아가다; n. 투쟁, 분투; 몸부림
If you struggle to do something, you try hard to do it, even though other people or things may be making it difficult for you to succeed.

break free idiom 떨쳐 풀다; 도망치다
If you break free from someone or something, you escape from someone or something that is trying to hold you.

spin [spin] v. (빙빙) 돌다; 돌아서다; n. 회전
If something spins or if you spin it, it turns quickly around a central point.

mimic [mímik] v. (mimicked-mimicked) ~을 모방하다; ~처럼 보이다; (남의) 흉내를 내다
If someone or something mimics another person or thing, they try to be like them.

복습 **speed** [spi:d] v. (sped-sped) 빨리 가다; 더 빠르게 하다; n. 속도
If you speed somewhere, you move or travel there quickly, usually in a vehicle.

복습 **ramp** [ræmp] n. (화물 적재·도로 연결 등을 위한) 램프, 경사로
A ramp is a sloping surface between two places that are at different levels.

복습 **launch** [lɔ:nʧ] v. 맹렬히 덤비다; 발사하다; n. 발사; 시작; 개시
If you launch yourself in a specific direction, you make a sudden energetic
movement in that direction.

복습 **land** [lænd] v. (땅·표면에) 내려앉다; 떨어지다; 놓다, 두다; n. 육지, 땅; 지역
When someone or something lands, they come down to the ground after moving
through the air or falling.

복습 **startle** [sta:rtl] v. 깜짝 놀라게 하다; 움찔하다; n. 깜짝 놀람
If something sudden and unexpected startles you, it surprises and frightens you
slightly.

복습 **cheer** [ʧiər] v. 환호성을 지르다, 환호하다; n. 환호(성), 응원
When people cheer, they shout loudly to show their approval or to encourage
someone who is doing something such as taking part in a game.

복습 **amaze** [əméiz] v. (대단히) 놀라게 하다; 경악하게 하다 (amazing a. 놀라운)
You say that something is amazing when it is very surprising and makes you feel
pleasure, approval, or wonder.

복습 **giggle** [gigl] v. 피식 웃다, 킥킥거리다; n. 피식 웃음, 킥킥거림
If someone giggles, they laugh in a childlike way, because they are amused,
nervous, or embarrassed.

복습 **meanwhile** [mí:nwàil] ad. (다른 일이 일어나고 있는) 그동안에
Meanwhile means while a particular thing is happening.

복습 **worm** [wɔ:rm] n. 컴퓨터 파괴 프로그램; 벌레; v. 꿈틀거리며 나아가다
A worm is a computer program that contains a virus which duplicates itself many
times in a network.

every inch idiom 전부 다; 완전히
Every inch of something is the whole of an area or place.

regenerate [ridʒénərèit] v. 재생시키다; (지역·시설 등을) 재건하다
If organs or tissues regenerate or if something regenerates them, they heal and
grow again after they have been damaged.

distance [dístəns] n. 거리; 먼 곳; v. (~에) 관여하지 않다
The distance between two points or places is the amount of space between them.

distract [distrǽkt] v. (주의를) 딴 데로 돌리다, 집중이 안 되게 하다
If something distracts you or your attention from something, it takes your attention away from it.

catch one's eye idiom 눈에 띄다; 눈길을 끌다
If something catches your eye, you suddenly notice it.

resemble [rizémbl] v. 닮다, 비슷하다
If one thing or person resembles another, they are similar to each other.

realize [ríːəlàiz] v. 깨닫다, 알아차리다; 실현하다, 달성하다
If you realize that something is true, you become aware of that fact or understand it.

inflatable [infléitəbl] a. (공기 등으로) 부풀게 할 수 있는
An inflatable object is one that you fill with air when you want to use it.

gorilla [gərílə] n. [동물] 고릴라
A gorilla is a very large ape. It has long arms, black fur, and a black face.

panic [pǽnik] v. 어쩔 줄 모르다, 공황 상태에 빠지다; n. 극심한 공포, 공황; 허둥지둥함
If you panic or if someone panics you, you suddenly feel anxious or afraid, and act quickly and without thinking carefully.

squirm [skwɔːrm] v. (몸을) 꼼지락대다; 몹시 당혹해 하다
If you squirm, you move your body from side to side, usually because you are nervous or uncomfortable.

detect [ditékt] v. 발견하다, 알아내다, 감지하다
To detect something means to find it or discover that it is present somewhere by using equipment or making an investigation.

recognize [rékəgnàiz] v. 알아보다; 인식하다; 공인하다
If you recognize someone or something, you know who that person is or what that thing is.

distribute [distríbjuːt] v. 분포시키다; 나누어 주다
To distribute a substance over something means to scatter it over it.

flash [flæʃ] v. (잠깐) 번쩍이다; 휙 나타나다; n. 순간; (잠깐) 반짝임
If a light flashes or if you flash a light, it shines with a sudden bright light, especially as quick, regular flashes of light.

break down idiom 고장 나다; 실패하다; 나누어지다
If something like a vehicle breaks down, it stops working because of a fault.

sputter [spʌ́tər] v. (분노·충격으로) 식식거리며 말하다; 털털거리는 소리를 내다
If you sputter, you speak or say something in a confused way, often while taking short quick breaths, for example because you are shocked or angry.

* **stable** [steibl] a. 안정된, 안정적인; 차분한; n. 마구간 (unstable a. 불안정한)
You can describe something as unstable if it is likely to change suddenly, especially if this creates difficulty or danger.

복습 **bolt** [boult] v. 달아나다; 빗장을 지르다; n. 번쩍하는 번개; 볼트
If a person or animal bolts, they suddenly start to run very fast, often because something has frightened them.

복습 **entrance** [éntrəns] ① n. 입구, 문; 입장, 등장 ② v. 도취시키다, 황홀하게 하다
The entrance to a place is the way into it, for example a door or gate.

복습 **boot** [bu:t] v. (컴퓨터를) 부팅하다; 세게 차다; n. 목이 긴 신발, 부츠
(reboot v. (컴퓨터를) 재시동하다)
If a computer or system reboots, or if someone reboots it, it starts again after it has been turned off.

복습 **exit** [égzit] n. (공공건물의) 출구; (고속도로의) 출구; 퇴장; v. 나가다, 떠나다; 퇴장하다
The exit is the door through which you can leave a public building.

복습 **urge** [ə:rdʒ] v. 재촉하다; 충고하다, 설득하려 하다; n. (강한) 욕구, 충동
If you urge someone somewhere, you make them go there by touching them or talking to them.

복습 **dust** [dʌst] n. 먼지, 티끌; v. 먼지를 털다; (고운 가루를) 뿌리다
Dust is very small dry particles of earth or sand.

crumble [krʌ́mbl] v. (건물이나 땅이) 허물어지다; 바스러지다; (힘·조직 등이) 흔들리다
If an old building or piece of land is crumbling, parts of it keep breaking off.

복습 **smash** [smæʃ] v. 박살내다; (세게) 부딪치다; 부서지다; n. 박살내기; 요란한 소리
If you smash something or if it smashes, it breaks into many pieces, for example when it is hit or dropped.

* **tower** [táuər] v. (~보다) 매우 높다; 솟다; n. 탑 (towering a. 우뚝 솟은, 높이 치솟은)
If you describe something such as a mountain or cliff as towering, you mean that it is very tall and therefore impressive.

skyscraper [skáiskrèipər] n. 고층 건물
A skyscraper is a very tall building in a city.

separate [sépərèit] v. 분리하다, 나누다; 갈라지다; a. 별개의; 분리된
If you separate people or things that are together, or if they separate, they move apart.

swerve [swəːrv] v. (갑자기) 방향을 바꾸다
If a vehicle or other moving thing swerves or if you swerve it, it suddenly changes direction, often in order to avoid hitting something.

beam [biːm] n. 기둥; 빛줄기; v. 활짝 웃다; 비추다
A beam is a long thick bar of wood, metal, or concrete, especially one used to support the roof of a building.

trap [træp] v. (위험한 장소에) 가두다; (함정으로) 몰아넣다; n. 함정; 덫
If you are trapped somewhere, something falls onto you or blocks your way and prevents you from moving or escaping.

rubble [rʌbl] n. (허물어진 건물의) 돌무더기, 잔해
When a building is destroyed, the pieces of brick, stone, or other materials that remain are referred to as rubble.

server [səːrvər] n. (컴퓨터의) 서버
In computing, a server is part of a computer network which does a particular task, for example storing or processing information, for all or part of the network.

spot [spat] v. 발견하다, 찾다, 알아채다; n. (특정한) 곳; (작은) 점
If you spot something or someone, you notice them.

wreckage [rékidʒ] n. 잔해
When something such as a plane, car, or building has been destroyed, you can refer to what remains as wreckage or the wreckage.

dodge [dadʒ] v. (몸을) 재빨리 움직이다; 기피하다; n. 몸을 홱 피함
If you dodge, you move suddenly, often to avoid being hit, caught, or seen.

debris [dəbríː] n. 파편, 잔해; 쓰레기
Debris is pieces from something that has been destroyed or pieces of rubbish or unwanted material that are spread around.

punch [pʌntʃ] v. 주먹으로 치다; (자판·번호판 등을) 치다; n. 주먹으로 한 대 침
If you punch someone or something, you hit them hard with your fist.

dive [daiv] v. (dove-dived) 급히 움직이다; 급강하하다; (물속으로) 뛰어들다;
n. 급강하; (물속으로) 뛰어들기
If you dive in a particular direction or into a particular place, you jump or move there quickly.

spill [spil] v. 쏟아져 나오다; (액체를) 흘리다, 쏟다; n. 흘린 액체, 유출물
If people or things spill out of a place, they come out of it in large numbers.

beg [beg] v. 간청하다, 애원하다; 구걸하다
If you beg someone to do something, you ask them very anxiously or eagerly to do it.

desperate [déspərət] a. 간절히 원하는; 필사적인, 극단적인 (desperately ad. 간절히)
If you are desperate for something or desperate to do something, you want or need it very much indeed.

flutter [flʌ́tər] v. (가볍게) 흔들다; 훨훨 날아가다; n. 흔들림; 소동, 혼란
If something thin or light flutters, or if you flutter it, it moves up and down or from side to side with a lot of quick, light movements.

thank goodness idiom 정말 다행이다!
You say 'Thank God,' 'Thank Goodness,' or 'Thank heavens' when you are very relieved about something.

relieve [rilíːv] v. 안도하다; (불쾌감·고통 등을) 없애 주다; 완화하다 (relieved a. 안도하는)
If you are relieved, you feel happy because something unpleasant has not happened or is no longer happening.

mess [mes] v. 엉망으로 만들다; n. (지저분하고) 엉망인 상태; (많은 문제로) 엉망인 상황
(mess up idiom 엉망으로 만들다)
To mess something up means to spoil it or do it badly.

dumb [dʌm] a. 멍청한, 바보 같은; 말을 못 하는
If you say that something is dumb, you think that it is silly and annoying.

sob [sab] v. (흑흑) 흐느끼다, 흐느껴 울다; n. 흐느껴 울기, 흐느낌
When someone sobs, they cry in a noisy way, breathing in short breaths.

sniffle [snifl] v. (계속) 훌쩍거리다; n. 훌쩍거림; 훌쩍거리는 소리
If you sniffle, you keep sniffing, usually because you are crying or have a cold.

fumble [fʌmbl] v. (말을) 더듬거리다; (손으로) 더듬거리다; n. (손으로) 더듬거리기
When you are trying to say something, if you fumble for the right words, you speak in a clumsy and unclear way.

★ **rescue** [réskju:] v. 구하다, 구출하다; n. 구출, 구조, 구제
If you rescue someone, you get them out of a dangerous or unpleasant situation.

★ **suspicious** [səspíʃəs] a. 의심스러워하는; 의심스러운; 의혹을 갖는
If you are suspicious of someone or something, you do not trust them, and are careful when dealing with them.

복습 **sigh** [sai] v. 한숨을 쉬다, 한숨짓다; 탄식하듯 말하다; n. 한숨
When you sigh, you let out a deep breath, as a way of expressing feelings such as disappointment, tiredness, or pleasure.

busted [bʌ́stid] a. (못된 짓을 하다가) 걸린
If someone is busted, they are discovered doing something that they should not be doing or saying something that is not true.

★ **attach** [ətǽʧ] v. 붙이다, 첨부하다; 연관되다 (attachment n. 부가 장치)
An attachment is a device that can be fixed onto a machine in order to enable it to do different jobs.

★★ **loose** [lu:s] a. 마음대로 돌아다니는; 흩어진; 꽉 죄지 않는
If people or animals break loose or are set loose, they are no longer held, tied, or kept somewhere and can move around freely.

복습 **harmless** [há:rmlis] a. 해롭지 않은, 무해한
Something that is harmless does not have any bad effects, especially on people's health.

복습 **defensive** [difénsiv] a. 방어적인; 방어의 (defensively ad. 방어적으로)
Someone who is defensive is behaving in a way that shows they feel unsure or threatened.

복습 **spy** [spai] v. 염탐하다; (갑자기) 보다, 알아채다; n. 스파이, 정보원
If you spy on someone, you watch them secretly.

★ **innocent** [ínəsənt] a. 무죄인, 결백한; 순진한; 무고한; 악의 없는
If someone is innocent, they did not commit a crime which they have been accused of.

복습 **ditch** [diʧ] v. 버리다; n. (들판·도로가의) 배수로
If someone ditches someone, they end a relationship with that person.

복습 **abandon** [əbǽndən] v. 버리다; 버리고 떠나다; 그만두다
If you abandon a place, thing, or person, you leave the place, thing, or person permanently or for a long time, especially when you should not do so.

fume [fjuːm] v. (화가 나서) 씩씩대다; 연기를 내뿜다; n. 연기; 화, 흥분
If you fume over something, you express annoyance and anger about it.

gasp [gæsp] v. 헉 하고 숨을 쉬다; 숨을 제대로 못 쉬다; n. 헉 하는 소리를 냄
When you gasp, you take a short quick breath through your mouth, especially
when you are surprised, shocked, or in pain.

pick up on idiom ~을 이해하다, 알아차리다
If you pick up on something, you react to something that has happened or that
you have noticed.

notice [nóutis] v. 알아채다, 인지하다; 주의하다; n. 신경 씀, 알아챔; 통지, 예고
If you notice something or someone, you become aware of them.

make one's way idiom 나아가다, 가다
When you make your way somewhere, you walk or travel there.

expire [ikspáiər] v. (기한이) 만료되다, 만기가 되다
When something such as a contract, deadline, or visa expires, it comes to an end
or is no longer valid.

discard [diskáːrd] v. (불필요한 것을) 버리다, 폐기하다
If you discard something, you get rid of it because you no longer want it or need it.

retrieve [ritríːv] v. 되찾아오다, 회수하다; 수습하다
If you retrieve something, you get it back from the place where you left it.

split [split] v. (split-split) 찢어지다, 쪼개지다; 분열되다; n. (길게 찢어진) 틈; 분열
If something such as wood or a piece of clothing splits or is split, a long crack or
tear appears in it.

mound [maund] n. 더미, 무더기; 언덕
A mound of something is a large rounded pile of it.

garbage [gáːrbidʒ] n. 쓰레기
Garbage is rubbish, especially waste from a kitchen.

idiot [ídiət] n. 바보, 멍청이
If you call someone an idiot, you are showing that you think they are very stupid
or have done something very stupid.

awful [ɔ́ːfəl] a. (정도가) 대단한, 아주 심한; 끔찍한, 지독한
You can use awful with noun groups that refer to an amount in order to emphasize
how large that amount is.

Check Your Reading Speed

1분에 몇 단어를 읽는지 리딩 속도를 측정해보세요.

$$\frac{938 \text{ words}}{\text{reading time (} \quad \text{) sec}} \times 60 = (\qquad) \text{ WPM}$$

Build Your Vocabulary

hub [hʌb] n. 중심지, 중추; (바퀴의) 중심
You can describe a place as a hub of an activity when it is a very important center for that activity.

mission [míʃən] n. 임무; 사명; v. 길고 험난한 여정에 나서다
A mission is an important task that people are given to do, especially one that involves traveling to another country.

chase [ʧeis] v. 뒤쫓다, 추적하다; 추구하다; n. 추적, 추격; 추구함
If you chase someone, or chase after them, you run after them or follow them quickly in order to catch or reach them.

clone [kloun] n. 복제품; 클론, 복제 (생물); v. 복제하다
If someone or something is a clone of another person or thing, they are so similar to this person or thing that they seem to be exactly the same as them.

horde [hɔːrd] n. 큰 떼거리; 무리
If you describe a crowd of people as a horde, you mean that the crowd is very large and excited and, often, rather frightening or unpleasant.

astonish [əstániʃ] v. 깜짝 놀라게 하다 (astonishing a. 정말 놀라운, 믿기 힘든)
Something that is astonishing is very surprising.

sight [sait] n. 광경, 모습; 보기; 시력; v. 갑자기 보다
A sight is something that you see.

army [áːrmi] n. 부대, 집단; 군대
An army of people, animals, or things is a large number of them, especially when they are regarded as a force of some kind.

take over idiom 장악하다, 탈취하다; (~을) 인계받다
If you take over a place, you fill it or use the whole of it so that other people cannot use it.

wreak [riːk] v. (큰 피해 등을) 입히다
Something or someone that wreaks havoc or destruction causes a great amount of disorder or damage.

havoc [hǽvək] n. 대파괴, 큰 혼란
Havoc is great disorder, and confusion.

^복_습 **announce** [ənáuns] v. 발표하다, 알리다; 선언하다 (announcement n. 발표)
An announcement is a statement made to the public or to the media which gives information about something that has happened or that will happen.

* **anchor** [ǽŋkər] n. 앵커; 닻; v. 닻을 내리다, 정박하다; 고정시키다
The anchor on a television or radio program, especially a news program, is the person who presents it.

^복_습 **assault** [əsɔ́ːlt] n. 공격; 도전; 폭행(죄); v. 폭행하다; (청각·후각 등을) 괴롭히다
An assault by an army is a strong attack made on an area held by the enemy.

* **massive** [mǽsiv] a. 엄청나게 심각한; (육중하면서) 거대한
Something that is massive is very large in size, quantity, or extent.

clog [klag] v. 막다
When something clogs a hole or place, it blocks it so that nothing can pass through.

^복_습 **server** [sɔ́ːrvər] n. (컴퓨터의) 서버
In computing, a server is part of a computer network which does a particular task, for example storing or processing information, for all or part of the network.

* **so-called** [souːkɔ́ːld] a. 소위, 이른바; 흔히 ~라고 일컬어지는
You use so-called to indicate that you think a word or expression used to describe someone or something is in fact wrong.

^복_습 **wreck** [rek] v. 파괴하다; 엉망으로 만들다; n. 충돌; 사고 잔해
To wreck something means to completely destroy or ruin it.

* **destructive** [distrʌ́ktiv] a. 파괴적인; 해로운
Something that is destructive causes or is capable of causing great damage, harm, or injury.

^복_습 **expert** [ékspəːrt] n. 전문가; a. 숙련된; 전문가의, 전문적인
An expert is a person who is very skilled at doing something or who knows a lot about a particular subject.

* **target** [tá:rgit] n. (공격의) 표적; 목표; v. (공격·비판의) 목표로 삼다
A target is something at which someone is aiming a weapon or other object.

spot [spat] v. 발견하다, 찾다, 알아채다; n. (특정한) 곳; (작은) 점
If you spot something or someone, you notice them.

thrill [θril] v. 열광시키다, 정말 신나게 하다; n. 흥분, 설렘; 전율
(thrilled a. 황홀해하는, 아주 흥분한)
If someone is thrilled, they are extremely pleased about something.

* **clue** [klu:] n. 실마리; (범행의) 단서 (have no clue idiom 전혀 모르다)
If you have no clue about something, you do not know anything about it or you
have no idea what to do about it.

delightful [diláitfəl] a. 정말 기분 좋은, 마음에 드는
If you describe something or someone as delightful, you mean they are very
pleasant.

* **courteous** [kə́:rtiəs] a. 공손한, 정중한
Someone who is courteous is polite and respectful to other people.

cherub [ʧérəb] n. 천사 같은 아이; (미술에서) 천사
A cherub is an attractive child, or one who behaves very well.

out of breath idiom 숨을 헐떡이며, 숨이 차서
If you are out of breath, you are breathing very quickly and with difficulty
because you have been doing something energetic.

autofill [ɔ́:toufil] n. 자동 완성
Autofill is a feature on a computer that adds information to forms automatically.

rapid [ræpid] a. (속도가) 빠른; (행동이) 민첩한 (rapidly ad. 빠르게, 신속히)
A rapid movement is one that is very fast.

bunch [bʌnʧ] n. (양·수가) 많음; 다발, 묶음
A bunch of things is a number of things, especially a large number.

blurt [blə:rt] v. 불쑥 내뱉다, 말하다
If someone blurts something, they say it suddenly, after trying hard to keep quiet
or to keep it secret.

* **appropriate** [əpróupriət] a. 적절한; v. (불법적으로나 무단으로) 도용하다
Something that is appropriate is suitable or acceptable for a particular situation.

* **shutter** [ʃʌtər] v. 폐쇄하다; 덧문을 닫다; n. 덧문; (카메라의) 셔터
To shutter means to close down a business or activity.

복습 **last** [læst] v. 오래가다; (특정한 시간 동안) 계속되다; 견디다; ad. 맨 끝에, 마지막에
If an event, situation, or problem lasts for a particular length of time, it continues
to exist or happen for that length of time.

복습 **bang** [bæŋ] v. 쾅 하고 치다; 쾅 하고 닫다; 쿵 하고 찧다; n. 쾅 (하는 소리)
If you bang on something or if you bang it, you hit it hard, making a loud noise.

복습 **stack** [stæk] v. (깔끔하게 정돈하여) 쌓다; n. 무더기, 더미
If you stack a number of things, you arrange them in neat piles.

복습 **pile** [pail] v. 쌓다; 집어넣다; 우르르 가다; n. 무더기; 쌓아 놓은 것, 더미
If you pile things somewhere, you put them there so that they form a pile.

* **barrier** [bǽriər] n. 장벽; 장애물; 한계
A barrier is something such as a fence or wall that is put in place to prevent
people from moving easily from one area to another.

hold back idiom ~을 저지하다; (진전·발전을) 저해하다
To hold someone or something back means to prevent them from moving forward
or from entering or leaving a place.

* **precise** [prisáis] a. 정확한, 정밀한; 엄밀한, 꼼꼼한 (precisely ad. 정확히)
Precisely means accurately and exactly.

복습 **blast** [blæst] v. 빠르게 가다; 쾅쾅 울리다; 폭발시키다; n. 폭발; (한 줄기의) 강한 바람
If you blast in a specified direction, you move very quickly and loudly in that
direction.

복습 **lunge** [lʌndʒ] v. 달려들다, 돌진하다; n. 돌진
If you lunge in a particular direction, you move in that direction suddenly and
clumsily.

* **furious** [fjúəriəs] a. 몹시 화가 난; 맹렬한
Someone who is furious is extremely angry.

erupt [irʌ́pt] v. 터뜨리다; 분출되다
If violence or fighting erupts, it suddenly begins or gets worse in an unexpected,
violent way.

break through idiom ~을 뚫고 나아가다, 돌파하다
If someone breaks through, they force their way through something that is
stopping them from moving forward.

barricade [bǽrəkèid] n. 바리케이드, 장애물; v. 방어벽을 치다
A barricade is a line of vehicles or other objects placed across a road or open space to stop people getting past, for example during street fighting or as a protest.

needy [níːdi] a. 자신감이 없는, 애정에 굶주린
If you describe someone as needy, they are needing emotional support or they are insecure.

clingy [klíŋi] a. 사람에게 매달리는
If you describe someone as clingy, you mean that they become very attached to people and depend on them too much.

unchecked [ʌntʃékt] a. 억제하지 않고 놔 둔
If something harmful or undesirable is left unchecked, no one controls it or prevents it from growing or developing.

slaughter [slɔ́ːtər] n. 대량 학살, 살육; 도살; v. (대량) 학살하다; 도축하다
Slaughter is the violent killing of a large number of people.

race [reis] n. 경주; 인종, 종족; v. 경주하다; 쏜살같이 가다; (머리·심장 등이) 바쁘게 돌아가다
A race is a competition to see who is the fastest, for example in running, swimming, or driving.

screw up idiom ~을 엉망으로 하다, 망치다
If you screw up, you make a serious mistake, or spoil something, especially a situation.

desperate [déspərət] a. 간절히 원하는; 필사적인, 극단적인
If you are desperate for something or desperate to do something, you want or need it very much indeed.

trigger [trígəːr] v. 작동시키다; 촉발시키다; n. (총의) 방아쇠
To trigger a bomb or system means to cause it to work.

immediate [imíːdiət] a. 즉각적인; 당면한; 아주 가까이에 있는 (immediately ad. 즉시, 즉각)
If something happens immediately, it happens without any delay.

query [kwíəri] n. 문의, 의문; v. 묻다, 질문하다; 의문을 제기하다
A query is a question, especially one that you ask an organization, publication, or expert.

therapy [θérəpi] n. 치료, 요법
Therapy is the treatment of someone with mental or physical illness without the use of drugs or operations.

alternative [ɔːltə́ːrnətiv] a. 대체 가능한, 대안이 되는; 대체의; n. 대안, 선택 가능한 것
(alternatively ad. 그렇지 않으면)
You use alternatively to introduce a suggestion or to mention something different
to what has just been stated.

archway [áːrʧwei] n. 아치 (지붕이 덮인) 길; 아치형 입구
An archway is a passage or entrance that has a curved roof.

district [dístrikt] n. 지구, 지역, 구역
A district is a particular area of a town or country.

security [sikjúərəti] n. 보안, 경비; 경비 담당 부서; 안도감, 안심
Security refers to all the measures that are taken to protect a place, or to ensure
that only people with permission enter it or leave it.

arch [aːrʧ] n. 아치형 구조물; 아치형; v. 아치 모양을 그리다; 동그랗게 구부리다
An arch is a structure that is curved at the top and is supported on either side by
a pillar, post, or wall.

at once idiom 동시에; 즉시
If a number of different things happen at once or all at once, they all happen at
the same time.

codependent [kòudipéndənt] a. (심리적으로) 종속적 관계가 되는
A codependent person is in an unsatisfactory relationship with someone who is
ill or an addict, but does not want the relationship to end.

exclaim [ikskléim] v. 소리치다, 외치다
If you exclaim, you cry out suddenly in surprise, strong emotion, or pain.

limo [límou] n. (= limousine) 리무진(대형 승용차)
A limo is the same as a limousine which is a large and very comfortable car.
Limousines are usually driven by a chauffeur and are used by very rich or
important people.

pull up idiom (차량·운전자가) 멈추다, 서다
If a vehicle or driver pulls up, they stop.

hop [hap] v. 급히 움직이다; 깡충깡충 뛰다; n. 깡충깡충 뛰기
If you hop somewhere, you move there quickly or suddenly.

damage [dǽmidʒ] v. 손상을 주다, 훼손하다; n. 손상, 피해; 훼손
To damage an object means to break it, spoil it physically, or stop it from working
properly.

gesture [dʒéstʃər] n. (감정·의도의) 표시; 몸짓; v. (손·머리 등으로) 가리키다; 몸짓을 하다
(empty gesture n. 무의미한 태도)
An empty gesture is a gesture that is not sincere, or has no effect.

willing [wíliŋ] a. 기꺼이 ~하는; 자발적인
If someone is willing to do something, they are fairly happy about doing it and
will do it if they are asked or required to do it.

demolish [dimáliʃ] v. 파괴하다; (건물을) 철거하다
To demolish something such as a building means to destroy it completely.

Chapters 19 & 20

1. What did Yesss say to Vanellope in the limo?

A. Ralph regretted all of his past decisions.

B. Ralph cared only about himself.

C. Ralph was going through a hard time.

D. Ralph became greedy because of his fame.

2. Why couldn't Yesss, Vanellope, and Ralph reach the Anti-Virus arch?

A. The Ralph clones crashed into the limo.

B. An ocean wave knocked the limo over.

C. The path to the arch was closed.

D. A building fell on top of the arch.

3. How did Ralph get Giant Ralph to put Vanellope down?

A. He scolded it for being a bully.

B. He talked to it in a sincere way.

C. He punched it repeatedly until it surrendered.

D. He begged it not to hurt his friend.

4. What did the Oh My Disney princesses do?

A. They invited Vanellope to join their group.

B. They congratulated Vanellope on discovering her dream.

C. They made Ralph land safely on the ground.

D. They rewarded Ralph with gifts for his bravery.

5. How were Ralph and Vanellope able to keep in touch?

A. They visited each other every weekend.

B. They left each other voice messages on their phones.

C. They sent each other long emails on their computers.

D. They called each other on their Buzzzy devices.

Check Your Reading Speed
1분에 몇 단어를 읽는지 리딩 속도를 측정해보세요.

$$\frac{1,945 \text{ words}}{\text{reading time } (\quad) \text{ sec}} \times 60 = (\quad) \text{ WPM}$$

Build Your Vocabulary

limo [límou] n. (= limousine) 리무진(대형 승용차)
A limo is the same as a limousine which is a large and very comfortable car. Limousines are usually driven by a chauffeur and are used by very rich or important people.

fume [fjuːm] v. (화가 나서) 씩씩대다; 연기를 내뿜다; n. 연기; 화, 흥분
If you fume over something, you express annoyance and anger about it.

extent [ikstént] n. 정도, 규모; 크기
If you are talking about how great, important, or serious a difficulty or situation is, you can refer to the extent of it.

I'm telling you idiom 정말로, 정말이야
You can say 'I'm telling you' to emphasize that what you are saying is true even though it may be difficult to believe.

comment [kάment] n. 논평, 언급; v. 논평하다, 견해를 밝히다
A comment is something that you say which expresses your opinion of something or which gives an explanation of it.

spew [spjuː] v. 뿜어져 나오다, 분출되다
When something spews out a substance or when a substance spews from something, the substance flows out quickly in large quantities.

horrible [hɔ́ːrəbl] a. 지긋지긋한, 끔찍한; 소름끼치는, 무시무시한
If you describe something or someone as horrible, you do not like them at all.

bunch [bʌntʃ] n. (양·수가) 많음; 다발, 묶음
A bunch of things is a number of things, especially a large number.

anonymous [ənάnəməs] a. 익명인; 익명으로 된
If you remain anonymous when you do something, you do not let people know that you were the person who did it.

* **bully** [búli] n. (약자를) 괴롭히는 사람; v. (약자를) 괴롭히다; 협박하다
A bully is someone who uses their strength or power to hurt or frighten other people.

복습 **fat** [fæt] a. 살찐, 비만인; n. 지방
If you say that a person or animal is fat, you mean that they have a lot of flesh on their body and that they weigh too much.

‡ **handle** [hændl] v. (사람·작업 등을) 처리하다; 들다, 옮기다; n. 손잡이
If you say that someone can handle a problem or situation, you mean that they have the ability to deal with it successfully.

복습 **hang one's head** idiom 낙담하다; 부끄러워 고개를 숙이다
If you hang your head, you are ashamed and discouraged.

‡ **ashamed** [əʃéimd] a. (~여서) 부끄러운, 창피한
If someone is ashamed, they feel embarrassed or guilty because of something they do or they have done, or because of their appearance.

복습 **treat** [tri:t] v. (특정한 태도로) 대하다; 여기다, 치부하다; n. 특별한 것, 대접, 한턱
If you treat someone or something in a particular way, you behave toward them or deal with them in that way.

* **conflict** [kənflíkt] v. 상충하다; n. 갈등, 충돌; 대립, 마찰
If ideas, beliefs, or accounts conflict, they are very different from each other and it seems impossible for them to exist together or to each be true.

복습 **dude** [dju:d] n. 놈, 녀석
A dude is a man.

복습 **obvious** [ábviəs] a. 분명한, 확실한; 명백한 (obviously ad. 분명히)
You use obviously to indicate that something is easily noticed, seen, or recognized.

복습 **pun** [pʌn] n. 말장난, 말재간
A pun is a clever and amusing use of a word or phrase with two meanings, or of words with the same sound but different meanings.

‡ **complicated** [kámpləkèitid] a. 복잡한, 이해하기 어려운
If you say that something is complicated, you mean it has so many parts or aspects that it is difficult to understand or deal with.

복습 **nod** [nad] v. (고개를) 끄덕이다, 까딱하다; n. (고개를) 끄덕임
If you nod, you move your head downward and upward to show that you are answering 'yes' to a question, or to show agreement, understanding, or approval.

clone [kloun] n. 복제품; 클론, 복제 (생물); v. 복제하다
If someone or something is a clone of another person or thing, they are so similar to this person or thing that they seem to be exactly the same as them.

instant [ínstənt] a. 즉각적인; n. 순간, 아주 짧은 동안 (instantly ad. 즉각, 즉시)
You use instant to describe something that happens immediately.

wreck [rek] v. 파괴하다; 엉망으로 만들다; n. 충돌; 사고 잔해
To wreck something means to completely destroy or ruin it.

chase [ʧeis] v. 뒤쫓다, 추적하다; 추구하다; n. 추적, 추격; 추구함
If you chase someone, or chase after them, you run after them or follow them quickly in order to catch or reach them.

needy [ní:di] a. 자신감이 없는, 애정에 굶주린
If you describe someone as needy, they are needing emotional support or they are insecure.

clingy [klíŋi] a. 사람에게 매달리는
If you describe someone as clingy, you mean that they become very attached to people and depend on them too much.

destructive [distrʌ́ktiv] a. 파괴적인; 해로운 (self-destructive a. 자멸적인, 자살적인)
Self-destructive behavior is harmful to the person who behaves in that way.

blame [bleim] v. ~을 탓하다, ~의 책임으로 보다; n. 책임; 탓
If you blame a person or thing for something bad, you believe or say that they are responsible for it or that they caused it.

break in idiom 끼어들다
To break in means to interrupt when someone is talking.

virus [váiərəs] n. (컴퓨터) 바이러스; 바이러스
In computer technology, a virus is a program that introduces itself into a system, altering or destroying the information stored in the system.

district [dístrikt] n. 지구, 지역, 구역
A district is a particular area of a town or country.

make it idiom 해내다; (힘든 경험 등을) 버텨 내다; 가다
If you make it, you are successful in achieving something difficult, or in surviving through a very difficult period.

make one's way idiom 나아가다, 가다
When you make your way somewhere, you walk or travel there.

^{복습} **arch** [aːrʧ] n. 아치형 구조물; 아치형; v. 아치 모양을 그리다; 동그랗게 구부리다
An arch is a structure that is curved at the top and is supported on either side by a pillar, post, or wall.

trail [treil] n. 자국, 흔적; 자취; v. 끌다; 뒤쫓다, 추적하다
(hot on one's trail idiom ~의 뒤를 바짝 뒤쫓아서)
If you are hot on the trail of a person or thing, you are trying hard to find them or find out about them.

^{복습} **cheer** [ʧiər] v. 환호성을 지르다, 환호하다; n. 환호(성), 응원
When people cheer, they shout loudly to show their approval or to encourage someone who is doing something such as taking part in a game.

^{복습} **celebrate** [séləbrèit] v. 기념하다, 축하하다
If you celebrate, you do something enjoyable because of a special occasion or to mark someone's success.

cluster [klʌ́stər] v. 무리를 이루다, (소규모로) 모이다; n. 무리, 집단
If people cluster together, they gather together in a small group.

ripple [ripl] v. 잔물결을 이루다; (감정 등이) 파문처럼 번지다; n. 잔물결, 파문 (모양의 것)
When the surface of an area of water ripples or when something ripples it, a number of little waves appear on it.

^{복습} **wave** [weiv] n. 물결; (손·팔을) 흔들기; v. (무엇을 손에 들고) 흔들다; (손·팔을) 흔들다
A wave is a raised mass of water on the surface of water, especially the sea, which is caused by the wind or by tides making the surface of the water rise and fall.

^{복습} **crash** [kræʃ] v. 부딪치다; 충돌하다; (컴퓨터를) 고장 내다; n. 요란한 소리; (자동차·항공기) 사고
If something crashes somewhere, it moves and hits something else violently, making a loud noise.

crawl [krɔːl] v. 기어가다; 우글거리다; n. 기어가기
When you crawl, you move forward on your hands and knees.

^{복습} **dust** [dʌst] v. 먼지를 털다; (고운 가루를) 뿌리다; n. 먼지, 티끌
When you dust something such as furniture, you remove dust from it, usually using a cloth.

curious [kjúəriəs] a. 궁금한, 호기심이 많은; 별난, 특이한 (curiously ad. 신기한 듯이)
If you are curious about something, you are interested in it and want to know more about it.

jaw [ʤɔː] n. 턱
Your jaw is the lower part of your face below your mouth.

gawk [gɔːk] v. 얼빠진 듯이 바라보다; n. 둔한 사람, 얼간이
To gawk at someone or something means to stare at them in a rude, stupid, or unthinking way.

gather [gǽðər] v. (사람들이) 모이다; (여기저기 있는 것을) 모으다
If people gather somewhere or if someone gathers people somewhere, they come together in a group.

enormous [inɔ́ːrməs] a. 막대한, 거대한
Something that is enormous is extremely large in size or amount.

terrify [térəfài] v. (몹시) 무섭게 하다 (terrifying a. 무서운; 겁나게 하는)
If something is terrifying, it makes you very frightened.

massive [mǽsiv] a. (육중하면서) 거대한; 엄청나게 심각한
Something that is massive is very large in size, quantity, or extent.

peer [piər] v. 유심히 보다, 눈여겨보다; n. 또래
If you peer at something, you look at it very hard, usually because it is difficult to see clearly.

rooftop [rúːftap] n. (건물의) 옥상
A rooftop is the outside part of the roof of a building.

unsettling [ʌ̀nsétliŋ] a. 동요하게 하는
If you describe something as unsettling, you mean that it makes you feel rather worried or uncertain.

insist [insíst] v. 고집하다, 주장하다, 우기다
If you insist that something should be done, you say so very firmly and refuse to give in about it.

grab [græb] v. (와락·단단히) 붙잡다; 급히 ~하다; n. 와락 잡아채려고 함
If you grab something, you take it or pick it up suddenly and roughly.

pushpin [púʃpìn] n. 제도용 압정
A pushpin is a pin with a small ball-shaped head, used to fasten papers to a bulletin board or to indicate positions on charts and maps.

beast [biːst] n. (덩치가 크고 위험한) 짐승, 야수; 짐승 같은 사람
You can refer to an animal as a beast, especially if it is a large, dangerous, or unusual one.

yell [jel] v. 고함치다, 소리 지르다; n. 고함, 외침
If you yell, you shout loudly, usually because you are excited, angry, or in pain.

wield [wi:ld] v. (무기·도구를) 휘두르다; (권력·권위 등을) 행사하다
If you wield a weapon, tool, or piece of equipment, you carry and use it.

club [klʌb] n. 곤봉; 클럽, 동호회; v. 때리다
A club is a thick heavy stick that can be used as a weapon.

swing [swiŋ] v. (swung-swung) (전후·좌우로) 흔들다; 휙 움직이다; 방향을 바꾸다;
n. 흔들기; 휘두르기
If something swings or if you swing it, it moves repeatedly backward and forward
or from side to side from a fixed point.

might [mait] n. (강력한) 힘; 권력; 세력 (with all one's might idiom 전력을 다하여, 힘껏)
If you do something with all your might, you do it using all your strength and
energy.

exit [égzit] n. (공공건물의) 출구; (고속도로의) 출구; 퇴장; v. 나가다, 떠나다; 퇴장하다
The exit is the door through which you can leave a public building.

pause [pɔːz] v. (말·일을 하다가) 잠시 멈추다; 정지시키다; n. (말·행동 등의) 멈춤
If you pause while you are doing something, you stop for a short period and then
continue.

force [fɔːrs] v. 억지로 ~하다; ~를 강요하다; n. 작용력; 힘; 영향력
If someone forces you to do something, they make you do it even though you do
not want to, for example by threatening you.

flick [flik] n. 재빨리 움직임; v. (버튼·스위치를) 탁 누르다; 튀기다; 털다
A flick is a sudden, quick movement.

colossal [kəlásəl] a. 엄청난, 어마어마한; 거대한
If you describe something as colossal, you are emphasizing that it is very large.

hurl [həːrl] v. (거칠게) 던지다; (욕·비난·모욕 등을) 퍼붓다
If you hurl something, you throw it violently and with a lot of force.

wince [wins] v. (통증·당혹감으로) 움찔하고 놀라다
If you wince, the muscles of your face tighten suddenly because you have felt a
pain or because you have just seen, heard, or remembered something unpleasant.

blaze [bleiz] v. (총을) 쏘아 대다; 눈부시게 빛나다; 활활 타다; n. 불길; 휘황찬란한 빛
If guns blaze, or blaze away, they fire continuously, making a lot of noise.

by a hair idiom 겨우, 아슬아슬하게
By a hair means just barely.

* **chuck** [tʃʌk] v. (아무렇게나) 던지다; ~을 그만두다
When you chuck something somewhere, you throw it there in a casual or careless way.

복습 **knock** [nak] v. 치다, 부딪치다; (문 등을) 두드리다; n. 문 두드리는 소리; 부딪침
To knock someone into a particular position or condition means to hit them very hard so that they fall over or become unconscious.

off-balance [ɔːf-bǽləns] a. 균형을 잃은; 허를 찔린
If you are off-balance, you are in an unsteady position and about to fall.

* **stagger** [stǽgər] v. 비틀거리다, 휘청거리다; 큰 충격을 주다
If you stagger, you walk very unsteadily, for example because you are ill or drunk.

* **sway** [swei] v. (전후·좌우로) 흔들리다; (마음을) 동요시키다; n. (전후·좌우로) 흔들림
When people or things sway, they lean or swing slowly from one side to the other.

복습 **site** [sait] n. (인터넷) 사이트; (사건 등의) 현장; 대지
A site is the same as a website which is a set of data and information about a particular subject which is available on the Internet.

* **cling** [kliŋ] v. (clung-clung) 꼭 붙잡다, 매달리다; 들러붙다; 애착을 갖다
If you cling to someone or something, you hold onto them tightly.

복습 **nearby** [niərbái] a. 인근의, 가까운 곳의; ad. 가까운 곳에
If something is nearby, it is only a short distance away.

복습 **grip** [grip] n. 꽉 붙잡음; 통제, 지배; v. 꽉 잡다, 움켜잡다; (마음·흥미·시선을) 끌다
A grip is a firm, strong hold on something.

dangle [dǽŋgl] v. 매달리다; (무엇을 들고) 달랑거리다
If something dangles from somewhere or if you dangle it somewhere, it hangs or swings loosely.

복습 **edge** [edʒ] n. 끝, 가장자리; 우위; v. 조금씩 움직이다; 테두리를 두르다
The edge of something is the place or line where it stops, or the part of it that is furthest from the middle.

hang on idiom 꽉 붙잡다; 잠깐 기다려, 멈춰 봐
If you hang on to something, you hold tightly to it.

* **tremble** [trembl] v. (가볍게) 흔들리다; (몸을) 떨다; n. 떨림, 전율
If something trembles, it shakes slightly.

clutch [klʌtʃ] n. 움켜쥠; v. (꽉) 움켜잡다
A clutch is a firm hold that you have on someone or something, usually because you are afraid or in pain, or do not want to lose them.

take off idiom (서둘러) 떠나다; 날아오르다
To take off means to leave a place suddenly.

dive [daiv] v. (dove-dived) 급히 움직이다; 급강하하다; (물속으로) 뛰어들다; n. 급강하; (물속으로) 뛰어들기
If you dive in a particular direction or into a particular place, you jump or move there quickly.

in time idiom 제때에, 시간 맞춰, 늦지 않게
If you are in time for a particular event, you are not too late for it.

crush [krʌʃ] v. 으스러뜨리다; 좌절시키다; 밀어 넣다; n. 홀딱 반함
To crush something means to press it very hard so that its shape is destroyed or so that it breaks into pieces.

helpless [hélplis] a. 무력한, 속수무책인 (helplessly ad. 어찌해 볼 수도 없이)
If you are helpless, you do not have the strength or power to do anything useful or to control or protect yourself.

scale [skeil] v. (아주 높고 가파른 곳을) 오르다; n. 비늘; 규모; 눈금
If you scale something such as a mountain or a wall, you climb up it or over it.

tower [táuər] v. (~보다) 매우 높다; 솟다; n. 탑 (towering a. 우뚝 솟은, 높이 치솟은)
If you describe something such as a mountain or cliff as towering, you mean that it is very tall and therefore impressive.

grunt [grʌnt] v. 끙 앓는 소리를 내다; (돼지가) 꿀꿀거리다; n. (사람이) 끙 하는 소리
If you grunt, you make a low sound, especially because you are annoyed or not interested in something.

meanwhile [míːnwàil] ad. (다른 일이 일어나고 있는) 그동안에
Meanwhile means while a particular thing is happening.

snag [snæg] v. 잡아채다, 낚아채다; (날카롭거나 튀어나온 것에) 걸리다; n. 문제; 날카로운 것
If you snag something, you get or catch it by acting quickly.

sensitive [sénsətiv] a. 민감한; 세심한; 감성 있는
If you are sensitive about something, you are easily worried and offended when people talk about it.

spy [spai] v. (갑자기) 보다, 알아채다; 염탐하다; n. 스파이, 정보원
If you spy someone or something, you notice them.

be about to idiom 막 ~하려는 참이다
If you are about to do something, you are going to do it immediately.

construct [kənstrʌ́kt] v. 건설하다; 구성하다; n. 건축물; 생각
(construction n. 건설, 공사; 건축물)
Construction is the building of things such as houses, factories, roads, and bridges.

block [blak] n. 사각형 덩어리; 구역, 블록; v. 막다, 차단하다; 방해하다
A block of a substance is a large rectangular piece of it.

catch up idiom 따라잡다, 따라가다; (소식 등을) 듣다
If you catch someone or something up, you go faster so that you reach them in front of you.

squeeze [skwi:z] v. (꼭) 쥐다; (좁은 곳에) 비집고 들어가다; n. (손으로 꼭) 쥐기
If you squeeze something, you press it firmly, usually with your hands.

squish [skwiʃ] v. 찌부러뜨리다, 으깨다
If something soft squishes or is squished, it is crushed out of shape when it is pressed.

plead [pli:d] v. 애원하다; 옹호하다, 주장하다
If you plead with someone to do something, you ask them in an intense, emotional way to do it.

that's it idiom 바로 그거야!; 그만해라
You use that's it to express agreement with or approval of what has just been said or done.

reassure [ri:əʃúər] v. 안심시키다 (reassuringly ad. 안심시키게)
If you find someone's words or actions reassuring, they make you feel less worried about something.

hold back idiom (진전·발전을) 저해하다; ~을 저지하다
If you hold someone or something back, you prevent the progress or development of them.

friendship [fréndʃip] n. 우정; 친선; 교우 관계
You use friendship to refer in a general way to the state of being friends, or the feelings that friends have for each other.

kid [kid] v. 놀리다, 장난치다; 속이다
You can say 'who is she kidding?' or 'who is he trying to kid?' if you think it is obvious that someone is not being sincere and does not mean what they say.

blink [bliŋk] v. 눈을 깜박이다; (불빛이) 깜박거리다; n. 눈을 깜박거림
When you blink or when you blink your eyes, you shut your eyes and very quickly open them again.

settle [setl] v. 결정하다; 자리를 잡다; 편하게 앉다
If something is settled, it has all been decided and arranged.

buddy [bʌ́di] n. 친구
A buddy is a close friend, usually a male friend of a man.

insecure [insikjúər] a. 불안정한, 안전하지 못한; 자신이 없는 (insecurity n. 불안정, 위험)
Something that is insecure is not safe or protected.

relieve [rilíːv] v. 안도하다; (불쾌감·고통 등을) 없애 주다; 완화하다 (relieved a. 안도하는)
If you are relieved, you feel happy because something unpleasant has not happened or is no longer happening.

swoop [swuːp] v. 급강하하다, 위에서 덮치다; 급습하다; n. 급강하; 급습
When a bird or airplane swoops, it suddenly moves downward through the air in a smooth curving movement.

rescue [réskjuː] v. 구하다, 구출하다; n. 구출, 구조, 구제
If you rescue someone, you get them out of a dangerous or unpleasant situation.

exclaim [ikskléim] v. 소리치다, 외치다
If you exclaim, you cry out suddenly in surprise, strong emotion, or pain.

spring [spriŋ] v. (sprang-sprung) 휙 움직이다; 튀다; n. 샘; 봄; 생기, 활기
If something springs in a particular direction, it moves suddenly and quickly.

freeze [friːz] v. (froze-frozen) 얼다; (두려움 등으로 몸이) 얼어붙다; n. 동결; 한파
If a liquid or a substance containing a liquid freezes, or if something freezes it, it becomes solid because of low temperatures.

slide [slaid] v. 미끄러지듯이 움직이다; 슬며시 넣다; n. 떨어짐; 미끄러짐
When something slides somewhere or when you slide it there, it moves there smoothly over or against something.

launch [lɔːnʧ] v. 맹렬히 덤비다; 발사하다; n. 발사; 시작; 개시
If you launch yourself in a specific direction, you make a sudden energetic movement in that direction.

include [inklúːd] v. 포함하다; ~을 (~에) 포함시키다
If one thing includes another thing, it has the other thing as one of its parts.

poison [pɔizn] n. 독, 독약; v. 독살하다; 나쁜 영향을 주다
Poison is a substance that harms or kills people or animals if they swallow it or absorb it.

chute [ʃuːt] n. (= parachute) 낙하산; 활송 장치
A chute is the same as a parachute which is a device which enables a person to jump from an aircraft and float safely to the ground.

mattress [mǽtris] n. (침대의) 매트리스
A mattress is the large, flat object which is put on a bed to make it comfortable to sleep on.

land [lænd] v. 떨어지다; (땅·표면에) 내려앉다; 놓다, 두다; n. 육지, 땅; 지역
When someone or something lands, they come down to the ground after moving through the air or falling.

plush [plʌʃ] a. 아주 안락한; 고급의; n. 플러시 천
If you describe something as plush, you mean that it is very smart, comfortable, or expensive.

comfy [kʌ́mfi] a. 편안한, 안락한
A comfy item of clothing, piece of furniture, room, or position is a comfortable one.

confuse [kənfjúːz] v. (사람을) 혼란시키다; 혼동하다 (confused a. 혼란스러워하는)
If you are confused, you do not know exactly what is happening or what to do.

journalist [dʒə́ːrnəlist] n. 기자
A journalist is a person whose job is to collect news and write about it for newspapers, magazines, television, or radio.

collective [kəléktiv] a. 공동의; 집단의, 단체의
Collective actions, situations, or feelings involve or are shared by every member of a group of people.

sigh [sai] n. 한숨; v. 한숨을 쉬다, 한숨짓다; 탄식하듯 말하다
A sigh is a slow breath out that makes a long soft sound, especially because you are disappointed, tired, annoyed, or relaxed.

mysterious [mistíəriəs] a. 기이한; 신비한; 비밀스러운 (mysteriously ad. 이상하게)
Someone or something that is mysterious is strange and is not known about or understood.

* **vanish** [vǽniʃ] v. 사라지다, 없어지다; 모습을 감추다
  If someone or something vanishes, they disappear suddenly or in a way that cannot be explained.

복습 **bench** [bentʃ] n. 벤치; 판사(석)
  A bench is a long seat of wood or metal that two or more people can sit on.

복습 **realize** [ríːəlàiz] v. 깨닫다, 알아차리다; 실현하다, 달성하다
  If you realize that something is true, you become aware of that fact or understand it.

astute [əstjúːt] a. 약삭빠른, 영악한
  If you describe someone as astute, you think they show an understanding of behavior and situations, and are skillful at using this knowledge to their own advantage.

* **observation** [àbzərvéiʃən] n. 관찰, 관측; 의견
  Observation is the action or process of carefully watching someone or something.

복습 **grin** [grin] n. 활짝 웃음; v. 활짝 웃다
  A grin is a broad smile.

복습 **giggle** [gigl] v. 피식 웃다, 킥킥거리다; n. 피식 웃음, 킥킥거림
  If someone giggles, they laugh in a childlike way, because they are amused, nervous, or embarrassed.

복습 **entrance** [éntrəns] ① n. 입구, 문; 입장, 등장 ② v. 도취시키다, 황홀하게 하다
  The entrance to a place is the way into it, for example a door or gate.

복습 **slaughter** [slɔ́ːtər] n. 대량 학살, 살육; 도살; v. (대량) 학살하다; 도축하다
  Slaughter is the violent killing of a large number of people.

복습 **joke** [dʒouk] n. 농담; 웃음거리; v. 농담하다; 농담 삼아 말하다
  A joke is something that is said or done to make you laugh, for example a funny story.

복습 **figure out** idiom ~을 이해하다, 알아내다; 계산하다, 산출하다
  If you figure out someone or something, you come to understand them by thinking carefully.

복습 **code** [koud] n. (컴퓨터) 코드; 암호, 부호; v. 암호로 쓰다
  Computer code is a system or language for expressing information and instructions in a form which can be understood by a computer.

^복_습 **regenerate** [ridʒénərèit] v. 재생시키다; (지역·시설 등을) 재건하다
If organs or tissues regenerate or if something regenerates them, they heal and grow again after they have been damaged.

^복_습 **speed** [spiːd] v. (sped-sped) 빨리 가다; 더 빠르게 하다; n. 속도
If you speed somewhere, you move or travel there quickly, usually in a vehicle.

Check Your Reading Speed
1분에 몇 단어를 읽는지 리딩 속도를 측정해보세요.

$$\frac{436 \text{ words}}{\text{reading time ( ) sec}} \times 60 = (\quad) \text{ WPM}$$

Build Your Vocabulary

station [stéiʃən] n. 역; 본부, 장소; 부서; 위치; v. 배치하다
A station is a building by a railway line where trains stop so that people can get on or off.

arcade [a:rkéid] n. 게임 센터, 오락실
An arcade is a place where you can play games on machines which work when you put money in them.

weird [wiərd] a. 기이한, 기묘한; 기괴한, 섬뜩한
If you describe something or someone as weird, you mean that they are strange.

wheel [hwi:l] n. (자동차 등의) 핸들; 바퀴; v. (바퀴 달린 것을) 밀다
The wheel of a car or other vehicle is the circular object that is used to steer it.

for starters idiom 우선 첫째로
For starters is used to say that something is the first in a list of things.

race [reis] v. 경주하다; 쏜살같이 가다; (머리·심장 등이) 바쁘게 돌아가다; n. 경주; 인종, 종족
(racer n. 경주 참가자)
A racer is a person or animal that takes part in races.

obnoxious [əbnákʃəs] a. 아주 불쾌한, 몹시 기분 나쁜
If you describe someone or something as obnoxious, you think that they are very unpleasant.

go on idiom 말을 계속하다; (어떤 상황이) 계속되다; 자자, 어서
To go on means to continue speaking after a short pause.

mention [ménʃən] v. 말하다, 언급하다; n. 언급, 거론
If you mention something, you say something about it, usually briefly.

^{복습} **surge** [sə:rdʒ] n. 서지(전압·전류의 급증); (갑자기) 밀려듦;
v. (재빨리) 밀려들다; (강한 감정이) 휩싸다
A surge is a sudden increase in electrical power that can damage equipment connected to it.

^{복습} **notice** [nóutis] v. 알아채다, 인지하다; 주의하다; n. 신경 씀, 알아챔; 통지, 예고
If you notice something or someone, you become aware of them.

★ **compliment** [kámpləmənt] v. 칭찬하다; n. 칭찬(의 말), 찬사
If you compliment someone, you praise or express admiration for them.

^{복습} **hang out** idiom 많은 시간을 보내다
If you hang out in a place or with a person or a group of people, you spend a lot of time in there or with them.

★ **host** [houst] v. 주최하다; 진행하다; n. (초대한) 주인; (TV·라디오 프로의) 진행자
If someone hosts a party, dinner, or other function, they have invited the guests and provide the food, drink, or entertainment.

set up idiom ~을 세우다; 준비하다; (기계·장비를) 설치하다
If you set up something, you build it or put it somewhere.

^{복습} **brick** [brik] n. 벽돌
Bricks are rectangular blocks of baked clay used for building walls, which are usually red or brown.

^{복습} **pile** [pail] n. 무더기; 쌓아 놓은 것, 더미; v. 쌓다; 집어넣다; 우르르 가다
A pile of things is a mass of them that is high in the middle and has sloping sides.

^{복습} **burn** [bə:rn] v. 태우다; 불에 타다; 상기되다; n. 화상
If you burn something that you are cooking or if it burns, you spoil it by using too much heat or cooking it for too long.

★ **grateful** [gréitfəl] a. 고마워하는, 감사하는
If you are grateful for something that someone has given you or done for you, you have warm, friendly feelings toward them and wish to thank them.

★ **hover** [hávər] v. (허공을) 맴돌다; 서성이다; 주저하다; n. 공중을 떠다님
To hover means to stay in the same position in the air without moving forward or backward.

^{복습} **device** [diváis] n. 장치, 기구; 폭발물; 방법
A device is an object that has been invented for a particular purpose, for example for recording or measuring something.

chat [ʧæt] v. 이야기를 나누다, 수다를 떨다; n. 이야기, 대화
When people chat, they talk to each other in an informal and friendly way.

disappoint [dìsəpɔ́int] v. 실망시키다, 실망을 안겨 주다; 좌절시키다
If things or people disappoint you, they are not as good as you had hoped, or do not do what you hoped they would do.

flash [flæʃ] n. 순간; (잠깐) 반짝임; v. (잠깐) 번쩍이다; 휙 나타나다 (in a flash idiom 순식간에)
If you say that something happens in a flash, you mean that it happens suddenly and lasts only a very short time.

halfway [hæfwéi] ad. 꽤 괜찮은; (거리·시간상으로) 중간에, 가운데쯤에
Halfway means reasonably.

decent [díːsnt] a. (수준·질이) 괜찮은; 적당한; 품위 있는
Decent is used to describe something which is considered to be of an acceptable standard or quality.

truckload [trʌ́klòud] n. 트럭 한 대 분량(의 화물)
A truckload of goods or people is the amount of them that a truck can carry.

daylight [déilait] n. (낮의) 햇빛, 일광
Daylight is the natural light that there is during the day, before it gets dark.

adieu [ədjúː] int. 안녕, 잘 가; n. 작별(인사)
Adieu means the same as goodbye.

fart [faːrt] v. 방귀를 뀌다; n. 방귀; 지겨운 인간
If someone farts, air is forced out of their body through their anus.

sorrow [sárou] n. 슬픔, 비통; v. 슬퍼하다
Sorrow is a feeling of deep sadness or regret.

so long idiom 안녕(작별 인사)
You can use so long as an informal way of saying goodbye.

stink [stiŋk] n. 악취; v. 좋지 않다; (고약한) 냄새가 나다
Stink means a strong unpleasant smell.

take in idiom ~을 눈여겨보다; 이해하다
If you take in something, you spend time looking at it.

pal [pæl] n. 친구; 이봐
Your pals are your friends.

bench [benʧ] n. 벤치; 판사(석)
A bench is a long seat of wood or metal that two or more people can sit on.

distance [dístəns] n. 거리; 먼 곳; v. (~에) 관여하지 않다
When two things are very far apart, you talk about the distance between them.

수고하셨습니다!

드디어 끝까지 다 읽으셨군요! 축하드립니다! 여러분은 이 책을 통해 총 20,864개의 단어를 읽으셨고, 1,000개 이상의 어휘와 표현들을 공부하셨습니다. 이 책에 나온 어휘는 다른 원서를 읽을 때도 빈번히 만날 수 있는 필수 어휘들입니다. 이 책을 읽었던 경험은 비슷한 수준의 다른 원서들을 읽을 때 큰 도움이 될 것입니다.

원서는 한 번 다 읽은 후에도 다양한 방식으로 영어 실력을 끌어올리는 데 활용할 수 있습니다. 일단 다 읽은 원서를 어떻게 활용할 수 있을지, 학습자의 주요 유형별로 알아보도록 하겠습니다.

리딩(Reading) 실력을 확실히 다지길 원한다면, 반복해서 읽어보세요!

리딩 실력을 탄탄하게 다지길 원한다면, 같은 원서를 2~3번 반복해서 읽을 것을 권합니다. 같은 책을 여러 번 읽으면 지루할 것 같지만, 꼭 그렇지도 않습니다. 반복해서 읽을 때 처음과 주안점을 다르게 두면, 전혀 다른 느낌으로 재미있게 읽을 수 있습니다.

처음 원서를 읽을 때는 생소한 단어들과 스토리로 인해 읽고 이해하기가 매우 힘듭니다. 전체 맥락을 잡고 읽어도 약간 버거운 느낌이지요. 하지만 반복해서 읽기 시작하면 달라집니다. 내용은 일단 파악해 둔 상황이기 때문에 문장 구조나 어휘의 활용에 더 집중하게 되고, 조금 더 깊이 있게 읽을 수 있게 됩니다. 좋은 표현과 문장을 수집하고 메모할 만한 여유도 생기게 되지요. 어휘도 많이 익숙해졌기 때문에 리딩 속도도 탄력이 붙습니다. 처음 읽을 때는 '내용'에서 재미를 느꼈다면, 반복해서 읽을 때는 '영어'에서 재미를 느끼게 되는 것입니다. 따라서 리딩 실력을 더욱 확고하게 다지고자 한다면, 같은 책을 2~3회 정도 반복해서 읽을 것을 권해드립니다.

리스닝(Listening) 실력을 늘리고 싶다면, 귀를 통해서 읽어보세요!

많은 영어 학습자들이 '리스닝이 안 돼서 문제'라고 한탄합니다. 그리고 리스닝 실력을 늘리는 방법으로, 무슨 뜻인지 몰라도 반복해 듣는 '무작정 듣기'를 선택합니다. 하지만 뜻도 모르면서 무작정 듣는 것은 엄청난 인내력이 필요합니다. 그래서 대부분 며칠 시도하다가 포기해버리고 말지요.

모르는 내용을 무작정 듣는 것보다는 어느 정도 알고 있는 내용을 반복해서 듣는 것이 더 효과적인 듣기 방법입니다. 그리고 이런 방식의 듣기에 활용할 수 있는 가장 좋은 교재가 오디오북입니다.

따라서 리스닝 실력을 향상시키길 원한다면, 이 책에서 제공하는 오디오북을 이용해서 듣는 연습을 해보세요. 오디오북의 활용법은 간단합니다. 그냥 MP3를 플레이어에 넣고 자투리 시간에 틈틈이 들으면 됩니다. 혹은 책상에 앉아 눈으로는 책을 보면서 귀로는 그 내용을 따라 읽는 것도 좋습니다. 보통 오디오북은 분당 150~180단어로 재생되는데, 재생 속도가 조절되는 MP3를 이용하면 더 빠른 속도로 재생이 가능하고, 이에 맞춰 빠른 속도로 듣는 연습을 할 수도 있습니다.

중요한 것은 내용을 따라가면서, 내용에 푹 빠져서 반복해 들어야 한다는 것입니다. 눈으로 책을 읽는 것이 아니라 '귀를 통해' 책을 읽는 것이지요. 이렇게 연습을 반복해서, 눈으로 읽지 않은 책도 '귀를 통해' 읽을 수 있을 정도가 되면, 리스닝으로 고생하는 일은 거의 사라질 것입니다.

이 책은 '귀로 읽기'와 '소리 내어 읽기'를 위해 오디오북을 기본으로 제공하고 있습니다.
오디오북은 MP3 파일로 제공되니 MP3 기기나 컴퓨터에 옮겨서 사용하시면 됩니다. 혹 오디오북에 이상이 있을 경우 helper@longtailbooks.co.kr로 메일을 주시면 안내를 받으실 수 있습니다.

스피킹(Speaking)이 고민이라면, 소리 내어 읽기를 해보세요!

스피킹 역시 많은 학습자들이 고민하는 부분입니다. 스피킹이 고민이라면, 원서를 큰 소리로 읽는 낭독 훈련(Voice Reading)을 해보세요!
'소리 내서 읽는 것이 말하기에 정말로 도움이 될까?'라고 의아한 생각이 들 수도 있습니다. 하지만, 인간의 두뇌 입장에서 봤을 때, 성대 구조를 활용해서 '발화'한다는 점에서는 소리 내서 읽기와 말하기는 큰 차이가 없다고 합니다. 소리 내서 읽는 것은 '타인의 생각'을 전달하고, 직접 말하는 것은 '자신의 생각'을 전달한다는 차이가 있을 뿐, 머릿속에서 문장을 처리하고 조음기관(혀와 성대 등)을 움직여 의미를 만든다는 점에서 같은 과정인 것이지요. 따라서 소리 내서 읽는 연습을 꾸준히 하는 것은 스피킹 연습에 큰 도움이 됩니다.

소리 내어 읽기를 하는 방법도 간단합니다. 일단 오디오북을 들으면서 성우의 목소리를 최대한 따라 하며 같이 읽어보세요. 발음 뿐 아니라, 억양, 어조, 느낌까지 완벽히 따라 한다고 생각하면서 소리 내어 읽습니다. 따라 읽는 것이 조금 익숙해지면, 옆의 누군가에게 이 책을 읽어준다는 생각으로 소리내서 계속 읽어나갑니다. 한 번 눈과 귀로 읽었던 책이라 보다 수월하게 진행할 수 있고, 자연스럽게 어휘와 표현을 복습하는 효과도 거두게 됩니다. 또 이렇게 소리 내어 읽는 것을 녹음해서 들어보면 스스로에게 좋은 피드백이 됩니다.

라이팅(Writing)까지 욕심이 난다면, 요약하는 연습을 해보세요!

최근엔 라이팅에도 욕심을 내는 학습자들이 많이 있습니다. 원서를 라이팅 연습에 직접적으로 활용하기에는 한계가 있지만, 역시 적절히 활용하면 유용한 자료가 될 수 있습니다.
특히 책을 읽고 그 내용을 요약하는 연습은 큰 도움이 됩니다. 요약 훈련의 방식도 간단합니다. 원서를 읽고 그날 읽은 분량만큼 혹은 책을 다 읽고 난 후에 전체 내용을 기반으로, 책 내용을 요약하고 나의 느낌을 영어로 적어보는 것입니다. 이때 그 책에 나왔던 단어와 표현을 최대한 활용해서 요약하는 것이 중요합니다.

영어 표현력은 결국 얼마나 다양한 어휘로 많은 표현을 해보았느냐가 좌우하게 됩니다. 이런 면에서 내가 읽은 책을, 그 책에 나온 문장과 어휘로 다시 표현해 보는 것이 가장 효율적인 방식입니다. 책에 나온 어휘와 표현을 단순히 읽고 무슨 말인지 아는 정도가 아니라, 실제로 직접 활용해서 쓸 수 있을 만큼 확실하게 익히게 되는 것이지요. 여기에 첨삭까지 받을 수 있는 방법이 있다면 금상첨화입니다.

또한 이런 '표현하기' 연습은 스피킹 훈련에도 그대로 적용할 수 있습니다. 책을 읽고 그 내용을 3분 안에 다른 사람에게 영어로 말하는 연습을 하는 것이지요. 순발력과 표현력을 기르는 좋은 훈련이 됩니다.

'스피드 리딩 카페'에서 함께 원서를 읽어보세요!

이렇게 원서 읽기를 활용한 영어 공부에 관심이 있으시다면, 국내 최대 영어원서 읽기 동호회 스피드 리딩 카페(http://cafe.naver.com/readingtc)로 와보세요. 이미 수만 명의 회원들이 모여서 '북클럽'을 통해 함께 원서를 읽고 있습니다.

단순히 함께 원서를 읽는 것뿐만 아니라, 위에서 언급한 다양한 방식으로 원서를 활용하여 영어 실력을 향상시키고 있는, 말뿐이 아닌 '실질적인 효과'를 보고 있는 회원들이 엄청나게 많이 있습니다. 여러분도 스피드 리딩 카페를 방문해보신다면 많은 자극과 도움을 받으실 수 있을 것입니다.

원서 읽기 습관을 길러보자!

일상에서 영어를 한마디도 쓰지 않는 비영어권 국가에서 살고 있는 우리에게 영어에 가장 쉽고, 편하고, 저렴하게 노출되는 방법은, 바로 '영어원서 읽기'입니다. 언제 어디서든 원서를 붙잡고 읽기만 하면 곧바로 영어를 접하는 환경이 만들어지기 때문이지요. 하루에 20분씩만 꾸준히 읽는다면, 1년에 무려 120시간 동안 영어에 노출될 수 있습니다.

영어원서를 꾸준히 읽어보세요. '원서 읽기 습관'을 만들어보세요! 이렇게 영어를 접하는 시간이 늘어나면, 영어 실력도 당연히 향상될 수밖에 없습니다.

아래 표에는 영어 수준별 추천 원서들이 있습니다. 하지만 이것은 절대적인 기준이 아니며, 학습자의 영어 수준과 관심 분야에 따라 달라질 수 있습니다. 이 책은 Reading Level 3에 해당합니다. 이 책의 완독 경험을 기준으로 삼아 적절한 책을 골라 꾸준히 읽어보세요.

영어 수준별 추천 원서 목록

리딩 레벨	영어 수준	원서 목록
Level 1	초 · 중학생	The Zack Files 시리즈, Magic Tree House 시리즈, Junie B. Jones 시리즈, Horrid Henry 시리즈, 로알드 달 단편들(The Giraffe and the Pelly and Me, Esio Trot, The Enormous Crocodile, The Magic Finger, Fantastic Mr. Fox)
Level 2	고등학생	Andrew Clements 시리즈 (Frindle, School Story 등), Spiderwick Chronicle 시리즈, 쉬운 뉴베리 수상작들 (Sarah Plain and Tall, The Hundred Dresses 등), 짧고 간단한 자기계발서 (Who Moved My Cheese?, The Present 등)
Level 3	특목고 학생 대학생	로알드 달 장편 (Charlie and the Chocolate Factory, Matilda 등), Wayside School 시리즈, 중간 수준의 뉴베리 수상작들 (Number the Stars, Charlotte's Web 등), A Series of Unfortunate Events 시리즈
Level 4	대학생 상위권	Harry Potter 시리즈 중 1~3권, Percy Jackson 시리즈, The Chronicles of Narnia 시리즈, The Alchemist, 어려운 수준의 뉴베리 수상작들 (Holes, The Giver 등)
Level 5	대학원생 이상 전문직 종사자들	Harry Potter 시리즈 중 4~7권, Shopaholic 시리즈, His Dark Materials 시리즈, The Devil Wears Prada, The Curious Incident of the Dog in the Night-Time, Tuesdays With Morrie 등등 (참고 자료: Renaissance Learning, Readingtown USA, Slyvan Learning Center)

'영화로 읽는 영어원서'로 원서 읽기 습관을 만들어보세요!

『주먹왕 랄프 2』를 재미있게 읽은 독자라면 「영화로 읽는 영어원서」 시리즈를 꾸준히 읽어보시길 추천해드립니다! 「영화로 읽는 영어원서」 시리즈는 유명 영화를 기반으로 한 소설판 영어원서로 보다 쉽고 부담 없이 원서 읽기를 시작할 수 있도록 도와주고, 오디오북을 기본적으로 포함해 원서의 활용 범위를 넓힌 책입니다.

『하이스쿨 뮤지컬』, 『업』, 『라푼젤』, 『겨울왕국』, 『메리다와 마법의 숲』, 『몬스터 주식회사』, 『몬스터 대학교』, 『인사이드 아웃』, 『빅 히어로』 등 출간하는 책들마다 독자들의 큰 사랑을 받으며 어학 분야의 베스트셀러를 기록했고, 학원과 학교들에서도 꾸준히 교재로 채택되는 등 영어 학습자들에게도 좋은 반응을 얻고 있습니다. (EBS에서 운영하는 어학사이트 EBS랑 www.ebslang.co.kr 교재 채택, 서초·강남 등지 명문 중고교 방과 후 보충교재 채택, 전국 영어 학원 정·부교재 채택, 김해 분성 초등학교 영어원서 읽기 대회 교재 채택 등등)

Chapters 1 & 2

1. D But each evening, after all the players had left and Mr. Litwak had closed the arcade, Vanellope and Ralph left their games behind and met up in Game Central Station. They would spend the rest of their time hanging out and goofing around together.

2. A For a moment, he thought back to before he met Vanellope, when he was wrecking buildings in Fix-It Felix Jr. and had no friends. "I mean, sure, it doesn't look so hot on paper. Y'know, I am just a Bad Guy who wrecks a building. And, yes, for twenty-seven years, I basically lived like a dirty bum without any friends . . . but now I got a best friend who just happens to be the coolest girl in this whole arcade."

3. B "So you're saying there's not one single, solitary thing about your life that you would change?" asked Vanellope, still thinking about what Ralph had said on the football field. "Not one. It's flawless," answered Ralph.

4. D "But really, the Internet is nothing to laugh at. It is new and it is different; therefore, we should fear it. So keep out."

5. C "Something wrong with your game?" asked Ralph. "No," said Vanellope. "It's just—every bonus level's been unlocked. I know every shortcut. I'd kill for a new track."

Chapters 3 & 4

1. A In the arcade, Nafisa urged Swati on. "Get back up there—you're going to lose!" Swati yanked the wheel hard to the left, trying to get Vanellope back onto the regular track, but it wasn't working. "What's wrong with this thing?" she said, struggling to control the Vanellope racer. She pulled hard at the wheel again, and this time the whole thing came right off!

2. C Outside the game, Mr. Litwak's face fell. "Well, I'd order a new part," he said to the crowd of kids now gathered around, "but the company that made Sugar Rush went out of business years ago." The kids were aghast. "I'll try to find one on the Internet," said one kid, looking down at his phone. All the kids dropped their heads as they began to do the same, searching their phones for a new steering wheel.

3. C Mr. Litwak adjusted his glasses as he read the information about the steering wheel on the phone. "Are you kidding me?" he scoffed. "How much? That's more than this game

makes in a year." Mr. Litwak sighed. "I hate to say it, but my salvage guy is coming on Friday, and it might be time to sell Sugar Rush for parts." The kids groaned as Mr. Litwak headed around to the back of the machine. Ralph's eyes popped. "Litwak's gonna unplug your game!" he shouted.

4. D Down below, Felix and Calhoun's apartment was packed with Sugar Rush characters, as well as some characters from other games. Felix addressed the group. "All right, we've found good homes for so many of our chums from Sugar Rush. And we're just hoping a few more of you will open your doors and your hearts to those in need."

5. B Ralph was excited. "That kid out in the arcade said there was a steering wheel part in the Internet at something called eBoy, or . . ." He grabbed his head as he tried to remember. "No, it was eBay. That's it—eBay!" he exclaimed. "Ralph, are you thinking about going to the Internet and finding that part?" asked Felix. "Getting that part's the only thing that's gonna fix the game, and that's the only thing that's gonna make Vanellope happy again."

Chapters 5 & 6

1. B They entered the router and looked around, expecting to see something amazing. But the space around them was mostly empty. There really wasn't anything going on. "Huh, the Internet is not nearly as impressive as how the hedgehog described it," said Ralph. "Yeah. I gotta admit, I'm underwhelmed," agreed Vanellope.

2. A Meanwhile, Mr. Litwak sat at his office desk, staring at his computer screen. He moved the mouse across the pad. "Okay, connect to network," he said, searching for the Wi-Fi icon on the menu bar. "Bingo. Password is HighSc0re, with a zero instead of an O. And we . . . are . . . online!" Mr. Litwak clicked on an icon. Suddenly, what appeared to be a little man who looked just like Mr. Litwak traveled at light speed from the computer to the Wi-Fi router. It was his avatar.

3. D "Come on, Ralph, let's follow him," Vanellope said, and ran after the tiny Litwak figure. Ralph and Vanellope watched as Litwak's avatar was encased in a small capsule. A voice read out a computer address with some numbers, and the friends gazed in awe as the capsule suddenly blasted through a tube, zooming away. Vanellope glitched onto the

launch pad, ready to go after him, and Ralph followed.

4. C On a quiet tree-lined street in suburbia, a woman sipped coffee as she stared at her computer screen. The letter B blinked as she began typing the word "ballet" on her keyboard. She spoke aloud as she typed, "Where can I find ballet—" "Ballet shoes? Ballet classes? Ballet folklorico?" KnowsMore blurted, eagerly trying to guess the rest of her request. "Ballet TIGHTS," said the woman as she continued to type. "Girls' size small," she added. "Oh, little Madeline's trying ballet now, is she?" said KnowsMore. "I hope this lasts longer than the soccer phase." The woman clicked the return button on her keyboard, and tons of results from KnowsMore's search popped up on the screen. "I found twenty-three million results for 'ballet tights, girls' size small,'" said KnowsMore.

5. B "Lemme try," said Vanellope. She typed in "eBay Sugar Rush steering wheel." She pushed the return button. "Oh, I only found one result for your query. Hmm, isn't that interesting," said KnowsMore as a photo of the Sugar Rush steering wheel on sale at eBay popped up.

Chapters 7 & 8

1. C Ralph looked over at Vanellope, utterly confused. "Are you understanding how this game works?" "I think all you have to do is yell out the biggest number and you win," replied Vanellope.

2. B A hologram of the Sugar Rush wheel appeared behind the auctioneer. A clock was ticking down, with only thirty-five seconds to go, and one avatar had already put in a bid! "Two-and-two-and-two-and-two-and-two-seventy-five," said the auctioneer. "And with thirty seconds left in this auction, we have two seventy-five. Do I hear three-and-a-three-and-a-three-and-a-three?"

3. A "Look," said Elaine, tired of dealing with their ridiculous behavior. "If you don't pay within twenty-four hours, you will be in violation of the unpaid-item policy, you will forfeit the bid, and you will lose this item."

4. B "Oh, there you are," said Ralph, walking up to him. "Thank goodness you're still here. Me and my friend here, we got twenty-four hours to make twenty-seven thousand and one dollars or she loses her game." "Yeah, so, can you please tell us how to get rich

playing video games?" asked Vanellope.

5. D "Slaughter Race is the most popular online racing game out there. However, it is wicked dangerous."

Chapters 9 & 10

1. A "Good day to you, madam," Ralph said to Shank. "Who are you?" asked Shank. "I'm here from the, ah, Department of Noise? And the thing is, we've been getting some complaints down at HQ—uh, Larry's the one who takes the calls. . . ." While Ralph distracted them, Vanellope tiptoed into the warehouse and hopped into Shank's car.

2. D "Whoa, Mother Hubbard, this lady can really drive," said Vanellope. As hard as she tried to lose her, Shank was able to keep up.

3. C "There are much better ways to make money on the Internet than stealing cars. Here," said Shank, taking the phone from Felony and handing it to Ralph. "Such as becoming a BuzzzTube star."

4. A "Friend of mine—chick named Yesss—she's the head algorithm over at BuzzzTube. Tell her I sent you. Yesss will hook you up."

5. B "I'm just sayin' that game was next level. The racing was awesome—and there's no one telling you what to do or where to go."

Chapters 11 & 12

1. D "I am the head ALGOrithm of BuzzzTube, which means I curate the content at the Internet's most popular video-sharing site," explained Yesss. "Which means I don't have time to trifle with every shoeless mouth-breathing hobo that trundles into my office. Yo, Maybe, call security."

2. D "What if you made a whole bunch of videos of me doing different things?" "You mean saturate the market," Yesss said, thinking. "That could get you a lotta hearts fast." "What exactly do you plan on doing in these videos?" Vanellope asked him. "I'll just copy whatever's popular," he answered.

3. B "I need you out there popping up and getting clicks at all the social media and entertainment websites. I'm talking Tumblr, Instagram, Mashable. . . . This isn't just a

marketing campaign! This is an all-out viral assault! Let's get this man his hearts!"

4. C Ralph's eyes widened as he saw the Slaughter Race icon appear on the map. That was the last place he wanted her to go. "Actually, why don't you send her somewhere a little more . . ." Ralph spun the globe, searching for the best and safest site for Vanellope. "How 'bout fan sites? She is technically a princess, so maybe you could send her to this one with the castle."

5. A Vanellope headed over to another crowd and managed to get more avatars to click. "It's almost too easy," she said to herself. But as she spun around to find more avatars, a security guard stopped her. "Hey, do you have a permit for that pop-up?" asked the guard. "Urm . . ." "That's unauthorized clickbait," said another guard. "You're coming with us."

Chapters 13 & 14

1. B "Have you ever had true love's kiss?" asked Snow White. "Ew! Baaaarf!" said Vanellope, gagging. "Do you have daddy issues?" asked Jasmine. "I don't even have a mom," said Vanellope. Nearly every princess in the room squealed, "Neither do we!" "And now for the million-dollar question," said Rapunzel. "Do people assume all your problems got solved because a big strong man showed up?" "YES!" Vanellope shouted without hesitation. "What is up with that?" "She is a princess!" they all exclaimed.

2. A "Right, of course," said Vanellope. "Important water. I stare at that and somehow magically I'll start singing about my dream? I don't think so, ladies." "You'll see," Belle said.

3. D "Oh, no, oh, no, no, no, no, no, no," said Yesss, her eyes fixed on her computer screen. A bright rainbow-colored wheel appeared, spinning and spinning. "OH, NO!" she shouted, frustrated. "Why are you angry at that lollipop?" asked Ralph. "What's going on?" "The file's not loading," Yesss answered.

4. C "Okay, well, hold on, now," said Yesss. "It's not all bad. The Internet can also be a place where you find a steering wheel at one website and make enough money to buy it at another one."

5. B "We're going home, kid! Our lives can finally go back to normal! Woo-hoo!" Ralph said, and hung up. "Wow. I can't believe it. I get to go . . . home?" Vanellope said quietly.

"I guess I do just want a steering wheel." Her excitement suddenly faded as the reality of going back to Sugar Rush set in. She knew she was supposed to feel happy, but for some reason, she didn't.

Chapters 15 & 16

1. C Ralph was shocked to see Vanellope sitting with Shank. "What are you doing in that awful game with her?" he said. But because the device was muted, Vanellope didn't hear him. She continued to chat with Shank. "The race will end right over there," Shank said. "It's gonna be so tight." "Wow. I love it," said Vanellope. Ralph realized they didn't notice his hologram and paused to eavesdrop. "Hey, can I tell you something that I don't think I could ever tell Ralph?" asked Vanellope. "Of course. What is it?" said Shank. "I know it sounds crazy . . . but the second I walked into this game, it felt, well, it felt like home. I mean, more than Sugar Rush ever did."

2. D "She's been brainwashed," said Ralph. "That's what this is. Cause the Vanellope I know would never abandon me. I gotta get her outta there right away."

3. A "Now, Gord here, he has dabbled in virus making. But his cousin, the guy we're going to see—big ol' son of a gun who goes by the name of Double Dan—this dude is a virus-making machine."

4. A "Crash it?" said Ralph. "No, no, no. I don't want anyone getting hurt." He watched nervously as Double Dan grunted and went to work, searching through various drawers and removing a variety of chemicals. "If there's a way to just, I dunno, make the cars go slow or something, just so the game is boring and my friend comes back home to me. That's all."

5. B "Are you stupid?" asked Double Dan. "Um—I . . . ," Ralph stuttered. "Because the only way anyone gets hurt is if you are stupid. All you have to do is make sure the virus stays in Slaughter Race." "Don't be stupid and let the virus out of Slaughter Race," repeated Ralph.

Chapters 17 & 18

1. D The worm squirming nearby detected Vanellope's glitch and recognized it as an

insecurity. It quickly copied the glitch and distributed it throughout the entire game! Suddenly, some of the buildings around her began to flash. She looked around, confused and shocked to see more and more parts of the game breaking down . . . and then everything was glitching!

2. B "Hey, how did you know to rescue me in Slaughter Race?" asked Vanellope, now suspicious that there was something Ralph wasn't telling her.

3. A While he sat alone, the virus worm squirmed through the firewall hole and exited Slaughter Race. It quickly picked up on Ralph, finding him to be one hundred percent insecure. Without anyone noticing, it copied Ralph's insecurity . . . and began to distribute it all over the Internet.

4. C Just then, the door blasted open and a Ralph clone lunged for Vanellope. She reached for a lamp and used it to hit him over the head. "Ow! It's me! It's me!" the clone shouted. But Vanellope hadn't heard the clones actually speak before. "Ralph?" "I'm so glad you're okay. I followed those things here. I think they're looking for you, kid," he said. It was the real Ralph after all! Vanellope was relieved, but still furious. "Yeah, ya think?" she shot back.

5. B "Either you put all of the clones in therapy, or," he said as he grabbed a book from his shelves, "alternatively, there's an archway in the Anti-Virus District made out of security software. If Vanellope could somehow lead the clones through that arch, the security software would delete them all at once."

Chapters 19 & 20

1. C "I've seen it a lot, actually," said Yesss. "Not to this extent, of course. But I'm telling you, reading the comments, listening to the hate those trolls spew—it can make a person do some crazy, horrible things." "Whaddaya mean? What comments?" "Oh, he didn't tell you? Ralph got trolled hard for those videos he made for you. Bunch of anonymous bullies calling him fat and ugly and useless, saying 'I hate you.'"

2. A The limo made its way to the Anti-Virus arch even though the Ralph clones were hot on their trail. "We're gonna make it!" cheered Ralph. But as they celebrated, the millions of clones clustered together and climbed on top of each other to form a giant, rippling

wave. The wave rose, then came down hard, crashing right into the limo, causing it to fly out of control and straight through a Pinterest window!

3. B Suddenly, Giant Ralph stopped to listen to what Ralph was saying. "You need to let her go. I know it's gonna hurt a little bit when you do. Heck, who am I kidding? It's gonna hurt a lot. But you're gonna be okay," Ralph said. Then he said to Vanellope, "And we're gonna be okay—right, kid?" "Of course we are," Vanellope said. "Always." Giant Ralph blinked as the words settled in. It lowered its huge hand and gently set Vanellope on top of a nearby website.

4. C Just before Ralph crashed into the ground, the Oh My Disney princesses swooped in and rescued him. "Look! Up there!" Belle exclaimed. "It's a big strong man in need of rescuing!" All the princesses sprang into action. They worked together to help, each one using her own special skill. Moana made a wave that Elsa froze so Ralph could slide down it before launching into the air again. With a variety of objects, including dresses, a poison apple, and a rope made out of hair, they had built a "hairachute" to slow Ralph's fall. "The hairachute is working, you guys!" Ariel said. Pocahontas used her wind power to push Ralph's chute toward a mattress website, causing him to land on top of a plush, comfy bed.

5. D Ralph was grateful. "I guess that's pretty much all the news I got for you." Vanellope smiled, her hologram hovering above Ralph's Buzzzy device as the two chatted. "Well, your stories never disappoint," she said.

주먹왕 랄프 2 : 인터넷 속으로(Ralph Breaks the Internet)

초판 발행 2019년 1월 21일

지은이 Suzanne Francis
기획 이수영
책임편집 김보경 정소이
콘텐츠제작및감수 롱테일북스 편집부
번역 정소이
마케팅 김보미 임정진 전선경 정경훈

펴낸이 이수영
펴낸곳 (주)롱테일북스
출판등록 제2015-000191호
주소 04043 서울특별시 마포구 양화로 12길 16-9(서교동) 북앤빌딩 3층
전자메일 helper@longtailbooks.co.kr
(학원·학교에서 본도서를 교재로 사용하길 원하시는 경우 전자메일로 문의주시면
자세한 안내를 받으실 수 있습니다.)

ISBN 979-11-86701-95-9 14740

롱테일북스는 (주)북하우스 퍼블리셔스의 계열사입니다.